THE
EVOLUTIONISTS

CRITICAL ISSUES IN HISTORY

Series Editor: Donald T. Critchlow

The British Imperial Century, 1815–1914: A World History Perspective
    by Timothy H. Parsons
The Great Encounter of China and the West, 1500–1800
    by D. E. Mungello
Europe's Reformations, 1450–1650
    by James D. Tracy
The Idea of Capitalism before the Industrial Revolution
    by Richard Grassby
The Unfinished Struggle: Turning Points in American Labor History, 1877–present
    by Steven Babson
A Concise History of the Crusades
    by Thomas F. Madden
America's Great War: World War I and the American Experience
    by Robert H. Zieger
Peter the Great
    by Paul Bushkovitch
Remaking Italy in the Twentieth Century
    by Roy Palmer Domenico
War and Genocide: A Concise History of the Holocaust
    by Doris L. Bergen
Conceived in Liberty: The Struggle to Define the New Republic, 1789–1793
    by Lance Banning
The Evolutionists: American Thinkers Confront Charles Darwin, 1860–1920
    by J. David Hoeveler

THE EVOLUTIONISTS

AMERICAN THINKERS CONFRONT CHARLES DARWIN, 1860–1920

J. DAVID HOEVELER

Rowman & Littlefield Publishers, Inc.
Lanham • Boulder • New York • Toronto • Plymouth, UK

ROWMAN & LITTLEFIELD PUBLISHERS, INC.

Published in the United States of America
by Rowman & Littlefield Publishers, Inc.
A wholly owned subsidary of The Rowman & Littlefield Publishing Group,
Inc.
4501 Forbes Boulevard, Suite 200, Lanham, Maryland 20706
www.rowmanlittlefield.com

Estover Road
Plymouth PL6 7PY
United Kingdom

British Library Cataloguing in Publication Information Available

Library of Congress Cataloging-in-Publication Data
Hoeveler, J. David, 1943–
   The evolutionists: American thinkers confront Charles Darwin, 1860–1920 /
J. David Hoeveler.
      p. cm. — (Critical issues in history)
   Includes bibliographical references.
   ISBN-13: 978-0-7425-1174-3 (cloth : alk. paper)
   ISBN-10: 0-7425-1174-X (cloth : alk. paper)
   ISBN-13: 978-0-7425-1175-0 (pbk. : alk. paper)
   ISBN-10: 0-7425-1175-8 (pbk. : alk. paper)
      1. Evolution (Biology)—United States—History. 2. Natural selection—
United States—History. 3. Religion and science—United States—History.
I. Title.
   QH361.H64 2007
   576.8—dc22   2006034795

Printed in the United States of America

♾™ The paper used in this publication meets the minimum requirements of
American National Standard for Information Sciences—Permanence of
Paper for Printed Library Materials,
ANSI/NISO Z39.48-1992.

For Charlie and Debbie

CONTENTS

INTRODUCTION ix

1 ALONG THE WAY TO DARWIN 1

2 DARWIN'S DANGEROUS IDEA 25

3 THE SCIENTIFIC RECEPTION
   Louis Agassiz and Asa Gray 51

4 PROTESTANT ORTHODOXY
   Charles Hodge and James McCosh 77

5 PROTESTANT LIBERALISM
   Henry Ward Beecher and John Bascom 103

6 SOCIOLOGY William Graham Sumner
   and Lester Frank Ward 133

7 FEMINISM Charlotte Perkins Gilman and
   Eliza Burt Gamble 157

8 METHODOLOGIES Thorstein Veblen
   and Oliver Wendell Holmes Jr. 179

9 PHILOSOPHY William James and
   John Dewey 211

CONTENTS

POSTSCRIPT, 2006   247

INDEX   251

ABOUT THE AUTHOR   265

INTRODUCTION

Charles Darwin's famous theory of evolution, introduced to the world in 1859, resonated widely in the United States. Indeed, this country became the preeminent Darwinian nation, at least by the measure of its multifaceted applications. No Western nation failed to register Darwin's influence in some way, and in countries like England and Germany, it gained some remarkable theoretical readings. American thinkers, from feminists to philosophers, found Darwinism an extraordinarily fertile concept. In the United States Darwinism helped shape the intellectual contours of modern liberalism and progressive politics. And, perhaps surprisingly, Darwinism, sometimes by inspiring fear of its implications, gave rise to a generation of liberal theologians who reshaped American Protestantism. In fact, in a perverse way, the United States is *the* Darwinian nation by the measure of the enduring fear of it and by the long-sustained effort to expunge it from our public schools and save Americans from its awful conclusions. Where in France is the counterpart of the 1925 Scopes trial? Where in England is the effort to teach "Creation Science" alongside Darwinism?

This book does not intend to adjudicate these controversies in their contemporary settings. Instead, it revisits a sixty-year period when evolution recharged American thinking and led it in fresh and exciting directions. It does so by looking at several categories of

American thought, subjects that reflected the new influence and gave it various applications. The reader will notice that evolution seldom served as a singular influence among the principals in this study; rather the thinkers here combined it with older notions, other systems of thought still current, and created new syntheses. Nonetheless, from a glance across the field, we see new structures of reality, or new social models, or new methodologies gaining our attention, the collective influence of evolutionary concepts.

I suspect that many people think of the Darwinian controversies as a well-defined battlefield. On one side stand defenders of religion, on the other the proponents of science. Or perhaps one would describe it as theists vs. naturalists. Battles of this kind did indeed rage. But matters were not that simple. I have structured this book in a manner that will show that *within* the different categories under study, fiercely oppositional views maintained. Scientists engaged in intense debates with each other over Darwin's form of evolution. Protestant clergy divided, adherents to orthodoxy resisting the theological accommodations of liberals. Another group of thinkers wanted to apply the lessons of evolution to society. Some used Darwinism to endorse a program of competitive laissez-faire and the minimal state, others, with thoroughly Darwinian credentials, also mapped programs of state planning and active government. In philosophy, where, many have argued, Darwinism inspired America's world contributions to this subject, in the form of pragmatism, we find major thinkers offering strikingly different versions.

To draw attention to this particular fact of the Darwinian revolution, I have arranged the chapters on the American thinkers by pairings. I prefer this alternative to a wider and more general discussion of such topics as science, religion, and sociology. What is lost in length of names and breadth of coverage will be gained, I hope, in depth and analysis. I hope, too, that the chapter pairings will add some human dimension to the discussion of ideas and theories. I have always believed that biography supplies the most useful vehicle of intellectual history. For me, it has been the most interesting. So I have tried here to show evolutionary thinking finding its way into a life history, a personality, sometimes an institutional setting.

Evolutionary theory has supplied a huge literature. For a book of moderate size I have had to make choices. I certainly concede that other authors would have made different selections—of individuals and of topics. I have highlighted the selections here because they seem to me to offer the most direct, or fruitful, or interesting engagements with the larger subject. I should say a word about the exclusion of race and related subjects like imperialism and war. Constraints of space are the main reason. But also, race views seem too often to me to be glosses on race prejudice, superficial applications of Darwinism designed to provide the putatively scientific sanction for older predispositions. Nonetheless, if this series on critical issues in American history had allowed for a larger book, I would have included this subject.

This book narrates the adventures of an idea, or at least part of such a chronicle. It begins in science—biology and geology—and moves into other fields. Evolution, as the first chapter shows, had received several formulations before Darwin added another. It had certainly acquired familiarity not just among intellectuals but extensively among the English reading public. Popular lecturers presented these ideas to library audiences and mechanics' institutes in Great Britain and elsewhere. But Darwin (and Alfred Russel Wallace) reshaped the discussion. Darwin believed he had discovered the mechanism of evolution, the explanatory key that demonstrated species transformation. The second chapter looks at Darwin's life and his route to that discovery and observes the reactions to it. The question then becomes, how did a theory that began with studies in animal life extend to so many other categories of intellectual interest? That course takes us through to the American philosophers who made Darwinism a model of reality itself.

The book's title references "the Evolutionists" and names Charles Darwin in the subtitle. Not all the evolutionists were Darwinians, to be sure. The liberal religionists, for example, embraced evolution but feared Darwin. But their actions nonetheless represented a "confrontation" with the British scientist; a theistic understanding of evolution served to co-opt Darwinian evolution, with its norms of chance and purposelessness, for an evolution that reflected intelligent design and divine imminence. Generally, the reader will find that the book, not by intelligent design at all, advances through thinkers that become more emphatically Darwinian, culminating in the premier Darwinian, John Dewey, who receives more space here than any other thinker. For more than any other thinker, Dewey brings Darwinian themes into a profound synthesis.

I wish to thank the excellent staff at Rowman & Littlefield for its work in producing this book. I would also like to thank a Milwaukee friend, Dennis Paul, who gave me the valuable gift of the complete published works of John Dewey.

I am pleased to dedicate this book to my brother, Charles Richard Hoeveler, and my sister, Deborah Bullard Campbell. We grew up together in Connecticut and now live in distant corners of the United States. We don't see each other as much as I would like, but this dedication expresses to each my enduring love.

Milwaukee, Wisconsin
July 2006

ALONG THE WAY
TO DARWIN

THE GREAT CHAIN OF BEING

Only one thing was certain: no consensus prevailed among those who pondered the evidence of earth history and animal life as that evidence multiplied in the eighteenth and nineteenth centuries. This fact will strike any student of this subject in the years leading to Charles Darwin's famous hypothesis; it will frustrate those who seek to measure the application of that thesis in the years after its publication in 1859. But such is the excitement of studying evolution, beginning with the scientists of the formative years and carrying through the religious thinkers, philosophers, and sociologists who strove to wring from it any and all useful applications. Before Darwin, catastrophists contended with uniformitarians. After Darwin, in Gilded Age America, one encounters social Darwinism and reform Darwinism. In philosophy one finds several varieties of pragmatism. In religion one finds Calvinist evolutionists and liberal Protestants. And on it goes.

At the outset, however, one useful generalization helps to launch this inquiry. Science and religion, through most of the eighteenth century, formed an entente cordiale in explaining why and how life began and what forms and shapes it had assumed since the first day of creation. Indeed, often one cannot readily differentiate scientific from religious thinking. Scientists believed that their discoveries illuminated God's creation, their increasing evidence serving to show the greater vastness of it and its glorious manifestations. Religious thinkers had every reason to welcome the new evidence. It confirmed such biblical events as the great flood described in Genesis. It demonstrated the order of Creation as presented in that account. Together, the contributions of both groups affirmed a Great Chain of Being that interconnected all of life. This idea provided the conceptual shorthand that facilitated and indeed motivated those who explored nature's forms, from their lowest to their highest configurations.

Intellectual historian Arthur Lovejoy showed the rich dimensions of this concept, the Chain of Being (sometimes referenced as the Scale of Being), in his famous study of 1936. He traced its beginnings in the works of Plato and Aristotle and recounted its extensions into the Middle Ages. It grew to its richest dimensions in the first half of the eighteenth century. The Chain of Being made certain postulations: All forms of life reflected God's original design of them; they remained unchanged since then; none has become extinct; they are separate creations, however similar they may seem. Furthermore, all forms of life belong to a hierarchy, or scale. They mark their positions in the scale by the degree of consciousness that characterized them, from God to the least sentient forms of life. Here is the testimony of the philosopher Leibniz: "All the different classes of beings which taken together make up the universe are, in the ideas of God who knows distinctly their essential gradations, only so many ordinates of a single curve so closely united that it would be impossible to place others between any two of them, since that would imply disorder and imperfection." Yet Leibniz does concede close proximity in the forms, "a principle of continuity," and he does acknowledge that all the orders of natural beings form but a single chain, in which the various classes are so closely linked as to appear merging one into the other. He felt confident that natural history would fill in the greater and lesser gaps that now exist.

The eighteenth century rested comfortably with the notion of "natural species." For these fixed forms implied nothing in the way of a phylogenetic relationship. Man might sit right next to the ape on the great chain, but none need fret because of the proximity. No genealogical connection tied man to the ape, and humans had no cause to worry about their ancestry. *Homo sapiens,* in fact, generally assumed a midposition in the scale. Man reflects the spiritual nature of the God who created him, but he shares a physiological life with the forms below. He resides below the more spiritual angels and archangels in this descending chain. The telescope and the microscope gave a new awe (and indeed intimidation) to those who pondered human beings' place in the universe—so small when measured against the expansive heavens, so immense when seen against the ubiquitous microorganisms that flourished without limit in the lower scale.

In 1691 the English clergyman and naturalist John Ray gave one among many illustrations of these ideas in his book *The Wisdom of God Manifested in the Works of the Creation.* According to historian John C. Greene, Ray set the dominant pattern of European science for the next two hundred years. All creation, Ray believed, represented "the Works created by God at first, and by Him conserved to this day in the same state and condition in which they were first made." No further inquiry about the origin of life need trouble anyone. As to why these forms took the shapes and showed the properties they did, one did not look to the climate or environment for answers; one need only acknowledge that they registered God's original intentions for them. Species might change because of local conditions but they never go so far as to blur the distinctions that mark them off one from the other. Nature does not reflect disorder or confusion. God's actions thus revealed his wise and benevolent intentions. He created with such perfection and foresight that we need assume no changes in any life forms since the creation.

But the clergy alone did not supply such readings of natural history. The Chain of Being received its most comprehensive and influential illustrations from the work of the great Swedish scientist Carolus Linnaeus (Carl von Linné). He was born in 1707 at Stenbrohult in southern Sweden, the son of a Lutheran pastor. Both his mother and father wished a career in the ministry for him, but Linnaeus had taken an early interest in the family gardens and developed a passion for botany. He prepared for a career in medicine through study first at the University of Lund and then at Uppsala. The course of study in medicine required much attention to botany, for doctors prepared and prescribed cures drawn from medicinal plants. Linnaeus undertook two botanical expeditions before going to the Netherlands in 1735, where he enrolled at the University of Leiden. The same year he published *Systema Naturae*, a famous work that would see many more editions and grow from pamphlet-size to a publication of several volumes. Three years later, Linnaeus returned to Uppsala and began the restoration of the university's botanical garden. His remaining career preserved his identification with that institution.

Linnaeus became known the world over as the great classifier. He effectively served modern science by use of the binomial nomenclature that he devised for the naming of plant and animal forms. He thus created considerable order from a confused and chaotic situation. Linnaeus established significant connections to England and he built on the work of John Ray, with which he reinforced the new nomenclature that filled his edifice. In the binomial arrangement, Linnaeus employed a generic name that indicated a general group of plants or animals that reflected visible likenesses. The second word, the adjectival designation, denoted a restricted group, or species. Hence, *Rosa canina* for the briar rose, *Canis lupus* for the wolf among canids, and the familiar *Homo sapiens*, the contribution of Linnaeus. In his extensive arrangement, Linnaeus originally grouped genera into orders, orders into classes, and classes into kingdoms. He had a passion to know and arrange everything. As Loren Eiseley wrote of Linnaeus: "It was basically the poetic hunger of [his] mind to experience personally every leaf, flower, and bird that could be encompassed in a single life which explains his gigantic labors. He was the naming genius par excellence, a new Adam in the world's garden, drunk with the utter wonder of creation." Of course, Linnaeus acknowledged biological changes, as in hybridization. But these categories did no violence to the primal patterns of life that arranged everything by divine fiat.

American naturalists well knew Linnaeus's work. The New World, of course, gave a great boost to European science. It provided abundant new examples of flora and fauna, and for years American naturalists sent vast varieties of plant and animal species to the Royal Society in London. Several Americans gained admission to that group, a prestigious recognition. Many became fascinated with Linnaeus's taxonomy, for it offered them insights to the natural forms that they discovered in the abundant wilderness of North America. To cite one example, Alexander Garden belonged to a community of scientists in Charleston, South Carolina. Born in Scotland, he had earned a medical degree at Edinburgh and arrived in America in 1752. He pursued his interests in botany in Charleston but left when the steamy climate began to impair his health. His trip north introduced him to other American scientists—the Quaker John Bartram and his son William, Cadwallader Colden of New York, and Benjamin Franklin. Garden collected plants and minerals in the Catskills and discovered Linnaeus's writings in Colden's library. They inspired new efforts on Garden's part and he took up a correspondence with Linnaeus. The Swede also sent some of his many students to the American colonies. One, John Ellis, made a connection with Garden, who in turn showed him a local species, the Cape jasmine. Garden found great satisfaction when Ellis, with Linnaeus's blessing, named it the *Gardenia*.

Linnaeus's passion also grew from his Christianity. He understood science in religious terms. He believed there had been one act of creation. The species one finds today would have also been found in the Garden of Eden or seen in pairs on Noah's ark. Within these fixed forms, though, Linnaeus saw, more than any in his time, the profound and various patterns of creation, the great diversity with which God created, yet withal so orderly. These glimpses into the supernatural inspired many who took to fields and woods to study nature in Linnaeus's time. And yet, as we shall see, Linnaeus succeeded too well. He would come to doubt his own system.

BATTLE OF THE SCHOOLS

Religion's partnership with science gained in depth as more inter-
pretive studies appeared later in the century. We can sample only
some for illustration, but one that commands attention focuses on
the seas. Indeed, the group known as Neptunists came to have a
dominating influence in scientific circles by the end of the century.
It would be no easy task to dislodge them from that position and the
effort to do so produced rival schools of thinking. Nor did charitable
relations between the parties rule the day. Each saw more at stake
than matters of earth history. The truths of scripture, the nature of
God, the direction of life on earth—all these questions stood at issue
in the scientists' investigations and the conclusions they drew from
them.

Abraham Gottlob Werner lived from 1749 to 1817. In 1775 this
German scientist assumed teaching duties at the Freiburg School of
Mines, and from that base he trained dozens of students who carried
his message to others. His study of rock formations led him to challenge the reigning opinion among the geologists he knew. They believed that rocks had an igneous origin, usually the product of volcanic activity. Werner dissented, and pointed instead to their
aquatic derivations. He theorized that nearly all formations that one
could find on the surface of the earth derived from crystallization
from the planet's oceans. In a publication in 1787, Werner listed four
categories of rocks. Only those in the volcanic group did he acknowledge to have derived from intense subterranean heat. All the
other categories—primitive, sedentary, and alluvial—came from the
other process.

And how did this happen? Werner conjectured that a vast briny
ocean once covered the earth, but that its waters had receded over
time. Rocks crystallized or formed from chemical precipitation.
Werner described further stages that formed the different categories
of rocks, but he also posited a recurring resurgence of the waters.
The different stages also concurred with succeeding life formations,
fish preceding mammals. Even allowing for a crude summary, the
Wernerian theory seems simplistic and implausible. Where did the

waters go? Into some cavernous openings at the bottom of the seas? What caused the waters to come rushing back, forming these "mighty inundations"?

That Werner and the "catastrophists" who carried his ideas had such an appeal takes us to critical questions in eighteenth-century science, for this interpretation gained wide religious sanction— church endorsements, in short. The Neptunists did not make great demands of time. They marked off earth history by dramatic events that brought sudden transformations. All this change might have occurred, then, within the assumed biblical framework of some six to ten thousand years of earth's existence. And for added measure, did not Wernerian science, with its watery stages of natural history, provide a parallel account, and in fact an endorsement, of the biblical account of the Flood? Indeed, here was an orthodoxy that science in the Christian era had not seen necessary to challenge. That era was about to expire, but for now, the Neptunists perpetuated a religious imposition on acceptable scientific theory.

Other ways of thinking about these matters were also gaining attention. A rival school, the uniformitarians, began to emerge. An important point of departure occurs with the bold presentations of a Frenchman, the imaginative Comte de Buffon. Born in 1707 as George Louis Leclerc, Buffon became a member of the Royal Academy of Sciences in Paris at age twenty-six. His travels in England gained him greater familiarity with Newtonian science, which he championed with translations of works that reflected that system. In 1739 he became intendant of the Royal Garden and keeper of the Royal Cabinet of Natural History.

Buffon's *Histoire Naturelle* appeared in 1749. In it, he specifically challenges Linnaeus's system. Any quest for a natural system of classification must meet defeat, Buffon believed. The very prospect, he said, was rooted in "metaphysical error," for it misconstrued the essential nature of life and its plant and animal forms. Classification, Buffon said, contained nature in fixed forms, abstract ideas in the mind of a Creator, and other intellectual principles that effectively froze it into hard and fast categories. "The error consists of a failure to understand nature's processes, which always take place by gradations," wrote

Buffon. For when one traverses Linnaeus's great scale, descending from the highest living forms to the lowest, one does so by imperceptible steps, Buffon asserted. One form differentiates itself from the next by the minutest of variations, Buffon observed. Thus, the recourse to designations by such demarcations as genera and species become wholly misleading and inherently inaccurate. Such convictions led Buffon to a key point: "There will be found a great number of intermediate species, and of objects belonging half in one class and half in another. Objects of this sort, to which it is impossible to supply a place, necessarily render vain the attempt at a universal system."

Buffon's significance lies not only in his speculations but in his methodology. Buffon, hostile as he was to the Christian depiction of Creation, proclaimed that the study of nature had reached the point where it should move away from religious influence. The true scientist, he averred, will leave the understanding of God to theologians and confine his activities to the most acute observations of nature. He charged contemporary scientists, such as William Whiston, with a fruitless preoccupation with the Flood and recourse to such catastrophic events as the key markings in the earth's chronology. Buffon made no biblical references in his treatise and furthermore argued that earth history had occurred by natural processes that any observer could recognize. Thus he wrote: "We ought not to be affected by causes which seldom act, and whose action is always sudden and violent. These have no place in the ordinary course of nature. But operations uniformly repeated, motions which succeed one another without interruption, are the causes which alone ought to be the foundation of our reasoning." In the successive chapters of his book, Buffon always shows how slow and gradual operations contributed to terrestrial changes over time, considerable time, in fact. He recognizes the effects of the ocean, but never allows dramatic events, such as the sudden rising and recession of the seas, to be the causal factor. The same laws, he insists, worked from the beginning of time down to the present; hence *uniformitarianism*. Buffon was laying the foundations of modern science.

In his helpful study of "Darwin's Century," Professor Eiseley shows how Buffon incorporated, however unsystematically, every important ingredient of Darwin's later evolutionary hypothesis. Buffon, for example, placed species heavily into their environmental milieu and described the struggle for survival that takes place in that setting. He recognized a tendency for animals (with their "unlimited fecundity") to reproduce faster than their available food supply. He saw that within a species (however slippery that term may be) there are variations. Buffon also perceived that mutations might be passed on to successive progeny. Then, too, Buffon speculated that the different varieties of forms that we see in profusion now do all reflect certain primal patterns that far antedate them. Eiseley saw a bold speculation here. Buffon wrote that "each family, as well in animals as in vegetables, comes from the same origin, and even that all animals are come from one species" which over time had produced "all the races of animals which now exist." Here we have a specific hypothesis of development, or what later scientists will call evolution.

Buffon made another key step in the direction of modern evolution when he expanded the duration of earth history. He tells his readers that it may have taken some seventy thousand years just for the earth to cool from a fiery state to the moderate temperatures necessary to sustain life. And another, roughly equal amount of time, may cool the earth to the point where it can no longer sustain life. No glorious millennium here. In fact, he warns, the cooling process may already have induced the expiration of some species. So in Buffon we also have a confirmation of extinction, also vital to Darwinian evolution.

Buffon had no easy time of it. His ideas scandalized the Catholic Church in France. He had somehow managed to get the first three volumes of his history published before he brought out the fourth. But then the church authorities compelled him to publish a retraction of those volumes. Also, the theological faculty at the University of Paris insisted that Buffon avow that he "had no intention of contradicting the text of Scripture" and that he personally believed everything that it said about Creation with respect both to time and the order of activity it described. A quarter century later Buffon issued his large-scale project, *Epochs of Nature*. He periodized the earth's history, but we note that he carefully selected six epochs, thus creating a scientific parallel to the six days that the book of Genesis assigned to God's schedule in creating the universe. Furthermore, Buffon took pains to point out that correspondence. However, the professors at the Sorbonne, still suspicious, did not buy it.

One other matter with respect to Buffon. As his studies blurred the distinctions between species, so he blurred the distinctions between man and ape. Although he did allow for a divine spirit in *Homo sapiens*, he also insisted on the stark proximity of the lowest form of human and the highest of the simians. Indeed, by the time of Buffon's death in 1788, the precise classification schemes were beginning to crumble. Jean-Jacques Rousseau and Lord Monboddo both conjoined man and the higher apes in the same species. Charles Bonnet closely compared the physical likeness and intelligence of the orangutan with humans. With respect to both matters, he said, "We are astonished to see how slight and how few are the differences, and how manifold and how marked are the resemblances." And finally Linnaeus himself reached these conclusions. Repeatedly he issued new editions of *Systema Naturae* and increasingly he had to narrow the gaps between species. But more, he saw new varieties appear spontaneously and "abnormal" plants derived from normal ones. He became convinced that new species could emerge from crossbreeding. In these later editions of his famous work, he discreetly expunged confidant references to the ancient origin of all species. The natural world now seemed far more in flux and unstable than it had a half-century before.

Before the century expired, however, it received its most impressive and resolute statement of the uniformitarian principles. James Hutton delivered the goods in 1795 with the publication of his *Theory of the Earth*, even though he had expressed his views, and seen them attacked, earlier. Hutton was a Scotsman, born in Edinburgh in 1726, the son of a merchant. He had the financial means to indulge his passion for geology and made several excursions to learn more about the earth's history. Given the prevalence of the Neptunists in European circles, Hutton's conclusions offered them a direct challenge. He concluded, in essence, that their theories were full of water. Instead, Hutton located the critical agency of terrestrial change in heat. In this account he described thermodynamic forces under the crust of the earth. They created stresses and pressures that induced gradual shifting and imperceptive movements of rock, soil, and sand. The expansive power of heat explained virtually everything for Hutton. He pointed to bent and tilted strata that, he insisted, could not be explained by the Wernerian recourse to the rising and falling of the seas. Hutton offered other reasons for the more convincing role of heat as opposed to water in explaining rock patterns under the earth. Buffon had dismissed the effects of a great flood; Hutton dismissed the very occurrence of it. There simply never had been a universal flood.

Hutton impaired his influence by his laborious and stilted writing style, but on occasion he could rise to high eloquence. He did so when he stood back to measure the collective impact of his *Theory*. Herewith his most quoted lines:

> Thus . . . from the top of the mountain to the shore of the sea . . . everything is in a state of change; the rock and solid strata slowly dissolving, breaking and decomposing, for the purposes of becoming soil; the soil traveling along the surface of the earth on its way to the shore; and the shore itself wearing and wasting by the agitation of the sea, an agitation which is essential to the purposes of a living world. Without those operations which wear and waste the coast, there would not be wind and rain; and without those operations which wear and waste the solid land, the surface of the earth would become sterile.

Despite the reaction against him, Hutton did not consider his ideas to be at all antireligious. Quite the contrary. The earth reflected for him a wonderful, self-perpetuating process, cyclical patterns that enabled the existence of life and its sustenance over millions of years, the assurance of a benevolent deity behind it all. Hutton belonged to a group of intellectuals in Edinburgh who were sustaining Scotland's remarkable Enlightenment in the eighteenth century. It had made its best achievements, and secured its widest influence, in philosophy. Francis Hutcheson and Thomas Reid at Glasgow University and Dugald Stewart at the University of Edinburgh provided that influence, to say nothing of the man who was also their great foil, David Hume. Adam Smith and Adam Ferguson also fortified the Scottish ranks. Several of these thinkers constituted a moderate party in the Church of Scotland that moved the Calvinist Presbyterianism of that church into a more rational theism and a human-based moral science. As such they reflected directions in religion elsewhere, especially in England where the latitudinarians in the church were fostering a rational Anglicanism. Hutton, indeed, was reinforcing the religiosity inspired by Sir Isaac Newton. Enlightenment thinkers, the deists, often described a God who was an ingenious creator, builder of the world machine, a deity who created with such perfection that things thereafter moved quite on their own.

Hutton certainly gave one that sense. The dissolution of rock, he explained, helped make the soil, the soil allowed plants to grow; the plants sustained life, feeding the animals that served human beings in their labor and their nourishment. Here Hutton saw a marvelous harmony, all the work of God, but for the benefit of man, too. "What a comfort to man," Hutton wrote, "for whom that system was contrived. . . . What a comfort, I say, to think that the Author of our existence has given such evident marks of his good-will toward man."

Hutton, however, had left the domain of orthodoxy, and would pay the price. For his theory, and indeed modern evolutionary thinking itself, required a vast extension of time. How otherwise could such gradual, painstaking change, secure such momentous transformations in natural history? Only by having limitless time to do so. Hutton made no speculations about the creation, but he knew that the earth must be millions of years old. We have, he wrote, "no vestige of a beginning—no prospect of an end." In fact, Hutton cannot be judged an evolutionist. He saw no reason to assume extinctions of species or successions of life after the original creation. Such was his strict uniformitarianism.

His religious affirmations notwithstanding, Hutton's theory met vehement criticism. Richard Kirwan, president of the Royal Irish Academy, assaulted the first offering of Hutton's idea, even before the *Theory* appeared. He expressed horror at Hutton's agnosticism respecting the origins of the world and asserted that the biblical account is all we need. Kirwan adhered to a strict Wernerian outline in making his case. Thus, he wrote, we have "darkness on the face of the day" at the primal moment, and the spirit of God moving on the face of the waters signifies "the great *evaporation* that took place soon after the creation, as soon as the solids began to crystallize." Interlaced among Kirwan's supposed science, ridicule of Hutton and misrepresentation of his presentation abounded.

Hutton registered eighteenth-century rationalism but the Enlightenment, in science and politics, had its radical side, too. Peter J. Bowler's studies describe how the various concepts of evolution, in this century and more so in the next, never stood aloof from the social and political matters of the day. "Radicals," hostile to the establishment of church and state, described the world as a product of random behavior, dissociated from any governing deity or supernatural design. Thus in 1748 Julien Offray de La Mettrie, in his treatise *Man a Machine*, provided a very materialistic reading of things. He dismissed mind, or soul, as distinct spiritual entities and related all such notions to the body. France provided radical pronunciations far more abundantly than did England. Baron D'Holbach and Denis Diderot, compiler of the famous *Encyclopedia*, challenged establishment science. They pictured a universe open, unstructured, and unregulated by any benevolent oversight. Life, Diderot insisted, reflects more of trial and error than a divine presence that assures progress and improvement. These more extreme views notwithstanding, we should bear in mind Bowler's admonition: The eighteenth century almost consistently avoided any implication of man with the lower forms of life. "The possibility that humans might have emerged from an animal ancestry was unthinkable for most eighteenth-century thinkers."

Wernerian science remained ascendant in Great Britain and even had its major voice in Hutton's own Edinburgh. Robert Jameson was regius professor of natural history at the university and keeper of its popular museum. He published his *System of Mineralogy* in 1804. Jameson also gave lectures on the campus that attracted many of the local citizens and thus disseminated Wernerian views to a large audience. Here again science seems to have been affected by the day's politics. Voices like Buffon and Hutton had a direct association with the liberal and radical ideas of the Enlightenment, which in turn now suffered amid the fears created by the French Revolution and the Terror that followed. Great Britain fell into a more conservatively religious mood and the catastrophists gained by offering a more dramatically supernatural version of contemporary science.

But the competition continued. And if Darwin later had his "bull-dog" in Thomas Huxley, Hutton had his in John Playfair. Hutton died in 1797, but Playfair immediately took up his cause. He was professor of mathematics and natural philosophy at Edinburgh and in 1802 presented *Earth Illustrations of the Huttonian Theory of the Earth*. He commands our attention not just for his defense of Hutton but because he tried to have modern science make a decisive turn. Playfair urged the full separation of science and religion. The Bible, he argued, spoke to man's moral duty and to human destiny. It did not and could not assume the burden of explaining natural history. Its pronunciations on matters of creation and its assumptions about time impose no demands on our understanding of nature, Playfair urged. We grant to the astronomer and the mathematician, he said, the "liberty of speculation" to pursue their studies, so why should the geologist not have the same freedom? Playfair saw the worst effects of this religion-science partisanship in the constraints scientists faced in investigating the age of the earth. Why should we try to cram all earth history into six thousand years? he asked. The effort, Playfair feared, became more absurd the more scientific research unraveled the facts of this subject. Playfair also suggested that this constraint distorted religion, too. We should not be obsessed with when things began, he urged, but should let the amazing facts of nature illustrate for us on their own the wonderful creativity and the beautiful artwork of God.

CLOSER TO DARWIN

There is a wonderful moment in Thomas Jefferson's *Notes on the State of Virginia*, a series of letters that he wrote to a friend in France in the 1780s. Jefferson, who smarted from the allegation of the Comte de Buffon that America produced smaller and inferior animals than did Europe, refuted him. He offered many proofs to the contrary. And then he added: "The bones of the mammoth [or mastodon] which have been found in America, are as large as those found in the old world." Later, when Jefferson instructed William Clark and Meriwether Lewis before their famous trip to explore the West, he urged that they look for the big mammoth. Nothing unusual here, perhaps. But we might note Jefferson's confidence that he could see such a beast in America, that if the bones were here then this species might also be flourishing somewhere in this part of the world. More importantly, we note that Jefferson seems not to have considered seriously the possibility that the evidence in question, these massive bones, might belong to a species now extinct.

The time was near, however, when a fossil record would assume central stage in the effort to understand natural history. Evidence was mounting rapidly that pointed to types of animal life that once existed on the earth but did no longer. As individuals explored more parts of the world, it seemed all the more demonstrable that these forms no longer inhabited the globe. The decisive turn came from an Englishman, William Smith. Smith made his living as an engineer and surveyor, a practical geologist who investigated coal deposits in the years of industrial expansion in England. Smith noticed that areas where he worked revealed different layers, or strata, of animal remains. In 1817, Smith, a reluctant writer, published his book *The Stratigraphical System of Organized Fossils*. He did not intend to enter the theoretical debates between the catastrophists and uniformitarians, and, to be sure, neither school had paid much attention to the fossil record. Smith did, however, confirm an epochal history. He wrote: "Each layer of these fossil organized bodies must be considered as a separate creation, or is an undiscovered part of an older creation." Smith then would seem to have given more persuasion to the catastrophists: "By the use of fossils we are carried back into a region of supernatural events," he added. For scientists, Smith dramatically exposed a whole new arena for investigating the record of life.

In England and France scientific thinking moved, however slowly, toward modern evolution. Among the contributors we find Charles Darwin's grandfather, Erasmus Darwin. He had written his widely noted *Zoonamia, or, the Laws of Organic Life* from 1794 to 1796. The elder Darwin suggested that animal drives of hunger and lust led to the accumulation of physiological assets that secure these needs. He exemplified the process: "Beasts of prey have acquired strong jaws or talons. Cattle have acquired a rough tongue and a rough palate to pull off the blades of grass." Erasmus postulated a "Great First Cause," an original organic form endowed with the capacity to acquire new components by which it continued to improve "by its own inherent activity," passing on new beneficial traits to its posterity on a course of continued improvement.

Actually, Charles paid his grandfather's ideas little heed. Some believe that Erasmus anticipated another individual whom Darwin took more seriously—the Frenchman Jean-Baptiste Lamarck. At Edinburgh Darwin had in Professor Robert Grant an appreciative follower of Lamarck. Born in 1744, the Frenchman was older than Erasmus by thirteen years. He came from a family with more of title than of means and his work led to his appointment as botanist to King Louis XVI in 1781 and, after he survived the Revolution, to the position of professor of zoology at the Museum of Natural History in Paris. Lamarck did clearly make contributions to the advancing idea of evolution. He strongly contended for mutability of species and made the environment a critical factor in the process. The Chain of Being took another hit from Lamarck; it became a viable notion, he said, only because Linnaeus and others could not supply the recent data that were now filling the gaps between the sharp rungs of the ladder, which in fact now looked more like a slide. Darwin would take a great interest in Lamarck because, like Buffon, he highlighted the environment as the force behind organic changes. Lamarck clearly took evolution in the naturalistic direction that marks the shift from the eighteenth to the nineteenth century.

"Lamarckism" would later become a kind of stigma, however, because of the Frenchman's theory of acquired characteristics. Lamarck postulated that organisms, in adjusting to their environments, can acquire structural changes and in turn pass them on to their young. The classic Lamarckian case references the giraffe, whose stretching to reach fruit atop the trees from which it feeds, elongates its neck, a change passed onto its progeny. How species confront their environment thus determines their physical shapes; needs will determine the appearance of an animal's organs. Inactivity also yields change, Lamarck believed. Bears lose their teeth because they swallow their food whole. Although Lamarck described a hierarchy of life, he suggested that a tree provides a better analogy of life history and animal varieties. Survival of the fittest also figures in Lamarck's ideas. He cited the "rapid multiplication of the small species," and especially of the less perfect ones. They would have impaired the species' collective survival "if nature had not taken precautions to restrain [their] multiplication." But animals devour each other, except the "stronger and the better equipped." In the long run, Darwin found Lamarck unsatisfactory, but he did say that "Lamarck was the Hutton of geology," a man of profound judgments but few clear facts.

Enter the remarkable Georges Cuvier. He would make of the fossil record a comprehensive construction that none in his day could rival as he advanced the new science of comparative anatomy. Cuvier was the son of a Swiss army officer, had studied in Germany, and had come to Paris in 1796. There he began his extensive publications, including his *Theory of the Earth* in 1815. "The task assigned me," as Cuvier described his work, led him to reconstruct the past in all its varieties, bone by bone. His reconstruction efforts amazed his contemporaries, for Cuvier needed but a few pieces to visualize and replicate the whole animal. He furthermore knew that he was entering into a very distant past, of species long vanished from sight, and revealing therefore a whole extended record of the plan of life.

What did he conclude? First, the evidence he offered demonstrated for him a catastrophic earth history, and Cuvier's writings, as Charles Coulston Gillispie summarized them, constituted "the scientific bible of Catastrophism." "The lands once laid dry," Cuvier wrote, "have been reinundated several times." He believed that either the risings of the seas or transient floods did the work. Lands where people now lived had earlier sustained quadrupeds, birds, plants, and "terrestrial productions of all types." Furthermore, Cuvier concluded that these events were "revolutions" of the earth, not gradual changes. Cuvier acquired these convictions by observing that some animals that he had found still bore pieces of flesh, skin, and hair on their skeletons. In other words, they had had no chance to putrefy or decompose by exposure to the air. Here in Cuvier is catastrophism fully on display: "Life in those times was often disturbed by these frightful events. Numberless living things were victims of such catastrophes: some, inhabitants of the dry land, were engulfed in deluges; others, living in the heart of the seas, were left stranded when the ocean floor was suddenly raised up again; and whole races were destroyed forever, leaving only a few relics which the naturalist can scarcely recognize." Cuvier confirmed the reality of extinction, and he postulated a very distant past in the animal creation. He enhanced the case for catastrophism, to be sure, but the era had dawned when one could no longer secure a precise match with the biblical record. Cuvier insisted that scientific and religious knowledge in no way informed each other. He made no reference to scripture, or even to God, though for many years the churchgoing Cuvier served as vice president of the Protestant Bible Society of Paris. Nor did Cuvier miss any opportunities to fault the materialistic thinking of Buffon and others. For Cuvier, fossils disclosed an ancient history. He nonetheless believed that the present race of humans could not have existed more than six thousand years.

Cuvier brings science closest to Darwinism in his views respecting the patterns of life. On the one hand, the extinct species impressed him by the connections they revealed with living forms. Thus for Cuvier the "same continuity of design" as we see in life now extends across the "enormous time gulfs of the past." However, for Cuvier the Great Chain of Being could no longer hold. Cuvier saw continuity, but perceived it within several distinct patterns, not one single pattern that conjoined all species. Specifically, he recognized four such separate groups: the Vertebrates, the Mollusca, the Articulata, and the Radiata. These did not fit into one another and not into one ascending interconnection. With this allowance, Cuvier did observe transition, but he rejected transmutation, and ridiculed his rival Lamarck for arguing for it. The pattern of change over time, he believed, denoted one of transitions toward increasing complexity in each of the historic epochs and within each category. Cuvier thus provided a critical advance toward modern evolution by this notion of biological progressionism, or organic succession, but, with his insisting on sharp breaks and well-defined eras, he fell short of it on the crucial matter of descent. Edward J. Larson writes: "In all his extensive study of fossils, Cuvier perceived only distinct species that persisted without change, never a gradual blurring of one type into another."

However, in this subject, we are forever in the realm of uncertainty and dissent. Charles Lyell became another important step to Darwinism, but he stood emphatically athwart the views of Cuvier. Lyell was a Scotsman by birth. He practiced law for a while but pursued his greater interest traveling and gathering information that led to publication of his three-volume work, *Principles of Geology*, beginning in 1830. Lyell, far less the "hands on" investigator than Smith or Cuvier, built upon a large accumulation of evidence since Hutton and it all confirmed in his judgment the validity of uniformitarianism. In fact, Lyell upheld it with a vengeance and enhanced it with the emerging record of the fossils. For that record did not reveal for Lyell, as it did for Cuvier, physical laws that operated then differently from the way they do now. "All former changes of the organic and inorganic creation are referrible to one interrupted succession of physical events, governed by laws now in operation," Lyell wrote.

Lyell seemed to recoil from everything that threatened the uniformitarian prescription. It alone, he believed, assures a reasonable and not a capricious God who prevails over nature. A deity who keeps changing the way things work commanded no reverence from Lyell. In his major study he expressed the hope that his work would "sink the diluvialists, and in short, all the theological sophists." Lyell, however, had no truck for the religious detractors, like the French skeptics of the previous century; Voltaire, he said, misread science in order to discredit scripture. Lyell wished essentially that religion and science kept to their respective domains, for when they extend them they only distort the true record. He lamented that popular misconceptions with respect to time had long impeded scientists in gaining credibility for their views. In one of his letters Lyell refers to the "liberal" camp in geology. He meant those who did not view earth history from within the long reach of the biblical story. If a great flood had occurred, he wrote, it was but a local one, probably from a lake. And, showing an apparent deference to the scriptures, he then recalled that a dove had returned to the ark bearing an olive branch. Hence, the flood could not have covered all the earth.

Historians of science have often observed that Lyell had all the evidence he needed to formulate a modern theory of evolution. He recorded the great age of the earth and of the life histories on it. He knew that species had become extinct. He even perceived the key factor of environmental influence and change: Ecological changes may explain readjustments of fauna over wide areas, he thought. They may also be the key factor in extinction of species. Human beings, he surmised, might have had an exclusive place of origin, one where physically stronger species did not exist, thus allowing time for the human advance in intellect to occur. And, in a struggle for existence, Lyell noted, stronger species move into one environment and destroy those inhabiting it. Darwin read Lyell with great fascination.

Lyell, however, rejected Cuvier's progressionism and used the fossil record to discredit any idea that species succeed one another over time. Here, Lyell's aggressive uniformitarianism proved an obstacle. For Lyell succession threatened the great continuity of design on which his system seemed to depend. However, he had to overlook his own evidence and he addressed the matter rather vaguely. The uniformitarians could be as inflexible as the catastrophists, but, we shall see, each contributed to the Darwinian formulation, and this despite the fact that the first group would generally line up on Darwin's side and the second group against him. Catastrophism did, however, reflect a distinctly more supernatural quality than uniformitarianism in the minds of those individuals, from scientists to the general public, who contemplated and reacted to these two schools.

This chapter concludes with a brief look at two very speculative thinkers: Robert Chambers and Herbert Spencer. Robert Chambers produced a book in 1844 titled *Vestiges of the Natural History of Creation*, and it changed the discussion concerning evolution. Religious voices all over Great Britain reacted in outrage against it. Scientists were intrigued, but unconvinced. Chambers certainly did get attention. This Scotsman, who came from the Peebles region south of Edinburgh, had a curious beginning. He and his brother William were both hexadactyls, born with six digits on their hands and feet. The two entered the publishing business in Edinburgh and produced works full of local history and color that had a sizeable readership among the literate working classes in the Mechanics' Institute in their city. *Chambers' Edinburgh Journal* exemplified the democratic intellect of Scotland in the middle nineteenth century. Its articles and essays, many of them written by the brothers, addressed various subjects, from industry, to science, to morality. The journal's appeal convinced Robert Chambers that his audience would welcome some bold new ideas.

Chambers retreated to Aberdeen in the northeast, telling only a few people about his enterprise, and there wrote *Vestiges*, which he published anonymously. In it, Chambers hypothesized a "single origin" of all earthly life. He employed the term "development," which for a while was the word of choice for "evolution." Chambers gave progressionism a strong statement; each higher form of life emerges from a lower form, he claimed. Lest that notion seem startling to his readers, Chambers appealed to ontogeny, the embryonic growth of an organism, as likened to phylogeny, the history of life forms antedating the particular species in question. (Hence, "ontogeny recapitulates phylogeny.") And Chambers included man within this process. *Homo sapiens*, he said, are the highest form of life, the ultimate stage, the end point of development, to date. He called man "the type of all types of the animal kingdom." He went even further. He rejected the idea that humans have a dual nature, that they have both a biological and a spiritual being. Chambers related all the "higher faculties" of humans to the improving sensory powers of lower forms, with which they share a qualitative identity. Man did thus emerge from the lesser species on the scale of being.

Did Chambers think his theory offensive to religion? By no means. In fact, he wanted to give a religious assurance to any troubled by the new views in science. The entire process of "development," he asserted, celebrated the genius and foresight of the Creator. His system constituted a kind of deism with progression. God created with foresight, and nature goes on to complete his great design. Development anticipates its high point in man's emergence, also its crowning point. And as such, man reflects God's nature, for God creates this perfected species in his own image. No degradation attaches to humans' development from lower forms, in Chambers' view. Does not the human embryo pass through the lower stages? he reiterated. Chambers' theory was thus emphatically teleological; natural history proceeds with an end in view, and all in an orderly manner. God created by an act of mind and with a plan in view; all holds true to form thereafter. Chambers thus offered this assurance: "When all is seen to be the result of law, the idea of an Almighty Author becomes irresistible, for the creation of a law for an endless series of phenomena—an act of intelligence above all else that we can conceive—could have no other imaginable source."

Despite the overwhelming rejection of Chambers' ideas by other scientists, he did bring evolutionary thinking closer to Darwin. His book got a huge public reading and, as historians like Peter J. Bowler believe, prepared the way for the acceptance of Darwin. *Vestiges* prompted people to think of the long procession of life and at least consider the possibility of not only its extended interconnections but the derivation of one form from another. Darwin's explanation for why derivation occurred differed fundamentally from Chambers' theistic and teleological formulation, of course. And therein lay Darwin's dangerous idea.

By the middle century, evolutionary thinking had attained such currency as to write itself into formal philosophy. It took the prolific Herbert Spencer, however, to render it into a vast and inclusive system. Spencer first outlined his laissez-faire ideal in *Social Statics*, his book of 1851. He coined the expression "survival of the fittest" in

1864. (Darwin had not employed these terms.) Spencer saw all existence locked in a competitive struggle that guaranteed the progress and improvement of the species if permitted to take a natural course. The British thinker eagerly applied his outlook to human society and became a champion of laissez-faire economics, the libertarian doctrine of the minimal state, and an ethics of individualism. These applications will concern us more later. But Spencer did more. In a seemingly endless parade of volumes, he wrote his *Synthetic Philosophy*. Its details have little relevance here, save for the overriding characteristic of the system, its cosmic outlook. Spencer integrated all life into a grand unity and conjoined all to a scheme of nature that worked within its own vehicle of assured progress. Spencer, favorably impressed by Lamarck, adhered to a teleological vision of the universe and belonged to the late pattern of grand metaphysical thinking that flourished in the eighteenth and nineteenth centuries. Life had clear and knowable ends, a purposeful direction.

Darwin would influence a different kind of evolutionary thinking. In fact, he and Spencer registered starkly different habits of thought. Darwin read Spencer and remained unmoved and uninfluenced by him. He remarked in his unpublished autobiography that "I am not conscious of having profited in my own work by Spencer's writing. His deductive manner of treating every subject is wholly opposed to my frame of mind." Where Spencer saw purpose and plan, Darwin saw contingency and chance, openness and flux, and blind mechanical processes. Darwin did not initiate what F. D. David, Ian Hacking, and other scholars have recently come to call the "probabilistic revolution" in Western thought, but he influenced greatly the new direction in antideterminist thinking, and no more significantly than among American thinkers that will receive attention later.

BIBLIOGRAPHY

Bowler, Peter J. *Evolution: The History of an Idea*. 3rd ed. Berkeley: University of California Press, 2003.

Eiseley, Loren. *Darwin's Century: Evolution and the Men Who Discovered It.* Garden City, NY: Doubleday, 1961.

Gillispie, Charles Coulston. *Genesis and Geology: A Study in the Relations of Scientific Thought, Natural Theology, and Social Opinion in Great Britain, 1790–1850.* New York: Harper & Row, 1951.

Greene, John C. *The Death of Adam: Evolution and Its Impact on Western Thought.* Ames: Iowa State University Press, 1959.

Larson, Edward J. *Evolution: The Remarkable History of a Scientific Theory.* New York: The Modern Library, 2004.

Lovejoy, Arthur O. *The Great Chain of Being: A Study in the History of an Idea.* New York: Harper & Brothers, 1936.

Young, David. *The Discovery of Evolution.* Cambridge: Cambridge University Press, 1992.

DARWIN'S DANGEROUS IDEA

A YOUNG MAN'S INTELLECTUAL WORLD

In his book *Darwin's Dangerous Idea*, Daniel C. Dennett wrote: "In due course, the Darwinian Revolution [like the Copernican and Galilean] will come to occupy a . . . similarly secure and untroubled place in the minds—and hearts—of every educated person on the globe, but today, more than a century after Darwin's death, we still have not come to terms with its mind-boggling implications." This is a bold statement. In some quarters Darwinism remains as controversial and as contested as it was at the time Darwin died. It will take a mighty shift of opinion to effect the kind of universal consent that Dennett so confidently anticipates. We must confine ourselves in this study to little more than a half century of intellectual ferment after the publication of Darwin's *Origin of Species* in 1859, and our focus on the United States will supply plenty of material to consider. We do well, however, to begin with a look at this remarkable book, how Darwin came to write it, and the controversies that ensued.

Charles Darwin did not find his way easily to his career in science. No one in his immediate family encouraged him to follow such a path. Little in his formal education inspired him to study the natural world. As with his famous theory itself, there is more accident than plan in his becoming the great theorist he was. Darwin's life does, however, constitute one of the most significant intellectual biographies of modern history. He did not discover evolution; by this date, as we have observed, the literature on the subject was vast. But Darwin got the world's attention, and he has kept it, because he dramatically changed the terms of discussion. From now on attention would focus not so much on the evidence of biological change as on the means by which the change occurred. Everything in the literature, Darwin believed, failed in this one respect: It did not explain, it did not describe a process, a mechanism of evolution. By the end of the 1830s, Darwin knew he was on to something. Two decades later he would tell the world what it was.

The Darwins came from the Lincolnshire area of England. We first take note of them in the 1500s, a yeomen family in this region. Charles's grandfather Erasmus, as noted, became the first to win recognition for this line. He himself contributed ideas about evolution and pursued a spectacularly successful career as a country doctor in the several towns of the Midland sections near Birmingham. His son—Charles's father, Robert Waring Darwin—also became a country physician, and also enjoyed success and prosperity. Born in 1776, the fourth of five children and the only one from Erasmus's first marriage to survive into maturity, he established his practice in Shrewsbury, but also enhanced his income through private money brokering. Robert married Susanna Wedgwood, from a family famous for its china plate ware that had worked their way to wealth in this classic era of English industrialization. Susanna brought a large sum of money into the marriage. As Janet Browne writes: "[Charles] Darwin's parents typified everything that is known about the emergent entrepreneurial society of early industrial England, a classic example of the way wealthy merchants of the professional and manufacturing classes created a significant niche for themselves in a changing world."

Robert Darwin had fast Whig political loyalties but few religious allegiances. Information about Susanna yields a scant record, however. She gave birth to Charles, the fifth of her six children, on February 12, 1809. (Darwin shares a birth date with Abraham Lincoln.) Charles lost his mother eight years later. Robert, never at ease in expressing his emotions, withdrew even more into himself in reaction to the loss. Gertrude Himmelfarb, one of Darwin's biographers, paints a consistently unhappy portrait of relations between Charles and his father. Robert was "tyrannical and unsympathetic," she writes, exercising an imperious authority in the family and seeking to manage all details of his children's lives. From the time he started school, and perhaps in reaction also to his mother's death, Charles went on long walks by himself, deep in thought as he strolled the countryside.

School failed to capture young Darwin's interest. The year after his mother's death, Charles switched from a day school in Shrewsbury to a more respected boarding school in that town. Here he confronted a program laden with classical studies. Throughout the week students read the Greeks: Thucydides and Plato, Aristotle and Demosthenes, Aeschylus and Sophocles, and Homer. And throughout the week the students also read the Romans: Cicero and Virgil, Tacitus and Horace, Juvenal and Longinus. Charles found all these studies remote and irrelevant to his interests. Nor did his later life alter a stark and negative judgment of this education. "Nothing could have been worse for the development of my mind," he wrote, "than Dr. Butler's school, as it was strictly classical, nothing else being taught, except a little ancient geography and history. The school as a means of education to me was simply a blank." So Charles forged his own interests. He loved to go hunting and increasingly he found an enthusiasm for animals and also for the rocks he observed on his country strolls. He started to collect specimens—different kinds of rocks, different kinds of insects. His father believed more than ever that he had reared a useless son. "You care for nothing but shooting, dogs, and rat-catching," he told him, "and you will be a disgrace to yourself and all your family."

But Robert did not give up on Charles. He had his son work with him in his medical practice and then resolved that he go north to Edinburgh to take up studies at the University Medical School. Robert himself had studied there and so also his father, Erasmus. Now, in 1826, Charles joined his brother, who remained for him at the university his best, indeed, virtually his only close friend. The new undertaking, however, reflected no commitment on Charles's part. He had learned to do his father's will and not to question his judgment in any way. Charles would quickly determine, however, that medicine had too much blood and gore, and this sensitive young man now swore it off. He did not disavow science, however, and these years slowly forged for him a new intellectual world. Edinburgh flourished with the controversies in geology that produced the heated debates between the two schools. Charles enrolled in Robert Jameson's course, though he found it boring almost to distraction. But Jameson did have a magnificent natural history museum, with collections among the most impressive in all of Great Britain. From Jameson, Darwin got a full dose of catastrophism. His professor had founded the Wernerian Natural History Society in 1808, and in fact had studied under the German professor in Freiburg. But Charles also heard opposing views from the Vulcanist professor Thomas Hope, with whom at this time Charles sided, if for no other reason than the fact that he found Hope's lectures illustrative and exciting. However, Charles did not inspire confidence among his teachers, certainly not to the point that anyone would encourage him to augment and continue his studies in science. The next decision for Charles came, again, from his father.

Robert Darwin now believed that Charles should become a minister. He would send his son to Cambridge University. Charles accepted the decision without complaint. To be sure, he had no love for religion, but neither did he have a skepticism that might have made him balk at such a program of study. To Charles, so uncertain about his future anyway, it occurred that he might become a country parson and still live the life of a gentleman and aristocrat, indulging all the while his love for the study of nature. Anglican clergy were not universally known for their religious piety, and some pursued science as an avocation; some even made worthy contributions to it. The prospects of clerical leisure, which he would put to the discipline of study, best defined Charles's hopes as he studied the classics once again in the summer of 1827, preparing for Cambridge. Early in 1828 he headed off to the university.

Charles entered Christ's College, "a college that catered to men with much money and little liking for discipline." Students at

Christ's, and at Cambridge generally, inclined to debauchery. They drank much and they gambled heavily. They spent lavishly and took advantage of whatever maidservant in their quarters they could. Charles eluded this crowd, but scarcely reflected any enthusiasm for his academic work. Had he been an inquiring mind with respect to questions of religion he might have at least found some liking for his theological studies. He seems, however, to have simply accepted the points of Anglican Protestantism as presented. He would write that he did not "in the least doubt the strict and literal truth of every word in the Bible." Other pursuits, however, still attracted him. When the summer of 1828 came around, Charles caught the beetle craze that was then sweeping England. Books on entomology sold briskly at the stands and excursions for collecting took students to various parts of Britain in search of exotic species, all in a spirit of competition, one group against another. Above all, it was wealthy gentlemen with leisure who fueled the new fad. Charles Darwin thought he might just like this kind of life.

But one should not overlook Darwin's intellectual world at Cambridge. It had lasting influences. First, there was Professor John Stevens Henslow, thirteen years older than Darwin, and soon to become both teacher and friend. Henslow taught mineralogy but also joined causes with a group of academic and political reformers. Together with another professor that Darwin came to know well, Adam Sedgwick, Henslow and his circle represented an activist Anglicanism, the "Broad Church" party of liberal theology. Henslow and Sedgwick had started the Cambridge Philosophical Society in 1818. It gave a rededication to a long tradition, going back to Richard Hooker in the late sixteenth century, of rational religion and Anglicanism's sustained identification with natural theology. To find God, look to nature and nature's laws. William Paley, with his book *Natural Theology* in 1802, had provided the great, recent statement of this axiom. And at Cambridge, Darwin fell into this circle, at least on a social basis, and under the wing of Henslow. At club meetings and private parties, and on Sedgwick's "equestrian" outings, Darwin mingled with William Whewell and John Herschel. He even took time to read some of their works. At Cambridge, religion and science knew no enmity. Charles Darwin certainly did not see any.

Darwin's record of academic indifference at Cambridge stands, however. He needed to graduate and now that issue seemed in doubt. After two years, he stood on the brink of academic failure. He picked up the slack enough in his third year, though, made it through, and even earned a ranking of tenth among 178 students. Such was the intellectual achievement of the young Cambridge "scholars"! But what now to do?

A VOYAGE OF DISCOVERY

In December 1831 a ship departed England and headed out into the Atlantic, bound for South America. It had no military conquests in mind and planned no imperialistic adventures for the mother country. Ostensibly, it had a thoroughly prosaic purpose—to survey the lands at the tip of the continent, a project financed by the Admiralty Department in London. Of course, that design made the trip not entirely innocent. Britain, in its era of international expansion, needed information to facilitate the work of its merchant fleet, vanguard of the colonial apparatus. Anything one might learn about mineral and coal deposits would also be welcome. We know that when Captain Robert FitzRoy brought his crew into Tierra del Fuego, he inquired about possible metallic ore in this mountainous region. Not for these reasons, however, did this voyage become one of the most significant in modern history.

This ship had the name *Beagle* and Charles Darwin found himself onboard as its botanist. He had received the invitation to make the trip from John Stevens Henslow, and George Peacock, professor of astronomy at Cambridge. Darwin found the letters of invitation upon a return from North Wales and rejoiced at this opportunity. Ever dutiful, he asked his father for permission to respond affirmatively. Robert Darwin judged the prospect absurd in the extreme and detailed a lengthy list of reasons why his son should not yield to this folly. For one thing, he told Charles, it would damage your reputation as a clergyman. But he offered an escape clause. If Charles could find one person of common sense who would endorse this idea, Robert would acquiesce in it. So Charles turned to his uncle, Josiah Wedgwood, who could find no fault with the project. Perhaps what persuaded the father was Josiah's suggestion that such a trip might instill in Charles some "habits of application." Charles prepared for the voyage. "Wo unto ye beetles of South America!" he proclaimed.

The *Beagle* departed England on December 27. In the course of the long voyage, Darwin kept voluminous records. And he made discoveries that sparked his thinking. The *Beagle* made an early stop at St. Jago island, among the Cape Verde outposts some 450 miles from the African coast. Approaching the island, Darwin observed in the bluffs a white horizontal band, some forty feet above the shore, a distinctive geological mark. He studied it closely and discerned a light layer of rock formed from corals and sea shells between other layers of volcanic rock. The deductions that Darwin made convinced him that a long and gradual process described the island's history, one perfectly understandable by Lyell's theories. Darwin became a confirmed uniformitarian. Perhaps he may have been prejudiced in that direction at that time. Darwin had onboard the *Beagle* a gift of Charles Lyell's first volume of the *Principles*, a presentation to him by Captain FitzRoy. The other volumes reached him along the way.

Where did Darwin travel on the *Beagle*? It departed with a crew of seventy-three, the young naturalist among them. Charles quickly became seasick. The ship arrived at the port of Santa Cruz on Tenerife Island on January 6, 1832, but the crew stayed onboard because of a cholera outbreak in England. Ten days later the ship made the Cape Verde Islands stop and then it headed out into the full Atlantic, arriving in Salvador, Brazil, on February 28. The ship set sail again in early April to Rio de Janeiro, where the crew received its first mail from England. Here Darwin had his first opportunity to explore and he headed into the tropical forest. He returned with a collection of insects and plants that dazzled his imagination, for he saw hundreds of varieties not known to Europe. Captain FitzRoy began his surveying work in August while the ship sailed along the Patagonia coastline.

Darwin was now collecting fossils and confounding his captain when he brought onboard so many samples of "useless junk."

In December the *Beagle* passed through the strait of Le Maire at Tierra del Fuego and anchored at Good Success Bay. In March it traveled out to the Falkland Islands, which the British had just taken from Argentina. FitzRoy then took his ship back to Montevideo, Uruguay, and Darwin went down to Bahia Blanca, Argentina, in August 1833 and on to Buenos Aires. He celebrated his twenty-fifth birthday in February 1834, and to honor the occasion Captain FitzRoy named the highest mountain in the region Mount Darwin. Finally, in early April the *Beagle* sailed around Cape Horn and into the Pacific Ocean by way of the Strait of Magellan. In July it arrived at Valparaiso, Chile, near Santiago, as the surveying assignment continued. At Valdivia Darwin saw the massive destruction wrought by a huge earthquake, nearly all buildings in the area destroyed. Horrified, but also curious, Darwin detected that areas of land had risen a few feet as a result of the earthquake. The data confirmed for him Lyell's theory that landmasses rose in very small increments over extensive periods of time. That recognition also confirmed for him the great antiquity of the earth.

Darwin also explored this region of the Andes Mountains before moving with the expedition north to Lima, Peru, in July 1835. Then in September, the *Beagle* brought the party to the Galápagos Islands, which Darwin would memorialize with the multitude of evidence it provided him for the later development of his theory. On October 20 the *Beagle* set out into the expansive Pacific, heading for Tahiti. Good winds carried the voyagers some 3,200 miles to the island. What followed were stops in New Zealand in December and Sydney, Australia, in January of the next year. Tasmania and the Cocos Islands followed and then a sail around Cape Town at the southern tip of Africa. The crew now eagerly anticipated its return to England, but spirits fell when FitzRoy, fearing that he had taken faulty measurements in Bahia (Salvador), announced the need to return. He finished that work in August and the ship headed directly for England. It arrived back on October 2, 1836. A projected voyage of two years had taken four years, nine months, and five days.

The published accounts of Darwin's trip are a vast and diverse accumulation. They constitute a record of scientific observation of flora and fauna, to be sure, but they do more. Darwin encountered new people, new ways of life, and an era of history redefining the part of the world in which he moved. His memoirs of the voyage therefore make fascinating reading. His chronicles give us one of the great narratives of the travelogue genre of the nineteenth century.

In Tierra del Fuego, Darwin directly encountered the natives of South America. He gave anything but a favorable report and echoed what certainly would have been standard for English people of his day. Darwin reported in his journal and also addressed the matter in a letter to Henslow in 1833:

> The Fuegians are in a more miserable state of barbarism than I had expected ever to see a human being. In this inclement country they are absolutely naked, and their temporary houses are like what children make in summer with boughs of trees. I do not think any spectacle can be more interesting than the first sight of man in his primitive wilderness.

Darwin judged negatively the social egalitarianism he perceived among the Fuegians and contemplated how to improve this people; most plausible, he concluded, would be to reform a few at the top and start some progress among this race than to attempt redemption of them all. Darwin supported missionary work, but judged it useless, and dangerous besides, to attempt it among these natives. Yet even in these observations, one finds an evolutionary insight. The Fuegians, Darwin pronounced, were as wretched, as ugly, as forbidding as the climate and terrain in which they dwelled. And Darwin judged them well adopted and even happy to this extent. But he could not avoid a harsh judgment, one to which he would recur later in explaining natural selection: "I could not have believed how wide was the difference, between savage and civilized man." Later Darwin would make that gap greater than that between savage man and higher simian.

Of course, the longer significance of Darwin's travel came from the natural specimens he studied and brought back to England with him.

The beauty of the tropics, with its lush botanical life and the new discoveries awaiting him, overwhelmed and inspired him. And the Galápagos Islands! Such a contrast to the bleak and barren terrain of the land's end to the south. Reptiles of massive size. Tortoises so big that one man alone could barely move one. Lizards two to three feet long, black as the lava rocks with which they blended. Darwin also discovered an enthusiasm for "geologizing" and plunged more into that work upon his return. Altogether he had enough samples and data to busy himself for years to come. He pondered them all. On the various islands, located at some distance from the Central America mainland, Darwin observed something curious. The governor had tipped him off. The gigantic tortoises found on the various islands looked a little different, one island's group from another's. Then Darwin noticed that the same differentiations maintained among the birds, the finches in particular. They had beaks of slightly different lengths. Why so? Darwin did not figure it out fully until after he returned to England. But clearly, he now recognized, the tortoises and birds, after many years' habitation separate from their original, shared location on the mainland, had adapted to the particular environments of the separate islands where they had since dwelled.

TOWARD THE THEORY

Darwin had much to occupy him when he returned from the *Beagle* voyage, and his new life gave him the means to use that time fruitfully. Along the way, important personal changes occurred. In early 1839 Darwin married his cousin Emma Wedgwood, a devout Anglican, in a ritualistic Anglican service for which Darwin had little enthusiasm. Indeed, Charles had carefully kept from Emma his growing religious indifference. Emma gave birth to their first child, William, in December 1839. In all, she would bear ten children, nine within the first twelve years of their marriage. The family lived on Upper Gower Street in London; a team of servants attended to the household maintenance. Although recurringly infirm, Darwin pursued his scientific studies. He published steadily, but his work focused mostly on geology. In a paper presented to the Geological Society in 1838, Darwin argued that the Andes Mountains emerged to their heights by volcanoes and earthquakes at work over a long period of time. These operations, he said, had slowly forced the continents up from the seas; one did not need recourse to great cataclysms to explain earth history. In 1844, the growing family relocated to the country, purchasing a large but not ostentatious home at Downe, a small village in Kent, only twenty miles by coach to London. And with money from his grandfather and father, Darwin had at last realized a dream; he had become a country gentleman of means and put himself under a disciplined regime of work. And here, the man who had traveled five years around the world settled in for the remainder of his days.

In 1838 Darwin had read Thomas Malthus's *Essay on the Principle of Population*, "for amusement," as he said. He considered Malthus a major influence on him. Malthus's work had appeared in 1798 and in it Malthus described the extraordinarily productive power of nature, so prolific that biological and botanical forms would swamp all livable space on earth if other factors did not intervene to curtail the growth. One would otherwise find dandelions and frogs everywhere. Of course, predators, disease, and above all the limited food supply provide those interventions. The food supply matter especially troubled Malthus and prompted his dire prognostications about the future of humans. They also forced Darwin to wonder, why did some individuals survive and not others? Here Darwin made a key shift. While Malthus focused on the competition for existence among the different forms of life, the particular species, and the collective traits that gave them certain advantages, Darwin now looked to different individual members of the same species. Thus, the owl hunting for field mice in a given area also competes with other owls seeking the same prey. What might make one organism in that group fare more successfully than another in the same group? Darwin would now begin to focus on biological change within individual organisms.

Malthus made his study of populations a prophecy of doom for the human race: Human reproduction would outstrip the food supply.

His calculations were wrong and misleading, as Darwin well saw, but nonetheless he significantly helped Darwin toward his theory in a second way. For through Malthus, Darwin saw a vast mechanical principle at work in life. Himmelfarb effectively states this point:

> What [Darwin] took from Malthus was more than a simple mechanism for the origin of species. It was a principle governing all the processes of nature: a natural, mechanical principle operating without the conscious intervention of either human or divine agents, a principle that was self-explanatory, self-sufficient, and self-regulating. As Malthus assumed that population was always adjusting itself, without the knowledge or even against the will of men, to the inexorable pressures of space and food, so Darwin saw men, animals, and plants, responding involuntarily to the competitive conditions of life and hence involuntarily contributing to the evolutionary process, the creation of new species.

That species were mutable now became Darwin's strong conviction and the focus of his work. His notebooks, which he began in 1837, disclose parts of the full-blown theory that he formulated later. He speculated that mutations in one organism might eventually yield a new species. Furthermore, if species change in this manner, then the different species we see today must have common ancestors. If we dare to "let conjecture run wild," he wrote, then even human beings are caught in this genealogy. Our "brethren in pain, disease, and death, suffering, and famine," as he put it, "may partake our origin in one common ancestor—we may be all melted together." Upon his return from the *Beagle* expedition, Darwin had communicated with Lyell. Now in 1842, Darwin, who actually shied from telling fellow scientists his emerging thoughts, disclosed them to Lyell. He got no encouragement there. Darwin now recognized how radical a notion he harbored. He dared not discuss it even with his wife.

Darwin always feared what the public would think of his ideas, but he could not grasp why scientists shunned so simple a theory as natural selection. Now convinced that new species could emerge from accumulations of small changes over many generations, he hoped to make his explanation more convincing by the examples of selective breeding. Pigeons supplied him his best case in point. Pigeon fanciers, he showed, had over time produced remarkable new varieties, so differentiated one from another that an innocent observer, seeing them in the wild, might classify them as separate species altogether. Darwin thought this example precisely paralleled natural selection; birds with the desired traits were permitted to reproduce while the others were not. "Artificial selection" simply illustrated a conscious process that natural selection achieved unconsciously.

By the middle of the 1850s, Darwin had committed to natural selection more than ever. Some extraneous factors pushed him closer to a full disclosure of his thesis. One came from the scientific community itself. William Whewell supplied Darwin with his most outrageous example. Whewell was a professor at Cambridge and Darwin knew of him from his days there, though he did not study with him. He became president of the Geological Society, a catastrophist, who nevertheless renounced the idea of a deluge. Whewell gave the notion of "adaption" a peculiar twist when he suggested that the length of days on earth represented an "adaptation" to the normal duration of human beings' sleep. Darwin recoiled in disbelief from the very notion, and even more from the credibility which some intelligent people gave to this foolish idea. But how then might they react to so bold an idea as his own?

In 1851 Darwin suffered the death of his beloved daughter Annie, who succumbed to a long and painful illness. The tragedy took Darwin another step away from religion. However, that movement had been long underway. Darwin's notebooks from 1837 to 1844 reflect his growing naturalism. He did not describe a "soul" in human beings, but was already relating human mental and emotional habits to those of lower species. Human morality, he believed, simply registered a programming effected by natural selection. And the more Darwin saw blind chance and a process of trial and error as dominant in evolution, the less he could relate them to any notion of a careful designer or benevolent overseer in the universe. Now, the tragedy of Annie's death left Darwin without faith.

Biographers Michael White and John Gribben write: Darwin now lost "any remaining vestige of religious faith he may have had. From that moment on, Darwin was a total, uncompromising atheist: his only god was rationality, his only savior logic and science; to that end he would continue to dedicate his life. There was no meaning to existence other than a culmination of biological events. Life was selfish and cruel, headless and heartless. Beyond biology there was nothing."

Certainly little remained of any idea, on Darwin's part, that human beings reflected a special creation by some divine likeness. Darwin now saw a species barely lifted from the brutes, gaining ascendancy only by a careful process of civilizing, not by any primal enhancements. For the highest form of animal life lacked little that savage man could claim. Perhaps Darwin drew from the stark observations he had made of the Fuegian natives on his *Beagle* tour. But long after that experience Darwin made some references to the orangutan. Darwin saw a noble beast—emotionally expressive, intelligent. Consider then the sorry picture of savage man, he wrote, "roasting his parent, naked, artless, not improving yet improvable; and then let [man] dare to boast of his proud pre-eminence." Darwin then put the matter pointedly: "Man in his arrogance thinks himself a great work, worthy the interposition of a deity. More humble and I believe true to consider him created from animals."

By now, Darwin had resolved on a published version of his ideas. And despite his own reservations about these ideas, it was Lyell who encouraged Darwin to write a book rather than settle on a paper offered to a scientific society. Lyell did find a major objection to Darwin precisely on the point just considered, the place of human beings in the evolutionary scheme. Lyell could not contemplate their inclusion with the animals. Also, in 1856, Darwin outlined the essence of his theory to the American scientist Asa Gray, who urged his going forward. The next year Darwin decided that he would have the intelligentsia as his audience. He also feared that some other scientist might be developing a theory similar to his own, and he wanted to come forth with a full treatise on the subject.

NATURAL SELECTION AND THE CONTROVERSIES

It was Alfred Russel Wallace who energized Darwin finally to present his theory to fellow scientists. One day in June 1858, Darwin received a package from the remote island of Ternate in the West Indies. It came from Wallace and in his handwriting the essay within spelled out Wallace's thoughts about evolution. They coincided precisely with Darwin's. "I never saw a more striking correspondence," Darwin said, in despair. He was completely taken aback, and really did not know what to do. Darwin wrote to Lyell: "All my originality, whatever it may amount to, will be smashed." Lyell and Joseph Hooker arranged to have both Darwin's and Wallace's views read at a scientific meeting. But Darwin had the advantage. He was better connected to the scientific "establishment" in England; Wallace, an outsider and product of lower social circumstances than Darwin, was not advised of the arrangement. In fact, however, Darwin had arrived to his theory well ahead of Wallace, and he could show it by his correspondence with others in England and with Asa Gray in the United States. Some believe that it would have required several years more for Wallace to supply his paper of 1858 with the abundance of evidence that Darwin had accumulated over decades.

Darwin and Wallace treated each other very cordially. Neither wanted to foster a competition. In fact, Wallace wrote to Darwin in 1867, saying, "As to the theory of Natural selection itself I shall always maintain it to be actually yours and yours only." The years after 1859 furthermore show that Darwin and Wallace had quite different intellectual temperaments. As Darwin moved to a more emphatic naturalism, Wallace acquired supernatural convictions. By the late 1860s he had developed an interest in spiritualism and calculated that if the spirit could survive the body there must have been some spiritual intervention in the evolutionary process. Nor could he make the mental dimension of human life square with a strict explanation by way of natural selection. Humans clearly had superior intellects, an original endowment—as, for example, the capacity for abstract reasoning—that primitive society did not utilize.

Wallace now posited a late stage of evolution marked by supernatural direction and moving the human race over time toward advanced civilization.

Charles Darwin published his book *On the Origin of Species* in London in 1859. It won immediate attention, in England, Europe, and the United States. From the beginning it enjoyed a large readership, for the public, too, took an interest in Darwin's ideas. The rest of this study will consider Darwinism as an intellectual phenomenon in the United States, but it remains in this chapter to review the main ideas associated with this book and the reaction to it in England. The *Origin* would have, eventually, six editions, as Darwin constantly refined and elaborated his thesis in the face of challenges to it. In 1873 he addressed the subject of human evolution with his book *The Descent of Man.*

In explaining his understanding of evolution Darwin stated that no offspring is the exact duplicate of its parents and some changes, chance mutations, may denote a significant difference. Then Darwin set forth his key concept of natural selection. For all along he had found other accounts of evolution inadequate because they could not postulate a persuasive explanation as to why species change; in other words, these theories lacked the critical causal factors. Darwin intended through his idea of "natural selection" to make up that deficiency. By that term he simply meant that nature "selects" those changes in an organism that may improve its chances of survival, and then that organism passes them on to successive generations. Nature winnows out those organisms that are less fit by virtue of their not having these assets. "All these results," wrote Darwin, "follow from the struggle for life." Among birds, for example, a longer beak may prove advantageous in penetrating the bark of trees to reach insects; in other cases a short, heavy beak may give advantages with different kinds of trees. These facts reflect a long history of physiological change, the adaptation process, that mark the creation of new species. Thus, survival of the fittest. This process of change, recurring in successive generations, may, over a long period of time, produce a new species altogether. In fact, Darwin wrote, each newborn is potentially an "incipient species." The biological record convinced Darwin that most forms of life we see today had experienced a long history of change.

Herewith the "how" of evolution. Darwin marveled at the system, accentuating that "the innumerable species inhabiting this world have been modified, so as to acquire that perfection of structure and coadaptation which justly excites our imagination." (Note: The quotations cited are from the sixth edition of the *Origin*.) To make his point more effectively to his readers, Darwin personified nature. "It may be metaphorically said," he wrote, "that natural selection is daily and hourly scrutinizing, throughout the world, the slightest variations; rejecting those that are bad, preserving and adding up all that are good; silently and insensibly working, *whenever and wherever opportunity offers*, at the improvement of each organic being in relation to its organic and inorganic conditions of life. We see nothing of these slow changes in progress, until the hand of time has marked the lapse of ages." Darwin later regretted the anthropomorphism in this description; it smacked too much of teleology, or conscious purpose in nature.

Darwin always tried to clarify his thesis against previous ones. Robert Chambers and Herbert Spencer supplied him with two examples of grand and speculative theorizing, which he rejected. Chambers' *Vestiges of Creation* offered a system of development, but it paid no attention to the role of environment in determining how organic change passed from one generation to the next. The author of the book, Darwin charged, could assume only that species emerged perfect and in the form that we now see them. Darwin wanted to discredit that notion root and branch. Natural selection, he asserted, will "banish the belief of the continued creation of new organic beings" by way of such larger cosmic design or grand scheme of "development." Only the power of "preconceived opinion," he said, could lend any credence to the idea that at certain periods of history "certain elemental atoms" just happened to combine in "some miraculous act of creation" to form new categories of life.

On the other hand, Darwin insisted that some scientists had emphasized external causes exclusively. Organisms, contrary to Lamarck, do not will themselves into beings configured perfectly to the external conditions they face. "Naturalists," Darwin said, "continually refer to external conditions, such as climate, food &c., as the only possible source of variation." These factors do have some role, he conceded, "but it is preposterous to attribute to mere external conditions, the structure, for instance, of the woodpecker, with its feet, tail, beak, and tongue, so admirably adapted to catch insects under the bark of trees." Only the long history of chance mutations, internal causes as opposed to external, and the careful screening process attending their full incorporation into the species, or into new species, sufficed to explain such transitions, Darwin insisted. Variation, he said, would occur even if the environment remained in a steady state.

Of course, Darwin in this way considerably muddied the waters of species history. Now the lines seemed not clear at all. Species of the same genera, he said, must, in many cases, have descended from "some other and generally extinct species." What we see among us in nature today may not, millions of years ago, have looked at all like what an observer roaming the earth would have noticed then. For if life moves forward in the direction of greater change and diversity, it must look backward to fewer forms and ultimately to perhaps only a few primal ones. Darwin was setting forth one of the most controversial of his ideas, controversial among other naturalists and more so among religious thinkers. He wrote: "Probably all the organic beings which ever lived on this earth have descended from some one primordial form, into which life was first breathed."

The reaction, feared all along by Darwin, came right soon. Only a half year after the publication, the British Association for the Advancement of Science, meeting in Oxford in June 1860, produced the first verbal battle. Darwin did not attend, and in fact in the years ahead, as the battle waged, he held a sideline position, mostly as observer. The science meeting, however, brought forth the first of his field commanders, who would stage the campaign for Darwin hereafter. One was the naturalist Joseph Hooker, another was Thomas Huxley, and the third was Charles Lyell—Darwin's "Three Musketeers." Curiously, it was Robert Chambers who encouraged Huxley to take the lead for Darwin. Huxley had written a highly critical review of Chambers' *Vestiges* some years before and now the two had a chance meeting in Oxford. Both, however, had a common foe in Samuel Wilberforce, bishop of London, who, they knew, would also be attending the meeting. Huxley especially had no truck for the religious establishment represented by Wilberforce, and now took on a personal crusade to defend naturalism against theism of any kind. He saw in Wilberforce only ignorance and arrogance.

Among the Darwinian polemicists none seemed to relish the controversies more than Thomas Huxley. He played two major roles. First, he wanted Darwin's ideas, and his methodologies, to shape a new program for science in England. Huxley, born in 1825 near London, grew up in an environment of religious orthodoxy, from which he recoiled early, almost in horror of its threats to the unfaithful. Huxley trained in surgery and entertained a great interest in botany and biology, marked by a long voyage to Australia aboard the *Rattlesnake* in 1847. He won election to the Royal Society at the age of twenty-six. Huxley, of course, followed with interest, but without conviction, the prevailing theories of evolution. Darwin's explanation, however, persuaded him, because he saw immediately that Darwin supplied the mechanism that the other speculations lacked. "How extremely stupid not to have thought of that!" he reacted when brought into the light. What most inspired Huxley was his great hope that Darwin could now refashion a discipline too long dominated by theology and religious thinking. Liberated from that injurious alliance, Huxley believed, science would now become an autonomous profession, with its own strictly empirical standards. He now took up the crusade to win other scientists to like thinking about their work, and indeed Huxley's efforts figure largely in the emerging professionalization of science in England and Europe.

Second, Huxley did not shy from adding his own input to the Darwinian debates, and with the intention of making evolution a thoroughly materialistic view of nature. He saw evolution as all of a piece, with no quantitative or qualitative differences between organic and inorganic substance. Repeatedly on the lecture circuit he made that point. Thus, all thought represented only an electric circuit that travels the nervous system. Huxley to this extent also closed the "gap" between man and ape and amassed as much evidence as he could, from the fossil record on down, to connect the species. He put his views together in his book of 1863, *Man's Place in Nature*. Huxley saw no degradation in conjoining humans to the "lower" forms of life and indeed, with his vigorous prose, rendered *Homo sapiens* a glorious achievement of nature's long and diligent work.

Of all people, Darwin certainly wanted the endorsement of Charles Lyell. The two corresponded at length and Lyell enthusiastically urged his younger friend to get his ideas and data organized for publication. Before other scientists, in a major address in Aberdeen just prior to the publication of Darwin's book, Lyell promised that it would shed new light on key questions in current science and provide an explanation of evolutionary change "for which no other hypothesis has been able, or has attempted to account." But enthusiasm did not necessarily mean endorsement. Although Lyell took a paternalistic interest in Darwin's advancing career, and although Darwin's evidence did change Lyell's mind on transmutation of species, Lyell did have one deep reservation about Darwin's theory. He could not include humans in natural selection. Thus, when Lyell wrote his book *The Antiquity of Man*, also in 1863, he did locate human origins far back from the Genesis account, but stated his preference for human creation as a special act, a sudden leap, or saltation, that took *Homo sapiens* out of the ordinary record of life. Lyell revealed religious beliefs here; he believed human characteristics— spiritual, intellectual, moral—marked off the species and must register the intervention of a like force. Historian William Irvine informs that Lyell "pleaded pathetically with Darwin to introduce just a little divine intervention" into his explanations. Darwin, however, would entertain no such notion and reacted with great disappointment, even anger, to Lyell's book.

Heavy opposition to Darwin came, of course, from church leaders, which is not to say, however, that all religious opinion weighed in against him. It is instructive, in fact, given today's continuing controversy, to observe that hardly any of the skepticism about Darwin's ideas focused on the biblical story of earth's creation. The scientific literature of the last seventy years had familiarized the informed public of earth's great antiquity and few felt any need to judge Darwin by the first chapter of Genesis. Nonetheless, skepticism and outright opposition abounded. Wilberforce above all has earned a lasting reputation as Darwin's most vociferous critic. His essays in the *Quarterly Review* inveighed against natural selection. Wilberforce did not demand that science corroborate scripture, but religion had an interest in science, he said, and the necessity to intervene when science undermined the notion of God and the divine activity in creating and sustaining life. Darwin went out of bounds, he believed, in applying natural selection to human beings. For, said Wilberforce, here he upends what we know above all, that "the moral and spiritual condition of man" distinguishes him from the animals and places him above them. Wilberforce could not abide "the degrading notion of the brute origin of him who was created in the image of God." However singular his public outspokenness against Darwin, Wilberforce expressed what became the conventional religious opposition to Darwinian evolution.

Darwin recognized his slim odds against winning over the religious voices, but he hoped greatly to persuade the scientific community. Here too Huxley made a valuable contribution. It was no easy task. One could site extensive literature here, but we shall consider one case. Richard Owen, as much as any, represented the scientific "establishment" of England, a prolific scholar and certainly the most formidable comparative anatomist and taxonomist of his time. Indeed, he became known as "the English Cuvier." Born in Lancaster in 1804, Owen, like Darwin, had studied in Edinburgh. He prepared for a career in medicine, but his work in cataloging the vast anatomical specimens belonging to the famous physician John Hunter redirected his interest. He made major contributions to morphology, as a later chapter will note. Owen's work also connected him to the English court as he taught natural history to Queen Victoria's children and became a close friend of Prince Albert. His prickly and often vindictive personality complicated all relations with him, but he spoke authoritatively, and he came forth with one of the first responses to Darwin's book, appearing in the *Edinburgh*

Review in April 1860. (As per custom, Owen published the review anonymously and thus one finds that he quotes "Professor Owen" frequently!)

From Owen Darwin surely expected no help and he got none. Owen dismantled Darwin's book almost page by page, faulting even his literary style. Owen was already bristling from personal animosities involving Darwin's friends Huxley and Lyell, but the natural selection theory proffered by Darwin easily sufficed to raise Owen's review to high pique. Owen did not adhere to a rigid notion of species and conceded that no scientist any longer considers species unchanging. But he warned against rash speculation respecting the causes of their transformation. The worst sin, of which Darwin proved guilty, according to Owen, was to "assume an indefinite capacity to deviate from a specific form." To that extent, though opinion remained unsettled on species change, Darwin, with his theory of natural selection, had lapsed into "purely a conjectural basis." As a result, Owen charged, he propelled himself into the outlandish notion that all forms of life could well have had but a single common ancestor. Owen rejected both the scientific and theological implications of this speculation. One detects the sarcastic tone, and the incredulity, of Owen, in summarizing Darwin on this point: "He leaves us to imagine our globe, void, but so advanced as to be under the conditions which render life possible; and he then restricts the Divine power of breathing life into organic form to its minimum of direct operation. All subsequent organisms henceforward result from properties imparted to the organic elements at the moment of their creation, preadapting them to the infinity of complications and their morphological results, which now try to the utmost the naturalist's faculties to comprehend and classify." Owen's critique left Darwin very angry; "malignant," he labeled it. He could barely muster the forbearance not to retaliate, but managed restraint.

This issue will recur in this study. It raises the question, just how orderly is nature? Darwin himself, in citing some objections to his own theory of natural selection, pondered what kept evolution from becoming utterly chaotic, producing new form after new form. He knew that it did impose checks on itself, but he could not successfully explain why. Those like Owen who feared Darwin's ideas on such grounds adhered to some form of ideal types, created by some intelligent designer. Louis Agassiz, as we shall see in the next chapter, clung tenaciously to a view of nature so conceived. Owen believed strongly that all living forms in one way or another, and at least to some degree, reflect dominant archetypes. Organisms derive from not one, but several archetypes, and, although these organisms always undergo some changes, they remain within the design parameters of the original type that produced them. Hence, Owen wrote: "The most numerous living beings now on the globe are precisely those which offer such a simplicity of form and structure, as best agrees . . . with that ideal prototype from which, by any hypothesis of natural law, the series of vegetable and animal life might have diverged." Nature, Owen, and many like-minded naturalists in Darwin's time, believed, truly respected pattern. Genus, family, order, class, and so on reflected nature's adherence to form, structure, design, and purpose. Anything less, or anything more, raised the specter of a meaningless, fortuitous universe. For Owen, then, it was no small matter, that Darwin redefined "species" from a precise category of nature to a "mere creature of the brain."

And as for Darwin himself? What did he make of the order of nature he was describing now for a fascinated audience? He was of unsettled opinion. At one point, viewing all "these elaborately constructed forms," so different from each other, "and so complex in their relations to each other," he felt in awe of them. "There is a grandeur in this view of life," he wrote, "with its several powers, having been originally breathed into a few forms or into one; and that whilst this planet has gone cycling on according to the fixed law of gravity, from so simple a beginning endless forms so beautiful and most wonderful have been, and are being evolved." But awe could also assume a more frightful tone. Later he wrote to a colleague: "What a book a Devil's chaplain might write on the clumsy, wasteful, blundering, low & horridly cruel works of nature. My God how I long for my stomach's sake to wash my hands of it—for at least one long spell." This other view, in the long run, won out in Darwin. He simply could not reconcile nature's violence, its brutal competitiveness, its prolific death, with any notion of a benevolent God.

One could review the scientific discussion of Darwin's book at great length and it supplies a compelling body of writing. No consensus prevailed. For most participants, Darwin's theory had profound implications, the ones that religious thinkers and philosophers pondered. William Irvine makes the arresting comment concerning all these exchanges about the theory that "scientists themselves did not know whether to reply to it with science or theology." For two prominent American scientists the two subjects were similarly inseparable.

BIBLIOGRAPHY

Appleman, Philip, ed. *Darwin: A Norton Critical Edition*. New York: Norton, 1970.

Browne, Janet. *Charles Darwin: The Power of Place. Volume II of a Biography*. Princeton: Princeton University Press, 2002.

——. *Charles Darwin: Voyaging, a Biography*. Princeton: Princeton University Press, 1996.

Dennett, Daniel C. *Darwin's Dangerous Idea: Evolution and the Meanings of Life*. New York: Simon & Schuster, 1991.

Himmelfarb, Gertrude. *Darwin and the Darwinian Revolution*. New York: Norton, 1959.

Hull, David L. *Darwin and His Critics: The Reception of Darwin's Theory of Evolution by the Scientific Community*. Cambridge, MA: Harvard University Press, 1973.

Irvine, William. *Apes, Angels, and Victorians: The Story of Darwin, Huxley, and Evolution*. 1955. New York: Time Reading Program Special Edition, 1963.

Kohn, David, ed. *The Darwinian Heritage*. Princeton: Princeton University Press, 1985.

Mayr, Ernst. *One Long Argument: Charles Darwin and the Genesis of Evolutionary Thought*. Cambridge, MA: Harvard University Press, 1991.

Ruse, Michael. *Darwin and Design: Does Evolution Have a Purpose?* Cambridge, MA: Harvard University Press, 2003.

——. *The Darwinian Revolution: Science Red in Tooth and Claw*. Chicago: University of Chicago Press, 1979.

Watson, James D., ed. *Darwin: The Indelible Stamp: The Evolution of an Idea*. Philadelphia: Running Press, 2005.

White, Michael, and John Gribbin. *Darwin: A Life in Science*. 1995. New York: Penguin, 1997.

Wilson, Edward O., ed. *From So Simple a Beginning: The Four Great Books of Charles Darwin*. Boston: Norton, 2005.

THE SCIENTIFIC RECEPTION

Louis Agassiz and Asa Gray

A CAREER IN SCIENCE

Science is never an exact science. Interpreting nature and the multitude of data it furnishes succumbs to the same individual beliefs, predispositions, and prejudices as do other fields of inquiry, like history or literature. Darwin's ideas found their way immediately to the United States and immediately they produced controversy, and no more so than in Darwin's own domain, the field of science. Darwin hoped above all to win the opinions of his peers. Eventually, he gained a consensus among most scientists, especially younger ones in Britain and the United States. But the *Origin of Species* also produced an intense debate between two American scientists, two men of great stature, and from the same institution. For in the person of Louis Agassiz, Darwin had his greatest detractor among scientists. In Asa Gray he had his foremost American champion. The engagement constitutes an important intellectual episode. It signified old science against new, European thought against American, and it illuminated two contrasting views of the world.

Louis Agassiz was born in the local parsonage at Moutiers, Switzerland, in 1807. His father, Rodolphe, served as assistant pastor in this area of longstanding Protestant strength. Louis grew up among the regional beauty of Moutiers, which looked out onto the imposing

Bernese Alps. His mother Rose, an energetic and engaging woman, had given birth to four children previously; Louis was the first to survive into youth. He showed an early interest in nature. He gathered local materials—insects, small animals, fish—and mastered their Latin names. Louis kept notebooks that recorded and classified his abundant samples. His curiosity extended widely, as he read of explorers, ancient and contemporary, who were expanding knowledge of the world. He also sought something more. He wanted to know the essential, underlying structure of nature. Nature had for the young boy, as it would for the mature man, a profound metaphysical and religious significance.

Agassiz pursued a university education in typical European fashion, by attending several institutions and studying with different men of reputation. His tour took him to Zurich, Heidelberg, Munich, Erlangen, and Paris. These travels and studies immersed Agassiz in the dominant intellectual current in Continental science, especially in Germany, *Naturphilosophie*. As Michael Ruse writes, "In Germany, a whole new system of morphology—called *Naturphilosophie*, or natural philosophy—was springing up." This system affirmed "underlying forms or ideas as informing the structure of organisms." After study at Heidelberg, Agassiz, in the summer of 1827, read the work by the German naturalist and philosopher Lorenz Oken, titled *Lehrbuch der Naturphilosophie*. At Munich, Agassiz studied with Oken and with Friedrich Schelling, another expounder of *Naturphilosophie*. Oken described a great unity in nature, with man the key to that unity. *Homo sapiens*, Oken tried to show, contained all the organic forms found in the rest of the animal kingdom. Thus, all that had appeared in the lower species could be discerned in the human structure. Oken believed that animals modeled the fetal stages of the human. This depiction gave Oken's writing a holistic and symbolic dimension; nature moves toward an ideal type, man. Through his early career, this *Naturphilosophie* inspired Agassiz. It confirmed an intelligent Creator.

Agassiz moved to Paris to study with Georges Cuvier, shortly before Cuvier died in 1832. Agassiz made a great impression on the famous paleontologist, who bequeathed his sketches and research materials to the younger man. Agassiz now began the daunting work of organizing them. Cuvier impressed on Agassiz the fact of stark, separate categories among life forms. These features also confirmed to him their separate creation. Agassiz always affirmed these categories and he would remain forever in the Cuverian frame of mind to this extent. Furthermore, Agassiz followed Cuvier in resisting a *Naturphilosophie* that would suggest the transition of one life form into another. In 1844 he became an immediate, strong critic of Robert Chambers' *Vestiges of Creation*. Agassiz rejected any derivation of one species from another. Cuvier had impressed Agassiz with the fact of divine intervention in the earth's long history. Cuvier's conviction that life forms reflected ideal, or immaterial, forms, helped keep Agassiz within the *Naturphilosophie* tradition.

Agassiz contributed a major work in his first publication, on the fishes of Brazil, and then attained international stature with his contributions to glacial theory. He took up this study in 1836, observing evidence of glaciers in his native Switzerland. He advanced his argument for the previous existence of a great ice age in his *Études sur les glaciers* in 1840 and in *Système glaciate* in 1847. These works, of course, showed Agassiz to be a confirmed catastrophist. Ironically (and Agassiz's life is nothing if not replete with irony), his evidence helped others who argued for evolution—the advancing and receding of glacial ice helped create the different features of flora and fauna in different regions, they argued. For Agassiz, however, the glacier demonstrated God's recurring and dramatic intervention in the earth's history. He referred to glaciers as "God's great plough." Agassiz always had a ready explanation for the fossil record of extinct forms: God had intervened according to his own arbitrary will and ended existing forms of life; he then began anew. Thus, however much some existing forms may resemble extinct ones, they cannot have a family connection by way of descent. Agassiz wrote: "There is . . . a complete break between the present creation and those [creatures] which precede it; if the living species of our time resemble those buried in the levels of the earth, so as to be mistaken for them, it cannot be said that they have descended in the direct line of progenitor, or what is the same thing, that they are identical species."

Agassiz traveled to the United States in 1846. He arrived in Boston that year to deliver the Lowell Lectures. He had a huge reception, some five thousand people attending to hear the noted scientist. Ostensibly, Agassiz also had the purpose of beginning a study of the natural history of North America and his work culminated in four volumes on that subject. He relished his new life in the United States, he wanted to write a natural history that would celebrate the new world marvels he saw here, and he wanted Americans to appreciate them. That inspiration yielded the lavish attention he gave to another American project: the creation of the Museum of Comparative Zoology at Harvard in 1859. Agassiz thoroughly enjoyed the limelight in which he found himself. We have his own immodest testimony to his influence. He wrote to a friend in Switzerland in 1855: "I have now been eight years in America, have learned the advantages of my position here, and have begun undertakings which are not yet brought to a conclusion. I am also aware how wide an influence I already exert upon this land of the future, an influence which gains in extent and intensity every year."

Harvard early saw an opportunity in Agassiz's American sojourn. A gift from Abbott Lawrence, cotton manufacturer and business associate of John Amory Lowell, led to the establishment in 1846 of the Lawrence Scientific School at Harvard. It represented an alliance of Boston industrialists, who knew well the value of advancement in science to the material progress of New England, and Harvard. Its creation coincided with an offer to Agassiz of a professorship in the new school. Indeed, Harvard created the school for him. Agassiz seized the opportunity. It began an American career that would make Agassiz a truly public individual. He established American connections quickly, with the industrialists and with former Massachusetts governor and now president of Harvard College Edward Everett. He made intellectual connections, too. Agassiz helped found the Saturday Club, a group that met for dining and discussion, and included Ralph Waldo Emerson, Nathaniel Hawthorne, Henry Wadsworth Longfellow, John Greenleaf Whittier, James Russell Lowell, Oliver Wendell Holmes Sr., and Charles Sumner. Soon Agassiz remarried. He had left his estranged wife in Europe and met Elizabeth Cabot Cary in 1848. Their marriage in 1852, it has been noted, "completed [Agassiz's] conquest of Boston society." Cary would become the first president of Radcliffe College.

Agassiz established himself at Harvard amid intellectual shifts at that institution. Since the late eighteenth century Harvard philosophy reflected the long reach of the Scottish Enlightenment, particularly in the classroom use of works by Thomas Reid and, after 1820, of Dugald Stewart. The Scottish system, with its confidence in moral truths introspectively knowable, sat comfortably with the rational Christianity of Unitarianism. Harvard had come under Unitarian dominance in 1805. After several decades of influence, though, new currents of thought challenged it. James Marsh at the University of New Hampshire introduced Americans to the Kantian intellectual system as processed in England by Samuel Coleridge. A young generation of Unitarian clergy, Ralph Waldo Emerson among them, seized on the German thinking with much excitement. Agassiz's *Naturphilosophie*, its own expression of idealism, gave it a larger representation and an important reinforcement. Older Unitarians attacked transcendentalism as the "latest form of infidelity." Agassiz got along very well with the Harvard Unitarians, though; partisans on both sides had a common cause in their antimaterialism.

One can examine Agassiz's American years in two stages—before and after Darwin's 1859 publication. Americans who took an interest in science, and there were many, certainly knew the general outline of Agassiz's thought. He had effectively familiarized people with it before his arrival in 1846 and afterward. Agassiz never detached science from a religious view of life. All creation, he believed, reflected the ideas of God, each form disclosing a separate divine thought. Agassiz, however, was not defending any particular religious system or tradition. He did not intend his views to underscore Judaeo-Christian teachings about the creation of the earth or its ensuing history. Thus, as Agassiz explained in an 1850 essay in the *Christian Examiner*, his views departed from the Genesis account of Creation. He also had to confront those who argued that Genesis confirmed a single creation of the human race, and in its entirety. Agassiz did not accept this view of the matter. His essay countered that Genesis referenced only those beings placed in the vicinity of Eden. Many other creations had followed this one, he said, and they explain the diversity of the natural record with respect to different geographical regions and with respect to both animal species and the different races of human beings. Agassiz maintained that "zoological provinces" thus reveal the forms of life peculiar only to that region in which God first planted them.

Here we come to another irony in Agassiz's career, and it concerns the subject of race. New Englanders lionized Agassiz, pleased to have so renowned a scientist join their company; but it was southerners—white southerners—who most eagerly applied his views to the great social question of the day. And, to be sure, Agassiz specifically helped them. Agassiz first encountered black people on his visit to Philadelphia shortly after his arrival to the United States. He reported his "painful impression": "As much as I try to feel pity at the sight of this degraded and degenerate race, as much as their fate fills me with compassion in thinking of them as really men, it is impossible for me to repress the feeling that they are not of the same blood as us." Agassiz went on to comment, in most unflattering terms, about the facial and bodily features of the city's black residents.

Agassiz's scientific views can explain his references to the distinctiveness of whites and blacks; like all forms in nature, they each had a separate, divine creation. It seems clear, nonetheless, that the race issue in turn reinforced these notions in Agassiz. It made him insist all the more on polygenism, or multiple creations, as opposed to monogenism. That view, Agassiz criticized, created a great kinship of all human life. (Note that Genesis again falls into this category, deriving all humans from an original pair.) Monogenesists, in more recent times, Agassiz also feared, looked to environment, that is, physical causes, to explain changes that have occurred over time. With monogenism, then, Agassiz associated materialism; with polygenism, he associated intelligence, forethought, immaterialism, and spiritual intervention in life history.

What Agassiz did say about the Negro race supplied intellectual ammunition for whites in the South and elsewhere. And, to be sure,

Agassiz lost appeal among northerners as a consequence. Some religionists faulted his pluralist views of creation because they did not conform to scripture. Others, though, took offense at what appeared to them as Agassiz's disparagement of a particular race. Possibly, Agassiz intended no denigration. He said as much, and his understanding of nature, well established before his arrival to the United States, did certainly lead consistently to his belief in the independent creation of the human types. Agassiz precisely applied Cuvier's scheme. He named eight primary human types: the Caucasian, Arctic, Mongol, American Indian, Negro, Hottentot, Malayan, and Australian. He associated each with zoological zones, the locations of their original, independent creations. All these categories together constituted the human race; they all belonged to the species *Homo sapiens*. But for Agassiz any idea along the lines of "the unity of the human race" simply defied scientific and divine fact.

These views did not necessarily lead to convictions of race superiority and inferiority. But Agassiz did little to prevent his ideas from endorsing such notions and he did lend his name to others who used them in these times of intense sectional conflict in America. When in Philadelphia and later in Charleston, South Carolina, Agassiz saw free Negroes and slaves, he recoiled in horror. Always the public man, Agassiz also addressed southern audiences on this subject. Thus in 1847 he opined that "the brain of the Negro is that of the imperfect brain of a seven months' infant in the womb of a White." Agassiz, of course, could never say that these differences derived from evolution; no, God created them that way. Races were immutable. In Mobile, Alabama, six years later, Agassiz told his audiences that the human race varieties represented a gradation, and more precisely, "a gradation parallel to the gradation of animals up to man." And climate, or physical conditions, had nothing to do with these rankings. Such disparity of rank, Agassiz urged on another occasion, should warn against the danger of sexual intercourse between blacks and whites, should confirm the wisdom of racial segregation, and should demonstrate the sound policy of denying blacks social equality. We should not be surprised that in 1854, when Josiah Nott and George Gladden published their contribution to white supremacy, a book titled *The Types of Mankind*, the first of two massive tomes, they placed at the beginning of the volume an essay they had solicited from Agassiz.

Just before Darwin published his book, Agassiz published in 1857 his "Essay on Classification." It constituted the greater part of volume one of Agassiz's *Contributions to the Natural History of the United States*. Richard Owen in England hailed the essay. Just as Darwin was about to shatter prevailing notions of design and intelligent creation in nature, Agassiz held forth on behalf of such convictions. Species represented God's independent acts of creation and the more we recognize the prolific number of species that research now reveals, the more we understand the immense and ongoing activity of God, Agassiz argued. Any suggestion that environmental change or other physical causes induced these varieties diminishes our notion of this powerful deity, he asserted. To draw one form from another, or to interconnect them into one all-embracing concept, assigned God to passivity. Here is Agassiz at his most eloquent: Nature, he wrote, "exhibits not only thought, it shows also premeditation, power, wisdom, greatness, prescience, omniscience, providence . . . all these facts . . . proclaim aloud the One God, whom man may know, adore, and love; and Natural History must, in good time, become the analysis of the thoughts of the Creator of the Universe, as manifested in the animal and vegetable kingdom, as well as in the organic world." Never did science do greater service to religion. And with these views in mind, one may well anticipate how Agassiz would receive Darwin's *Origin* two years later. He did not disappoint.

FIGHTING DARWIN

In November 1859 Louis Agassiz received a letter from Charles Darwin. Darwin announced that he was taking the liberty of sending Agassiz a copy of his new book, one dealing with the origin of species. The letter was quite direct. Darwin said that the views expressed in the book differed so much from Agassiz's that he feared

Agassiz might think he sent him the book just for spite. (Darwin had pronounced Agassiz's 1857 essay "utterly impracticable rubbish.") Darwin disavowed any such intention and asked only that Agassiz appreciate that he had made his best effort to get at the truth. When the book arrived, Agassiz read it carefully. He judged right away that Darwin had taken familiar ideas of development and simply given them a new mode of explanation. It made no difference to Agassiz. He wrote in the margins such comments as "This is truly monstrous!" Darwin represented to Agassiz but another attempt to merge all life into one vast unity. Heresy!

Agassiz reviewed Darwin's book in the June 1860 issue of the *American Journal of Science*. He first raised a matter of definition and logic, by posing the question, "If species do not exist at all, as the supporters of the transmutation theory maintain, how can they vary, and if individuals alone exist, how can the differences which may be observed among them prove the variability of species?" (Darwin, of course, had not put the matter that way.) Agassiz said one can avoid the confusion by recognizing the plain facts that each individual organism has a definite trajectory to follow from the time of its conception to the end of its life. During that time it never changes its relation to other individuals of the same species. Agassiz also insisted that the more one sees specimens of a species, the more precise the limits that mark off one species from another appear.

This review, however, signaled Agassiz's demise as a scientist of influence, if indeed that demise had not already begun. From now on he would stand as champion of the old ways of thinking while science moved into modernity with Darwin at the lead. Agassiz held forth as relentlessly as ever for permanence of forms. "It stands recorded now as never before," he wrote, "that the animals known to the ancients are still in existence, exhibiting to this day the characters they exhibited of old." Supposed intermediate forms, the transitional ones in new species formation, Agassiz dismissed as wholly "imaginary beings" summoned to support "fanciful theory." Agassiz, of course, found especially offensive Darwin's attributing evolutionary change to "accident." Agassiz's system of nature had no place for accident. Nature for him constituted a system, with each component

individually created, "an organic whole, intelligibly and methodi-
cally combined in all its parts."

Agassiz's review won attention among scientists; after all, he was
an international figure. But it did him little good. Over the next half
decade and more, younger scientists cast their lot with Darwin. Not
all of the older scientists resisted and Charles Lyell, as noted, came
to Darwin's defense, with a reservation. A generational fault line was
emerging nonetheless. Asa Gray led the pro-Darwinian forces in the
United States. Darwin learned from Gray that his book had caused
an immediate sensation in America and expressed amusement at
Agassiz's fierce critique. Gray even judged it an advertisement to
Darwin's benefit. Darwin seemed less certain. He wrote to Gray that
"Agassiz's name no doubt is a heavy weight against us." He did not
shy, though, from scorning Agassiz's review of his book. "How cooly
he assumes that there is some clearly defined distinction between
individual differences and varieties. It is no wonder that a man who
calls identical forms, when found in two countries, distinct species
cannot find variation in nature. . . . The whole article seems to me
poor; it seems to me hardly worth a detailed answer."

By the middle 1860s Agassiz's attempt to stop the Darwin band-
wagon approached desperation. Agassiz had secured his great reputation from his contribution to glacier studies, for which Darwin,
among many, had great respect. To Agassiz, as noted, glaciers exemplified God's manner of eradicating existing forms and starting creation anew. But if one restricts the Ice Age to North America the
idea loses plausibility. God should be starting all creation over again,
one could reason. So in 1864, as he finished a series of public lectures on glaciers, Agassiz proposed an expedition to Brazil to seek
out evidence of glacial history in South America. Businessman
Nathaniel Thayer found the idea intriguing and agreed to cover the
costs. The party that departed on the *Colorado* in March 1865 included Agassiz and his wife, and, among others, the young medical
student at Harvard, William James. When Agassiz returned in August 1866, he presented to the National Academy of Sciences his lectures on "Traces of Glaciers under the Tropics." He believed he had
cinched his case and concluded the series with his comment: "So

here is the end of the Darwinian theory." Agassiz did not convince scientists at all, however, and some thought he had made a spectacle of himself. Gray wrote to Darwin that Agassiz "was bent on covering the whole continent with ice."

In his fight against Darwin, Agassiz battled nearly to his last breath. In 1874, the year after his death, *Atlantic Monthly* published his piece titled "Evolution and Permanence of Type." Agassiz reviewed familiar turf, beginning the essay by telling his readers that he would address again the question whether "there is any process of evolution in nature." Few scientists at this time were even asking that question. Agassiz knew that the tide had turned, but he intended to reset the clock. He lamented that amid the "present ferment of theories" the basic, established tenets of animal life and history had fallen into neglect among scientists. By those tenets, Agassiz meant the precise and permanent categories that mark the animal kingdom. Agassiz complained that the in the new theories, these categories "are completely overlooked."

In the essay, Agassiz revisited the curious matter of recapitulation. Partisans of evolution (though not necessarily Darwin himself) often cited recapitulation to those critics who insisted that we have never seen evolution in action. In the embryonic development of human beings, the ontogenetic process, they said, we notice that the forms of the developing fetus successively resemble the chronological stages, the phylogenetic order, that mark the appearance of life forms over time. Thus, the human embryo resembles at first a tadpole, or aquatic organism, and later any of the simian species. Here, it was urged, we see "evolution," and we see an overriding pattern that connects all of life. Agassiz validated recapitulation as a real procedure in nature, and replied to the Darwinists that if embryonic change could occur so quickly, why did evolution supposedly require the immense amount of time that they said it did.

Agassiz, however, recognized recapitulation only within the severest limits. For the phenomenon occurs, he said, within only the four categories of life, those specified by Cuvier. Thus, Agassiz insisted, as soon as we see ontogeny in any instance, we know immediately to which category it conforms. He wrote: "Every living creature is formed in an egg and grows up according to a pattern and a mode of development common to its type, and of these embryonic norms there are but four." In others words, even recapitulation honors the sharp boundaries of life. It does not overleap them. The history of the type is actually the cause of the history of the individual. Thus final causes prevailed in nature. Agassiz therefore inscribed in all his writings his own formulation of *Naturphilosophie*.

So Agassiz's last word appeared in a literary magazine. He had for some time ceased to make useful contributions to science or to address scientists specifically, and certainly after 1859 he had lost influence. Philosopher David Hull wrote: "Prior to the publication of the *Origin*, Agassiz was considered to be slightly behind the times; after its appearance he became a living fossil."

ASA GRAY: AMERICAN SCIENTIST

In Asa Gray, Louis Agassiz had his great American antagonist. Gray was American born and bred, and it showed in his approach to science, in his quarrels with Agassiz, and in his reception of Darwin. One could hardly have scripted a more appropriate or more interesting coupling to view the clash of ideas over Darwin's scientific reception in the United States. The engagement generated much interest among intellectuals and among the public. Gray and Agassiz represented different views of science, but also different views of religion. Their rival opinions never amounted to a clash of science against religion, however. Thematically for the whole subject of evolution in the United States, they represented different accommodations of religion and science.

Gray came from upstate New York. He grew up ten miles from the Erie Canal and felt the enthusiasm for commercial growth and expansion that its construction signified for the country. Robert Gray represented the first in the American line of the family. An Ulster Protestant, he arrived in Boston in 1718, part of the growing mass of Scotch-Irish and Presbyterian immigrants who strongly shaped the texture of colonial America in the early eighteenth century. His group received a cold reception among New Englanders, fellow Calvinists though they were, and many moved west, most to the Pennsylvania frontier and south from there. Robert stayed in Worcester, Massachusetts, but Asa's grandfather Moses Wiley Gray established his residence in Sauquoit, New York. His eighth child with Sally Miller Gray, Moses, grew up there and apprenticed as a tanner, soon establishing his own business. He married Roxanna Howard in 1809. The couple had their first child, Asa, in November 1810.

Asa studied at local academies, absorbing a program heavily classical in content and creating little excitement in him. In fact, like Darwin's experience, little in Gray's early education inspired him and he made no plans to go to college. He discovered botany and was interested in it enough to think he might pursue a career in medicine, and with that prospect in mind he enrolled at the College of Physicians of the Western District, in nearby Fairfield. Through his instructor there, James Hadley, Asa gained a genuine enthusiasm for his work. The course in *materia medica*, especially, intensified his fascination for plants and that study now became his ruling passion.

Gray did take on a medical apprenticeship at Bridgewater. That situation allowed him time for adventures in the outdoors. He walked and explored and gathered plants. The collecting intensified and in 1830 Gray visited New York City, carrying with him a letter from Hadley and botanical samples. He went there to meet Dr. John Torrey, an illustrious name in American botany. He missed Torrey, absent from the city at the time, but left a letter and some specimens. Upon his return, Torrey viewed them and contacted Gray; he wanted to involve him in his project to study the flora of North America. Enthusiastic, Gray signed on and the first volume of *Flora of North America* was published in 1838. Gray, in the meantime, became a science teacher at the Utica Gymnasium, formerly the High School for Boys, beginning in 1832. Like Darwin at almost the same time, he abandoned a career in medicine.

In November 1839 Gray began a grand tour of England and the Continent. He landed at Liverpool and made his way to the home of the prominent British naturalist Joseph Hooker, where he stayed. Hooker introduced Gray to many other noted scientists, including Richard Owen and a younger friend, about Gray's age, Charles Darwin. In Germany, Gray visited great universities, now becoming the intellectual site of pilgrimages for Americans who had no place for advanced research in their own country. Gray went to Berlin, Freiburg, Tübingen, Dresden, and Halle. Back in the United States there followed an even more exciting turn for Gray. In April 1842, Asa Gray, the man without a college education, received an appointment to become the Fisher professor of natural history at Harvard College. He arrived at Cambridge in July.

At this point there occurred another event of lasting significance in Gray's life. Before his departure for Europe, Gray had been living near Torrey in New York City and in 1835 joined the Presbyterian Church on Bleeker Street. Until now, he had little of a religious identity, sharing a kind of Jeffersonian deism with the teachers he knew at Bridgewater. He now took on a church affiliation. Although he emerged from his "dark delusion," he adhered to a rational faith. His "conversion," if we use that word cautiously, did not signify a profound inner transformation, nor, in this era of Protestant revivalism, did it arrive with any emotional drama. Gray identified with the New Side wing of Presbyterianism. More evangelical in tone, to be sure, it was also moving away from the Calvinist orthodoxy of the Old Side, and it embraced a social reform outlook that carried many New Siders into the antislavery movement. Gray had no interest in theological speculation and never would. He believed in a God of Creation whose works nature reflected everywhere. Religion and science for him went hand in hand and this conversion in 1835 all the more inspired Gray for his work as a scientist. He now saw it as God's personal calling to him. Nature, in fact, always spoke more authentically to Gray's religiosity than did scripture, which, he believed, had no role in teaching scientific truth.

Religion was not a passing fancy with Gray. He took on Sunday school teaching of black boys in the city. He sent religious literature to his family. On his English tour Gray sought out dissenting churches, not always easy to find, and he made a special visit to the chapel of George Whitefield, the great preacher who had electrified the American colonies in the events that history describes as the great awakening of the middle eighteenth century. Evangelical scruples attended Gray. Thrilling though he did to the great cultural life of Europe, he made excuses for not attending the opera or the theater, institutions of moral taboo in American Protestantism. In moving to the Boston area, Gray also entered the heart of Unitarianism in the United States. In Boston Gray showed his preference for Congregationalism over Unitarianism by joining the Park Street Church. A colleague referred to him as a man "of orthodox faith." In 1848 Gray married Jane Lathrop Loring, daughter of Charles Greely Loring, a very prominent Boston attorney. In their marriage, which produced no children, they preserved their separate religious loyalties, hers to Unitarianism.

In 1846, Gray welcomed the appointment of Louis Agassiz to the Lawrence Scientific School of Harvard. He had no reason not to. At least not yet. Gray and Agassiz shared a strong antimaterialist bent in their science. Gray, who defined species as essentially marked by a pair's ability to bear like offspring, also, at this time, judged them the special and thus separate creations of a supreme being who had arranged them all according to plan and foresight. Also, Gray had read Agassiz's thoroughgoing criticism of the *Vestiges of Creation* and applauded it. He, too, recoiled from the notions of unity and common derivation pronounced by Chambers, and he judged man's long "development" from inert matter into spiritual being an affront to religion and science. When Chambers published a reply to his critics, Gray took him on directly in the pages of the *North American Review* in 1846.

Agassiz's views on another matter, however, did trouble Gray. That issue was race. Gray knew the work of Josiah Nott and George Gladden, who were trying to demonstrate the racial inferiority of Negroes. Gray had developed a strong aversion to slavery and soon saw how advocates of white supremacy were appropriating Agassiz's views on race for their political purposes. These ideas ran directly against Gray's evangelical Christianity and their concern for the moral value of every human being, but they violated his science, too. Gray's ideas on species and his knowledge of hybridization confirmed for him the unity of the human race. Here science and religion held a common ground in his thinking. (Incidentally, the later, frequent correspondence between Gray and Darwin showed Gray to be a staunch supporter of Abraham Lincoln's Civil War policies, including the Emancipation Proclamation. The abolitionist-minded Darwin faulted Lincoln for not acting sooner to end slavery.)

Gray's departure from Agassiz in matters of natural science became clear at the end of the 1850s, just before the publication of Darwin's *Origin*. Gray also proved of great value to Darwin in his new studies. He had become in the United States the nation's best-known botanist. People sent him all kinds of samples and expected responses from Gray about them. And Gray tried to oblige, so consuming his time that biographer A. Hunter Dupree speculated that Gray burdened himself with so much work of this kind that he had virtually none available to him for theoretical work. But he was acquiring data immensely valuable for his geographical comparisons. And now that field expanded to Japan, where Commodore Perry was opening up American commercial interests. Gray received from Japan an array of samples sent by Charles Wright and what he studied astonished him. Precisely, he found species from Japan that exactly resembled ones known in Europe and North America, and that, surprisingly, as Gray showed statistically, the region with the most resemblances was eastern North America. How was this pattern possible?

Gray found the answer in geological history. He concluded that in the Tertiary period a common flora covered all the northern portions of all the continents, extending unbroken from Asia to North America. The glacier propelled the flora south and sundered their continuity, establishing two new great branches. Similar rearrangements occurred with the receding of the glacier and the cooling period that followed. Dupree summarizes Gray's conclusions: "Thus an unbroken series of causes and effects accounted for the striking disjunction of plants in eastern North America and eastern Asia. What had been an a priori case for the double creation of species was completely and convincingly destroyed. Common ancestry and a single center of creation was established as the more reasonable assumption." Here was a dagger in the back of Agassiz. And Darwin, too, knew it.

Gray's shift measured his growing alienation from the older science. Sharp differentiation of species no longer made sense to him and simply had no value for scientific study. As Gray's convictions grew, he resolved to bring the matter before the Cambridge Scientific Club in December 1858. And then he outlined his ideas to a meeting of the American Academy of Science. Now, in seriously questioning Agassiz's explanations, Gray asserted that accounting for species creation by reference to divine will circumvented the inductive reasoning of science. One cannot begin with an ideal category and then fit all data into it, he said. And those data now seemed to confirm a genetic connection of all species. To be sure, Gray was offering hypotheses, but he also implicated Agassiz in bad scientific thinking. Agassiz's idealism, Gray was saying, imposed a priori thinking on bodies of evidence that demanded empirical analysis and inductive reasoning. Agassiz perceived the challenge and both he and Gray accepted an invitation from the Cambridge organization, in March 1859, to expound their thoughts. By this time, Darwin had brought Gray into an inner circle of scientists, Gray the only American, with whom he had discussed the electrifying theory he was only a few months away from introducing to the world. Gray even saw the Cambridge meeting as a trial run for his colleagues' receptivity toward Darwin's ideas.

These events merely brought out what had become serious differences between Agassiz and Gray. Agassiz relished the public limelight and lectured whenever he could to worshiping audiences. Gray believed that all this activity had "greatly injured" Agassiz. He was telling American audiences what they wanted to hear, Grey believed. Agassiz, as Gray also knew, enjoyed the company of the rich and famous of the Boston area as well as its renowned literati. Gray did not enjoy public lectures and did few of them. He did not connect with the socially powerful and had no company with the famous intellectual set. He certainly felt no affinity for their idealism. New England transcendentalism indicated to Gray the long reach of

European *Naturphilosophie* and its infecting of modern science. Although he lived in its midst, Gray stood aloof, not hostile but essentially indifferent, to the romantic movement in the United States. He needed to look no further than his Harvard colleague to see the bad effects. Gray was determined to push American science into a new era, but old habits impeded his progress. Gray helped open the way to the pragmatic era in American intellectual history. He endorsed design but allowed for chance and accident, for flux and change. He rejected brittle intellectual systems that conspired against an open, fresh, and empirical judgment of things. This scientist, product of no university, American or European, had come to conclude by 1857 that one might get along in science very well with no theorizing at all.

DARWIN AND DESIGN

Darwin first became acquainted with Gray's work when Joseph Hooker passed on to him a letter from Gray giving his opinions of Hooker's book of 1854, *Flora of New Zealand*. Gray recognized, and appreciated, that Hooker was moving significantly away from Agassiz's idea of species. Darwin saw from the review that Gray had valuable ideas available for the fight against Agassiz, the common enemy of all three scientists. So Darwin wrote to Gray and asked some pointed questions of him. Expressing his ignorance of botany, he asked Gray to clarify some points in his published writings about the flora of North America. Gray saw how astute was Darwin's interrogation and prepared new material on the subject. In 1856 his essay "Statistics of the Flora of the Northern United States" appeared in the *American Journal of Science*. Darwin rejoiced at Gray's methodology (statistical studies bolstered his own empiricism and would find application in the *Origin*), but he especially welcomed Gray's conclusions. "I have been eminently glad to see your conclusion in regard to species of large genera widely ranging: it is in strict conformity with the results I have worked out in several ways. It is of great importance to my notions."

Then in July 1857 Darwin wrote to Gray a significant letter. It was a general statement of his theory of natural selection. He had disclosed it heretofore only to Lyle and Hooker, he said. Darwin, after a general review, states: "But as an honest man I must tell you that I have come to the heterodox conclusion that there are no such things as independently created species—that species are only strongly defined varieties." Darwin urged that Gray inform no one of his theory. The world would know it soon enough.

Gray prepared to take up Darwin's cause in America and in May 1859, just before the publication of *Origin*, he presented an outline of Darwin's ideas to the Harvard University science club, where Agassiz reigned. He did so, Gray said to Darwin, "partly to see how it would strike a dozen people of varied minds and habits of thought, and partly, I confess, maliciously to vex the soul of Agassiz, with views so diametrically opposed to all his pet notions." Gray knew mostly what Darwin would say in the *Origin* and received an early copy when it appeared late in 1859. He read the work during the last week of the year. He also became the first to review the book in the United States, a fact of great significance, and he worked with Appleton's to arrange for the first (legal) American printing and all subsequent editions. Surely none was more disposed to give the book a fair consideration or to help it make sense to a reading public. Gray's review of *The Origin of Species* appeared in the March 1860 edition of the *American Journal of Science and Arts*. There would follow from Gray other important essays on Darwinism and evolution, and a collection, *Darwiniana*, that includes Gray's many offerings on that subject, in 1876. Darwin relied on Gray for scientific advice and criticism and they established an expansive correspondence. "I declare," Darwin wrote to Gray, "you know my book as well as I do myself."

Gray's review proceeded systematically. It summarized the conventional wisdom respecting species, that they have an independent creation and produce their like "from generation to generation." Most readers, Gray knew, would appropriately associate such views with Agassiz. Then Gray wrote: "From this generally accepted view the well-known theory of Agassiz and the recent one of Darwin diverge in exactly opposite directions." Darwin, he explained, traced all forms "from a single ancestor or pair," so that over a long history, new ones have emerged from the slightest variations from those identities that all offspring have in common with their parents. Thus, as Gray outlined Darwin, "the species we recognize have not been independently created, as such, but have descended, like varieties, from other species." Each organism is, then, an incipient, or possible new species.

Gray set himself a specific challenge: to persuade readers to perceive how Darwin's way of thinking made sense. He did not think it perfect in all respects, by no means. Darwin, however, at least thought like a scientist, Gray believed. Agassiz, with his ideal forms, Gray had to say, "may be said to be theistic to excess." "Darwin's aim and processes are strictly scientific," Gray wrote, "and his endeavor, whether successful or futile, must be regarded as a legitimate attempt to extend the domain of natural or physical science." How could Gray get his readers to shift their thinking? For one thing, he must de-radicalize Darwin. Gray anticipated the religious and scientific objections to Darwin's theory of species transformation. The derivation of one species from another, Gray wanted to assure, suggests nothing extraordinary, nothing we should find troubling.

Here Gray turned, as he often did in the review, to the *Origin* and quoted from it. Darwin analogized evolution to a growing tree. The green and budding twigs, he suggested, represent existing species. Those produced in previous years represent extinct species. Darwin went on: "At each period of growth all the growing twigs have tried to branch out on all sides, and overtop and kill the surrounding twigs and branches, in the same manner species and groups of species have tried to overmaster other species in the great battle for life." Thus Darwin pictured dynamic change and struggle within one system in which all parts were interrelated one with another. From biology to physics, he explained, we are learning more and more about the unity of force in nature. Scientists, he exemplified, speculate now that the universe derived from a common fluid mass. Gray threw his lot in with Darwin: "The mind of [our] age," Gray wrote, "cannot be expected to let the old belief about species pass unquestioned."

Gray knew, though, that he had to do more. This analogy would not assuage religious readers who saw Darwin as a threat. Gray could speak directly to their concerns because he himself had difficulties with Darwinian natural selection. Nature, he insisted, greatly protected the integrity of species. The offspring of mixed parents, as in the case of the horse and the jackass, are infertile, as in the mule. Nature does not permit indiscriminate creation of new forms. Gray made other observations in his review. Natural selection, he had to concede, could not account for all change. A huge gap, contrary to Darwin, he insisted, separates the lowest of humans from the highest of the apes. To the religious-minded, he offered another thought. Any scientific theory, Gray maintained, is potentially atheistic. But none complain about Newton's theory of gravity or the nebular theory of the universe. Why, then, should there be any fuss over natural selection?

With this exhortation for a fair hearing, Gray assured confidently that when all the evidence emerged, no triumph for atheism would result from evolution. Gray went on, in the review and in following essays, to argue that evolution confirmed design, that it demonstrated an intelligent universe overseen by a Creator. Gray meant to show that one did not have to go to Agassiz's extremes to fight materialistic views of evolution or to reconcile evolution with ideas of a benevolent universe. In *Origin*, Darwin, even though he described the harsh realities of the struggle for existence, nonetheless affirmed that a greater good was at work, that "the healthy and happy survive and multiply," and that nature works always toward greater perfections of all forms. Gray reminded his readers of those words.

Darwin may have thought to make his theory more palatable this way, but his melioristic posture lacked conviction. And to Gray personally in 1860 Darwin conveyed these somber thoughts: "I own I cannot see, as plainly as others do, and as I should wish to do, evidence of design and beneficence on all sides of us. There seems to me too much misery in the world." How could he reconcile the incessant violence, brutality, and horrible death with the existence of a beneficent God? Yet Darwin, as noted earlier, viewed the world, and the human race, too, with awe and wonder. He could not dismiss the creation as merely the product of brute force. To Gray he confided that the whole matter had left him in a terrible quandary. The problem, he felt, might be just too profound for the human intellect to resolve. "The more I think the more bewildered I become," he confessed to his American friend.

In England, both his defenders and his critics perceived Darwin as atheistic or materialistic. They could not see how an effective argument for design could be read into natural selection. Thomas Huxley, as noted, was leading the Darwinian circle away from association of evolution with any religious understanding of natural history. Gray saw the trend and worried about it. From the outset he feared that lines would break hard between outright materialists, who gave evolution no larger meaning than blind chance at work in all things, and those who recoiled from Darwin so extremely as to have recourse to a dogmatic religion that wholly bypassed the evidence of science. Both reactions would leave only unbreachable barriers between them, Gray feared, and no useful discourse on these important matters of nature and God.

This outcome Gray sought to prevent. He wrote assuredly in the review: "Even if the doctrine of the origin of species through natural selection should prevail in our day, we shall not despair; being confidant that the genius of an Agassiz will be found equal to the work of constructing, upon the mental and material foundations combined, a theory of Nature as theistic and scientific as that which he has so eloquently expounded." Some evolutionists, to be sure, did give Darwin a teleological reading and Gray was one of them. The review clearly made room for design and Gray fortified his efforts in an essay he titled "Natural Selection Not Inconsistent with Natural Theology," which appeared the same year in the *Atlantic Monthly*. Gray believed that Darwin had provided a teleological work. Natural selection did not exclude final causes, he insisted. This idea that the universe has ultimate ends that are to that extent the "cause" of the changes that occur in the progression of time toward those ends Gray accepted as an explanation of natural selection. At the simplest level, Gray asserted that if we may believe, with Agassiz and others, that the species were designed, then why not also the actual varieties of the species?

But Gray meant to do more. Natural selection as a mechanism of blind force, he said, strains credulity. Darwin must either admit a first cause, maker and perfecter of the many organisms, or disallow such cause and deprive the universe of an overriding intelligence. Then he challenged Darwin on a profound point: "If [Darwin] so misuses words that by the Creator he intends an unintelligent power, undirected force, or necessity, then he has put his case so as to invite disbelief in it. For then blind forces have produced not only manifest adaptations to specific ends—which is absurd enough—but better adjusted and more perfect instruments or machines than intellect . . . can contrive and human skill can execute—which no sane person will believe." In short, how, out of blind forces and chance, does order, precision, and accommodation emerge in nature? Gray concluded that Darwin should accept "the theistic view" for it dissolved an intellectual dilemma for him.

Gray had other doubts. Natural selection could not (at least not yet) account for gaps in the biological record. He continued to believe that the "missing link" between ape and man presented a serious challenge to Darwin. The ape-to-man nexus, achieved by the accidents of evolution, Gray could not accept. He clung to purpose and design. Gray wrote in his essay, "To insist, therefore, that the new hypothesis of the derivative origin of the actual species is incompatible with final causes and design, is to take a position which we must consider philosophically untenable." Gray knew that the committed atheist would not go along with him on the question of design, but he also knew that the unlearned religious dogmatist would reject evolution outright. He wanted to make his appeal to "the thoughtful theistic philosopher." He pursued the middle ground of accommodation and reconciliation.

Darwin could not go this far with Gray. If design accounted for the changes we see in evolution, then natural selection has no role to play, he told Gray. If one attributes design, or providential arrangement, to each variation, then natural selection becomes superfluous and we have left the realm of scientific explanation altogether,

Darwin warned. So he reiterated to Gray that variations in plants and animals "are due to unknown causes, and are without purpose, and in so far accidental." Later in 1869 when Darwin wrote his two volumes of *The Variation of Animals and Plants under Domestication*, he stuck to his guns. "However much we may wish it," he said, "we can hardly follow Professor Gray in his belief."

On one matter their discussions become more specific—on the subject of the eye. Darwin marveled in his studies how every existing feature of an organism, in its various parts, is so wondrously fitted to its existing circumstances. He found it improbable that it could have been made perfect, any more than a person could invent a machine perfect for all time and needing no improvements. But what about the eye? Darwin confessed that this item troubled him. For what good is an eye that is not already perfect? It is no good save in its final, complete form; so how could natural selection function in the early stages when the first changes that would produce this highly complex form had really no survival function at all? Here indeed is a general problem for natural selection, as Gertrude Himmelfarb has observed. What good does it do a giraffe to grow only one inch taller, that is, on its supposed way to becoming eight feet taller? The one inch, as opposed to the eight feet that will gain it access to the fruit at the top of trees and thus enhance its survival chances, gives it no special advantages and thus no special opportunity to pass on its acquired traits. On the matter of the eye, Gray also stood in awe, judging it one of nature's spectacular creations. What to make of it? Darwin's natural selection just did not give Gray a sufficient explanation for the production of this natural marvel. In the end, Gray could accept Darwin on natural selection only by adhering to a markedly different notion of that phenomenon than the one Darwin defended.

Philosophy aside, in contemplating such a marvel, any individual will probably go with his or her own imagination and impressions. Gray could not view the world and see in it only the chance operation of blind forces. "To us," he wrote, "a fortuitous cosmos is simply inconceivable. The alternative is a designed cosmos."

In concluding, we need to remember again that Gray addressed not only those among his scientist colleagues who veered with Darwin toward a materialistic account of life. He spoke also to those who might follow Agassiz and who offered only one alternative: God or Darwin. Gray rejected this false choice. Agassiz had allies in the Protestant clergy and in Francis Bowen, professor of moral philosophy at Harvard. To them, Gray urged that not every creation represented a supernatural event, and not only supernatural events showed God's activity. Gray believed that natural selection represented the secondary causes by which God worked his ways in nature. He even argued that the so-called accidental element in natural selection did not at all rule out design. But why, Gray wanted to know, does the religious person seem to look only for seemingly providential events, like huge floods, to confirm his sense of God? If the sexual union of two humans created a zebra, would it make us believe in a god of miracles? Gray urged a religious sensibility that marveled at the amazing order, continuity, and regularity of life, as confirmed by evolution. What more did a religious person need than an appreciation of the fact that out of an original form of life, or perhaps several primal forms, there had evolved such a complex, integrated, and orderly network of living forms? The strict Darwinian cannot explain it, the religious person should appreciate it, and the theistic evolutionist leads the way in understanding modern science.

Asa Gray retired from the Harvard faculty in 1872. He lived an active life for another sixteen years. He and Louis Agassiz tell us much about American science and they provide two key measures of the Darwinian reception in the United States. Repeatedly, their ideas involved questions of religion, too, for scientific thinking always led into religious categories. We now take up the subject of Darwin and religion. More controversy and more intellectual transformation lie ahead.

BIBLIOGRAPHY

Agassiz, Louis. *Essay on Classification.* Ed. Edward Lurie. 1857. Cambridge, MA: Harvard University Press, 1962.

Dupree, A. Hunter. *Asa Gray, 1810–1888.* Cambridge, MA: Harvard University Press, 1966.

Gray, Asa. *Darwiniana: Essay and Reviews Pertaining to Darwinism.* Ed. A. Hunter Dupree. 1876. Cambridge, MA: Harvard University Press, 1963.

Lurie, Edward. *Louis Agassiz: A Life in Science.* Chicago: University of Chicago Press, 1960.

Menand, Louis. *The Metaphysical Club: A Story of Ideas in America.* New York: Farrar, Straus and Giroux, 2001.

Nartonis, David K. "Louis Agassiz and the Platonist Story of Creation at Harvard, 1795–1846." *Journal of the History of Ideas,* 66 (2005): 437–49.

Ruse, Michael. *Darwin and Design: Does Evolution Have a Purpose?* Cambridge, MA: Harvard University Press, 2003.

PROTESTANT ORTHODOXY

Charles Hodge and James McCosh

Any reference to the "Darwinian controversy" invariably evokes the subject of religion. The controversy, to be sure, cut through many categories of thought; this book seeks to make that demonstration. But religion produced the most bitter quarrels, and not only between theists and secularists, but between theists of all kinds. It gave a new life to liberal Christianity; but some of its exponents had to endure heresy trials in denominational courts. The religious case against Darwinism went public and it produced one of the most famous trials of the twentieth century; and into the later twentieth century, state legislatures and school boards tried to discredit Darwinian evolution or diminish its influence on young minds. And from the moment of Darwin's reception in the United States, evolutionary naturalism ran smack against an American religious tradition of longstanding.

No religious system and no religious denomination had ever enjoyed a monopoly in this country. Colonial America had its regional religious establishments but complete conformity was the rule in none of them. The Calvinist theological tradition, however, had given a measure of unity to American Protestantism (six of the nine colonial colleges were founded under Calvinist auspices). Calvinism had survived many challenges and, even amidst its decline in the years after the Revolution, still maintained a powerful institutional influence. The Presbyterian denomination especially assured its durability. The Presbyterians, after establishing the College of New Jersey (Princeton) in 1746, led all other denominations in organizing new colleges in the nineteenth century. They enjoyed social prestige in the North and South, and they operated an influential religious press. This chapter, the first of two on religion, examines the complexities of the Darwinian challenge to American religious "orthodoxy." Presbyterians provided the most adamant religious critic of Darwin—Charles Hodge—and they produced the first well-known American religious leader to make an accommodation with Darwin—James McCosh.

THE PRINCETON WAY

For well over half his life, Charles Hodge had an association with Princeton Theological Seminary, the intellectual fortress of Calvinism in the United States of the nineteenth century. Hodge came from Philadelphia, born there in 1797. The family descended from the Scotch-Irish element that populated the American colonies in the early eighteenth century and gave Presbyterianism its major ethnic identity. Charles never really knew his father, a physician who died when Charles was only seven months old. His mother, Mary Blanchard Hodge, ran a boarding house to raise Charles and his older brother, with support from relatives. The family's strong Presbyterian loyalties sent the boys to Princeton to enroll Charles in the College of New Jersey. Presbyterian connections always mattered in Hodge's life. In this case, the college president, Ashbel Green, had previously served the Hodges' church in Philadelphia and knew the family well.

Charles entered college in 1812 and that year has a large significance for American Presbyterianism. The College of New Jersey, under the direction of Samuel Stanhope Smith, had taken a liberal and modernizing direction. It opened up to new ideas in science, including the contributions of Smith himself. The president in fact, was the son-in-law of John Witherspoon, Princeton's Scottish-born president from 1768 to 1788 and prominent leader in the American Revolution. Although New Side Presbyterians, partisans of the great awakening in the 1740s, had established Princeton, Witherspoon introduced it to the moderate Enlightenment. He drew from his own Scottish background and introduced the Scottish philosophers to his Princeton students. But in ensuing years this liberalizing direction brought conservative Calvinists into opposition against the college. Smith, who wanted to unite Christianity to Enlightenment ideas, bore the brunt of the disaffection. Ultimately, the stronger-minded Calvinists opted to establish their own institution, Princeton Theological Seminary, in 1812. It became immediately, and remained for decades thereafter, the citadel of American Calvinism.

Upon his graduation from the college, Hodge entered the seminary. He already knew Archibald Alexander, the first theology professor, and his studies with him trained Hodge thoroughly in the expansive repertoire of seventeenth-century Calvinist literature. Hodge graduated in 1819 and then returned the next year to teach biblical languages. Here began his long association with the seminary, one that lasted until his death in 1878. A remarkable career it was. Hodge trained more American pastors and theologians than any other individual in the nineteenth century. And he produced a prodigious amount of scholarship as well. From his editorship of the *Biblical Repertory and Princeton Review*, which he established in 1825, to the publication of his three-volume *Systematic Theology* in 1872, Hodge made himself the formidable proponent, protector, and prosecutor for Calvinism in America.

With respect to the array of competing ideas in his time, one could say that Hodge took on the world. His contributions to the *Princeton Review* confronted the new directions in religious thinking—the Oxford movement from England and the higher criticism from Germany. They measured the condition of Christianity by timely pieces on American religious writers—Nathaniel William Taylor and the "New Divinity," Charles Grandison Finney and revivalism, Andrews Norton and Unitarianism, Horace Bushnell and liberal Congregationalism, Philip Schaff and John W. Nevin on church history. They elaborated on traditional doctrinal matters—original sin, justification, the confessional standards. They reviewed denominational events with reports on the annual Presbyterian General Assembly meetings. The *Princeton Review* gave Hodge an outlet for his views on political and social questions—Sabbatarianism, temperance, slavery. And they brought under judgment the new ideas in another field—science.

When Hodge confronted the challenge posed by Darwin, he brought to his critique a particular kind of religious thinking. John W. Stewart has written of Hodge that his "sustained project was to interpret the world around him through his biblical, Augustinian, Calvinist, Westminister Confessional lens." His Christianity projected a powerful God and gave a large place to the Holy Spirit. For Hodge's writings could reflect the severe logic and rationality of Calvin, but they described an affectionate religiosity, too. They revealed the hard core of human sin that dominates all souls, but they showed also how the spirit connects us to a live and accessible God. Hodge recoiled from theologies that gave effective power to the individual will, and any that too easily narrowed the yawning gap between a magisterial God and a fallen humanity. And always against the temptations of speculative belief he evoked the inviolable standards of scripture. Here Hodge found his secure foundation and his supreme confidence. And thus, as James Turner writes: "Hodge behaved extraordinarily like Zeus, pronouncing his high judgments and hurling his thunderbolts accordingly on the inferior mortals below."

Early in his life Hodge found a lively and lasting interest in science. After his Princeton studies, he traveled widely in Europe and there met and engaged prominent men in that field. In 1822 he married Sarah Bache, granddaughter of Benjamin Franklin and a cousin of Alexander Dallas Bache, an important American scientist. Hodge also had a close friendship with Joseph Henry, first secretary of the Smithsonian Institution. The *Princeton Review* presented for its readers reviews of new directions in European science. As well it might. Much was at stake.

Hodge believed all his life that he bore an open and receptive posture toward science. "No sound-minded man," he wrote, "disputes any scientific fact." In his *Systematic Theology* he warned that "it is unwise for theologians to insist on an *interpretation* of Scripture which brings it into collision with the *facts* of science." And like the Puritans before him, he believed that nature reveled God's creativity and the grandeur of his designs. Religion and science, Hodge proclaimed, were "the twin daughters of heaven." Under Hodge's editorial leadership the *Princeton Review* accommodated science sometimes to the point that it earned the rebuke of religious conservatives. An 1841 essay in the journal, for example, addressed the "Relation between Scripture and Geology" and acknowledged that geological evidence should recast modern thinking about the biblical chronology. Other *Princeton Review* contributors insisted that scientific correctives simply helped one see the truth of scripture in a more informed way. No true conflict between religion and science existed. Before he wrote *What is Darwinism?* Hodge wrote confidently: "Let Christians calmly wait until [the] facts [of science] are indubitably established, so established that they command universal consent among competent men, and then they will find that the Bible accords with those facts." We have to ask the question, did Hodge retreat from this liberality when he later wrote his book about Darwin?

Hodge and the Princeton scholars believed that science and religion shared a common methodology. For Hodge that affinity had vast implications for both subjects. As Dwight Bozeman has shown, the Princetonians embraced a Baconian epistemology. Knowledge, it taught, begins with established facts, the empirical data from which we induce larger truths. For the scientist, this standard requires observation of visible evidence. For the theologian, it means that all religious truth derives from the "facts" of scripture. At Princeton Hodge embraced the idea that theology was a scientific enterprise. Princetonians followed Francis Bacon, the seventeenth-century English thinker, in his criterion for scientific truth and they made those standards applicable to theology. "The true method of theology," Hodge wrote, "is, therefore, the inductive, which assumes that the Bible contains all the facts or truths which form the content of theology, just as the facts of nature are the contents of the natural sciences." Hodge said of the theologian that "his business is simply to exhibit the contents of the Bible in a scientific form. His relation to

Scripture is analogous to that of the man of science to nature." Put another way, as Hodge did quite nicely in *Systematic Theology*: "The Bible is to the theologian what nature is to the man of science."

The Baconian methodology had strategical purposes for the Presbyterians. They wanted to fortify their denominational standards by a powerful hermeneutics rooted in the authoritative foundation of scripture. They had witnessed a dangerous drift from those standards in the United States, in the severe rationalism of Unitarianism and in the metaphysical excesses of transcendentalism. But they feared also a popular Christianity rooted in emotion. Baptists and Methodists were surpassing the Presbyterians in numbers and had refashioned American Christianity to democratic tastes, a pattern also evident in the politics of Jacksonian America. It evoked from Hodge the curt rebuke "the ascendancy of the rabble." The Presbyterians intended to uphold high intellectual criteria for their officers. They wanted to check dangerous, speculative tendencies in religion as well as popular excesses. Those goals embraced a biblical scholarship that was also "scientific" in the Baconian meaning of the term.

To this end they had the assistance of the Scottish Enlightenment that Witherspoon had introduced in the previous century. The Scottish philosophers like Thomas Reid and Dugald Stewart were Baconian to the core. They offered the advantage for Protestant America of employing an inductive method to confirm the dictates of common sense and the certitude of moral principles disclosed by the introspection of consciousness. Their philosophical dualism confirmed the differentiated realities of both a physical and spiritual realm of existence. Against the "heresies" of the day—the skepticism of David Hume, the idealism of George Berkeley, and the infidelity of the French *philosophes*—the Scottish thinkers rendered their enterprise an intellectual support system for Christian theism. At Princeton Theological Seminary, Archibald Alexander's course in moral philosophy was "virtually a transcript" of Reid and Stewart, an appropriation by no means exclusive, however, to that institution in the United States, or to the Presbyterians.

GENESIS AFFIRMED

Within Hodge's massive portfolio of theological commentary, one theme in particular has a special relevance to evolution. Both in Europe and the United States the rather static and mechanical conceptions of life prevalent in the eighteenth century were yielding to more dynamic ones. Change and transition, emergence and growth, flux and spontaneity, became more normative descriptions of the world human beings experienced and of nature's characteristics, too. Hodge had inherited an intellectual edifice that readily located God in his revealed word and in the handiworks of nature. But he saw increasingly the declining persuasion of these sources. He feared that the very notion of God was undergoing a terrible erosion. He also knew the culprits. Hodge's writings rail constantly against the German infection. Immanuel Kant, he lamented, had made a dangerous dislocation of the realm of science (phenomena) and the realm of religion (noumena). Post-Kantian philosophies, Hodge observed, gave rise to ideas of God as essentially unknowable, beyond the reach of intellectual conceptualizing. From Scotland Hodge encountered such expressions in Sir William Hamilton's philosophy, and from England in Henry Mansel's theology. And he recognized it most dangerously in Herbert Spencer, a direct link, he believed, to Darwinism.

But the German disease also derived from Hegel. With his large temporal trajectory, Hegel influenced religious thinking in the direction of process and development. Historicism, with its focus on the particularities of time and place, reflected the Hegelian perspective, and for Hodge, introduced a dangerous relativism. In David Strauss, author of *Das Leben Jesu* (*The Life of Jesus*) (1835), the whole biblical narrative broke into sections properly judged "mythical" and others that were essentially historical. Here biblical "facts" so important to Hodge lost their foundational authority. Strauss belonged to a movement known as the higher criticism, which in this case contextualized Jesus' life and rendered him a thoroughly historical and humanized figure. Hodge sharply rebuked such "violent exegesis" in the new scholarship as he readily perceived its inimical effects.

Nineteenth-century romanticism also raised for Hodge another threat to his Baconian methodology. Hegelian influence led many German thinkers to make history the vehicle of God's emerging presence in human affairs and often the institutional location of his continuing spiritual presence in the world. Such viewpoints had various expressions. The German romanticist August Neander, for example, described history as a dynamic process, a living reality generated by a live spirit. His system idealized the church as an organic unity denoted by growth, but also continuity. The Tractarians in England and the later Oxford movement also accepted history as an authority parallel to scripture. In the United States, Hodge had the examples of Philip Schaff and John Williamson Nevin, professors at the Mercersburg Theology Seminary in Pennsylvania, who revitalized church history as they recoiled from the stark individualism of American Protestantism. Invariably, these varieties of conservative romanticism in religion embraced high church forms, with a concentration on the liturgy and a faith in the spiritual power of institutional religion.

Hodge rejected all notions of truth as process or development. Against excessive speculation, in both science and religion, he posed the strict standards of the Baconian methodology, returning Christian truth to the "facts" of scripture. The Christian "system of doctrine," he wrote, "had been recorded in the Bible," "fully" and "clearly." And for this system "there can be no *development*." Hodge rejected as well all notions of the "organic development" of the church. He could not embrace any system that made truth a progressive realization. To that extent, as Stewart observes, Hodge stood "deeply at odds with the great intellectual drift of the nineteenth century." Hodge thus brought to evolutionary ideas in religion a profound skepticism. What might he think of the same ideas in science?

The answer came with force in Charles Hodge's book of 1874 *What Is Darwinism?* It delivered Hodge's famous response that "Darwinism is atheism." So summarized, the little volume suggests an easy dismissal of Darwin's ideas and a giant step in an emerging warfare between science and religion, even a look ahead to such landmark events as the "monkey trial" of 1925 in Dayton, Tennessee. But *What Is Darwinism?* is in many ways a remarkable book. It surveys a formidable amount of opinion on its subject, in Europe and the United States. Alfred Russel Wallace, Thomas Huxley, Ludwig Büchner, Ernst Haeckel, Louis Agassiz, Paul Janet, and others meet Hodge's critical assessments. And in the largest sense, of course, Hodge was right. Darwinism proffered a materialist interpretation of nature. It ruled out grand design and envisioned no teleological process in nature. So at a time when a new generation of American theists set out to accommodate religion and evolution, to read intelligence into development and preserve a theistic understanding of the big scientific question of the late nineteenth century, Hodge stood athwart that progression and flashed a large warning sign.

Hodge presented to his readers a man he much respected as a scientist. He recognized in Darwin "a careful and laborious observer, skillful in his descriptions." He labeled Darwin's book *Voyage of a Naturalist* "a very remarkable and delightful book." He also admired Darwin for his candor, for the scientist often acknowledged where his theory had difficulties or needed more evidence for a fuller verification.

After his opening review of opinions respecting evolution, Hodge turned in his book to confront Darwin's own interpretation. *What Is Darwinism?* appeared just shortly after Darwin had followed his *On the Origin of Species* in 1859 with his *The Descent of Man* in 1871. Hodge quoted key passages from these books to make clear where he would confront his rival. Thus, from the first volume: "Lower animals, especially the dog, manifest love, reverence, fidelity, and obedience; and it is from these elements that the religious sentiment in man has slowly evolved by a process of natural selection." And from the second, what Hodge takes to be Darwin's "grand conclusion": "Man (body, soul, and spirit) is descended from a hairy quadruped, furnished with a tail and pointed ears, probably arboreal in its habits. . . . He who denounces these views (as irreligious) is bound to explain why it is more irreligious to explain the origin of man as a distinct species by descent from some lower form, through the laws of variation and natural selection, than to explain the birth of the individual through the ordinary laws of reproduction."

Hodge combated these conclusions by employing three strategies. First, he offered his standard maxim that the religious person will accept the facts of science when authenticated. "Religious men admit all the facts connected with our solar system, all the facts of geology, and of comparative anatomy, and of biology," he wrote. That much Hodge would yield to the scientists. But then he asked, "must we also admit their explanations and references"? So with respect to Darwin's assertion, in the statement above, Hodge replied that transformations evidenced in embryology (ontogeny), have no necessary extension to the entire life histories of species (phylogeny). Does recapitulation confirm the notion that man was once a fish and then a dog and then an ape? Recurring patterns of shapes and forms from one species to another, as in vertebrates, do not confirm the evolution of one form from another or of all from some primordial germ, Hodge insisted. "It is to be remembered," he wrote, "that facts are from God, the explanation from men; and the two are often as far apart as Heaven and its antipode."

How, though, might one decide between two rival interpretations? Here Hodge used another strategy. Omitting reference to scripture, he appealed instead simply to the common sense of his readers, whether religious or secular. Hodge wanted them to conclude that Darwin's theory offered little persuasion to the intelligent reader. Once again, the problem of the eye emerged as an example. Darwin himself knew the difficulty of it, but believed one could explain the eye without recourse to a designing intelligence or some cosmic scheme. Natural selection suffices.

Hodge judged Darwin his own most trenchant critic. In this instance, Darwin's appeal to blind, physical causes alone in governing the eye's development, should, Hodge averred, appear to "any ordinarily constituted mind" as a sheer impossibility. It requires assumptions not evidenced in each step of this imaginary process, Hodge claimed. Moreover, he observed, as did others at the time, that Darwin could give no adequate account of the process without actually personifying nature. Darwin, as we have noticed, did use anthropomorphic language: He referred to nature as "intensely watching," "picking out with unerring skill," and "carefully preserving" those slight alterations that lead so assuredly, in a happy progression, over millennia, toward the perfected organ, the eye. Darwin himself, Hodge concluded, could not avoid using teleological language to explain his theory. And are we to believe, Hodge asked, that all the varieties of life, all the wondrously various forms, are the derivatives of a common germ? Repeatedly, Hodge asked his readers whether their common sense could sanction so unlikely a development. So when Hodge, in his book, wrote a section on "objections to Darwin," he began with this point: "The first objection to the theory is its *prima facie* incredibility."

So widely read, Hodge used what evidence he could from other scientists to query Darwin on natural selection. From George Campbell, Duke of Argyll, who wrote *The Reign of Law* in 1867, Hodge offered the problem of mutations. For Darwin, a mutation in one organism may pass to its progeny if it has survival value. But the variation, the Duke pointed out, would have no use for the individual organism unless other variations should occur at the right time in a careful coordination of change in nature. Thus the poison of a snake must acquire the chemical properties that render it lethal to another species that it intends to destroy. Moreover, the original mutation that evolves toward a permanent change in a species, or even a new species, may not have an initial advantage at all to the specific organism. In fact, it may actually be injurious or cumbersome to it. The wing of a bird, for example, in its beginning state had no advantages for swimming, walking, or flying and little use at all until it had evolved to its enlarged, functional state, achieved perhaps millions of years later, by Darwin's own calculating.

The objections stated here pointed to one overriding issue for Hodge, the question of design in nature. Here Hodge confronted the evolution question with clear peripheral vision, for he foresaw that the matter would be resolved, if ever it could be, on this battleground. In his book Hodge made teleology the subject of his chapter preceding his final topic of Darwinism and religion. For religion had every stake in that issue, he believed. Hodge went right to the point:

"The grand and fatal objection to Darwinism is [the] exclusion of design in the origin of species or the production of living organisms." This feature above all others, wrote Hodge, distinguished Darwin's theory and made it so formidable a challenge. Hodge was issuing a warning to his fellow religionists: Accommodation with Darwin was a death trap for theism. "The conclusion of the whole matter is that denial of design in nature is virtually the denial of God."

One does not get far in studying evolution without the necessary appeal to a designing intelligence, Hodge insisted. Darwin had to refer at times to the original act of the Creator, he noted. But if you admit the intervening creation of life by a god, Hodge said, why not then acknowledge the intercessory activity of a god in the creation of new species? "If the stupendous miracle of creation be admitted," Hodge wrote, "there is no show of reason for denying supernatural intervention in the operations of nature." But Darwin would have us believe, Hodge urged, that we can account for all the ordered change we see by reference to blind, physical forces, an impossible demand on our common sense. "The most credulous men in the world," Hodge proclaimed, "are unbelievers."

What, though, leads one person as opposed to another, to find Darwin generally plausible or implausible, persuasive or absurd? Many factors may count, as each individual brings to the subject his or her own life history and experiences, intellectual convictions, even emotions and prejudices. The matter may be resolved by intense empirical investigation, or it may be decided beforehand for any of the above influences. Hodge, we have noted, had long affirmed that religion should follow science in establishing the facts, the database of nature on which all thinkers may legitimately make their interpretations. Did Hodge himself, when confronted by Darwin's remarkable speculations, adhere to these standards? Or did his loyalty to the "facts" of scripture prevent him from accepting certain key points in the Darwinian account?

From the late eighteenth century, we have earlier observed, scientists, as evolutionary theories advanced, were extending their estimations of the earth's age. James Hutton in Scotland made such an extension and allowed a slow and painstaking nature to effect, slowly, the many changes evidenced in the geological record. So also did Charles Lyell and the catastrophist Georges Cuvier. Just a year *before* he wrote *What Is Darwinism?* Hodge spoke confidently on this matter in a quite remarkable passage: "Christians have commonly believed that the earth has existed only a few thousands of years. If geologists finally prove that it has existed for myriads of ages, it will be found that the first chapter of Genesis is in full accord with the facts, and that the last results of science are embodied on the first page of the Bible." But in *What Is Darwinism?* a different attitude prevails. In his last section, titled "Relation of Darwinism to Religion," Hodge is considering Darwin's assertions that changes in species are imperceptible and their accumulation so slow as to evade notice. And to that extent the time required to bring about species transformation must be counted "by millions or milliards of years." (Hodge's words.) Hodge responds: "Here is another demand on our credulity." Hodge does not allow any possible biblical reconciliation with Darwin's chronology. A little later in the book, he reacted even more emphatically in considering Alfred Russel Wallace's speculation that human history might go back one hundred thousand and even four hundred thousand years. This was simply too much for Hodge. "Of course we do not believe this," he wrote. And then, in a jarring contrast to his pre-Darwinian confidence, Hodge proclaimed, "We have little faith in the chronology of science."

One may conclude that Hodge's biblical faith, which had seen no conflict with science, finally, in encountering Darwin, had to make a reassessment. Darwin's evolution, rooted in naturalism, compelled Hodge to back off, to deny that Darwin could be reconfigured for biblical accommodation. When scientists like Darwin and Wallace so dramatically extended the age of man, perhaps it seemed to Hodge that giving credence to that possibility might do real damage to scriptural authority, so far did it seem from the "facts" of the Bible. The Darwinian chronology would have discredited those facts to the point that they lost an independent authority of their own. And the vast extension of time seemed to give Darwinian naturalism greater plausibility. Hodge favored a more "catastrophic" understanding of geology and biology.

Or, perhaps, another conclusion is possible. Darwin once noticed, in a letter he wrote to a friend, that his ideas had made very favorable impressions on younger scientists; older scientists did not readily endorse him. With respect to Hodge, he too, as Bruce Kuklick has observed, represented an intellectual era now fading from influence and yielding to another, represented by Darwin. Kuklick writes: "To put it briefly, Darwin-like biology was more conceptual than what had come before it. It gave greater emphasis to a hypothesizing mind than its empirical-minded predecessor, which demanded little in the way of human creativity in science." Hodge measured both biblical and scientific authority by a rigid Baconian factuality. It secured for him a static world of unchanging truths—the word of God revealed in scripture, nature's forms fixed and permanent. Hodge brought to his insights an immense erudition, evident in his imposing scholarship and his prolific reading. Ultimately, though, his methodology revealed Hodge's limitations. "Ironically," as Kuklick summarizes, "Hodge's devotion to the notion that science was only fact-driven put him in the position to disallow many facts, and, as matters turned out, all manner of science." His encounter with Darwin signified profound differences, on subjects like the nature of species and the ages of man. But they represented also a clash of intellectual systems.

FROM SCOTLAND TO AMERICA

James McCosh and Charles Hodge shared a common intellectual tradition. They were both lifelong Presbyterians and Calvinists. They both appropriated the Scottish Enlightenment and made it a critical component of their work. Indeed McCosh lived the Scottish philosophy firsthand and made himself a late contributor to the school. Both he and Hodge served the denomination in key academic roles, one at Princeton Theological Seminary, the other at Princeton College. Both fought to contain the German "bug," and confronted, head on, the challenge of evolution and the Darwinian formulation of it.

McCosh came from the lowland sections of Scotland, born in Patna, Ayrshire, in 1811. His father owned a large farm there and the young James helped with its operation, especially after the father's death when the son was nine years old. James attended the local parish school and then earned degrees at two of Scotland's universities—Glasgow in 1829 and Edinburgh in 1834. At the latter he gained a master's degree in divinity. The Edinburgh experience shaped McCosh's career thereafter. He studied with Thomas Chalmers, leader of the evangelical party in the Church of Scotland, and to which McCosh gave his firm loyalty. We note also, however, that McCosh attended lectures by the university's great philosopher Sir William Hamilton.

McCosh's education thus placed him within the two parts of Scotland's intellectual history. Hamilton represented the culmination of the Scottish Enlightenment of the eighteenth century, denoted by such individuals as Francis Hutcheson, and as we have seen, Thomas Reid and Dugald Stewart, but also Adam Smith and Adam Ferguson. Chalmers represented the evangelical movement, a revitalizing and popular direction in the church that was challenging the dominance of the Moderate Party, so called, and its control of the Scottish kirk. This group, influenced from the early eighteenth century by Hutcheson, had opened the church to rationalizing tendencies and had supported a "moderate" theology that loosened the church from its Calvinist roots. The Evangelicals believed that under the moderate persuasion Scotland had succumbed to an easy and comfortable religiosity, given more to "fashionable" pulpit eloquence than to moral exhortation and the fear of God. At Edinburgh, Chalmers introduced McCosh to the English Puritan writers of the sixteenth and seventeenth centuries and to the American Jonathan Edwards. McCosh cast his lot with the Evangelicals but for the rest of his life he sought to fortify the Reformed faith with modern knowledge. To that end he shared goals similar to Hodge.

McCosh took up the gospel ministry with a parish assignment in Arbroath, on the eastern coast of Scotland. By then, the breach in the Scottish Church, between Evangelicals and moderates, was breaking wide open. Now many of the Evangelicals, McCosh and Chalmers among them, were calling for a separation of their party from the established church. McCosh had removed inland to a parish in Brechin when the Disruption of the Church occurred in 1843. He and the Evangelicals now had to head new parishes that had no support from the state. The young minister had a heavy round of parish duties to conduct, but he saved time for intellectual pursuits. His efforts led to publication of his first book, *The Method of the Divine Government*, in 1850. It gained a sizeable readership in Scotland and in the United States and it led to McCosh's appointment as professor of logic and metaphysics at Queen's College in Belfast, Ireland. There he served from 1852 to 1868.

At Queen's McCosh did his first writing in science. Of course, he knew well the Scottish contributions in evolutionary theory, from Hutton in the late eighteenth century and his "bulldog" at Edinburgh, John Playfair. And while at that university McCosh attended the classes of Robert Jameson, who, against the uniformitarian views of the others, brought a catastrophist viewpoint to his field of geology. Then, while McCosh was at Brechin, Scotsman Robert Chambers offered his anonymous work *Vestiges of the Natural History of Creation*. We have noted the huge controversy surrounding Chambers' theory of "development."

McCosh's major work at Queen's came from his collaboration with colleague George Dickie, a book titled *Typical Forms and Special Ends in Creation*, published in 1855. Parts of the book dealt with a subject that McCosh had taken up previously—morphology, or the study of the biological structure and forms of organisms. In a presentation to the Botanical Society of Edinburgh, McCosh analyzed the pattern of leaf venation in different types of trees, some twenty varieties. He observed that the outline of the leaf's veins, including the angulation of the lesser stems to the central stem, in each type bears a structural resemblance to the naked outline—trunk and branches—of the mature tree itself. McCosh intended to draw attention to the continuity of design that prevailed in the different tree types. In their book he and Dickie extended their observations to other natural formations, botanical and animal.

In this manner, the two authors took up the question of design in nature. McCosh had long thought about it. The classic account of design remained Anglican William Paley's contribution in 1802, his book *Natural Theology: Or Evidence of the Existence of the Attributes of the Deity*. Paley offered his famous example of a watch. If one were to discover a watch lying in the road, one would conclude, upon inspection of its elaborate mechanical contrivances, that it must have had a designer. McCosh, however, judged Paley's argument too self-evident, and, more critically, too static to carry the weight for the theistic argument in an intellectual age denoted by the dynamics of romanticism and evolutionary science. His and Dickie's book does not constitute a contribution to evolution as such, but it offered two considerations that McCosh carried into his later dealing with that subject.

The first phenomenon the authors offered they called "collocation." In *Typical Forms* it carries on the argument for design in nature, but in a more complex presentation than the watch analogy of Paley. McCosh exemplified this term by the pollination of flowers. The procedure, he said, demonstrates the coordinated interrelationships of natural occurrences. Thus, in pollination, neither the seed-producing plant nor the nectar-drawing bee knows anything of the needs of the other, but a mutuality of interests exists and the bees' quest for nectar and their concurring distribution of pollen sustain both plant and insect. McCosh and Dickie cited these "mutual adaptations of different and independent" functions as evidence of design. They cannot proceed from chance for they show overwhelming evidence of a careful coordination of ostensibly unconnected occurrences. Collocation thus purported to give a more comprehensive and vigorous offering of the design argument than Paley had provided.

The two authors also gave attention to another pattern that had a particular relevance for the evolution question—homologies. McCosh had read with interest the book by Richard Owen, *On the Archetype and Homologies of the Vertebrate Skeleton*, published in 1848, and he had written a lengthy review essay about it. Owen had studied the progressive appearances of the same organ in different animals. He drew his comparisons widely across species. And he narrated a record of progressive change: Forelimbs become fins in fishes, wings in birds, claws in reptiles. One example in particular intrigued McCosh. The five-part division of the whale's fin, Owen suggested, is akin to the pendactyl hands and feet of *Homo sapiens*. Now in describing these forms, Owen adhered to the familiar design account of Paley; that is, he specified their utilitarian function for the successive organisms in question. Owen's account rendered an avowedly theistic interpretation, as homologies, he took pains to argue, showed the careful design and intelligence of a single Creator. Homologies, in fact, provided a key component of *Naturphilosophie*.

McCosh learned much from Owen's book, as the review clearly showed. Owen had written that each species was created perfect "in relation to the circumstances and sphere in which it was destined to exist." But he wondered whether Owen might not have overlooked something of greater significance in his materials. He wondered if the continuity of design that Owen described might not reveal a greater scheme of planning than the merely local and utilitarian incidents that Owen, à la Paley, specified. For McCosh believed that structure did not always reveal function. So with respect to the whale's fin and its later connections to the human hand he wrote: "It is a curious circumstance that every segment and almost every bone present in the human hand and arm, exist also in the fin of the whale, *though they do not seem required for the support and movement of that undivided and inflexible paddle*." (Emphasis added.) In other words, it was not clear that the five-part segmentation of the whale's fin had a functional purpose at all. For how did that division assist the mammal in its watery passages? Yet, McCosh asserted, continuity of design, from whale to human, was evident all along the intermediate stages. McCosh then conjectured that nature was anticipatory. Owen held to a narrow teleology, or so McCosh alleged, and McCosh wanted to describe a more expansive one. Thus the appearance of the division in the whale's fin, though of no consequence to this organism itself, was nonetheless crucial to the later emergence of man and to the distinguishing and vitally functional pendactyl features of *Homo sapiens*. Homologies for McCosh thus enhanced the theistic argument by design. He wrote: "The Supreme [Being] could see that which was to come, and which he had preordained. . . . Man appears as the final and foreseen product of the one mighty plan."

Again, McCosh advanced a dynamic view of nature, one that acknowledged the integration of the species, though not necessarily their transmutation. To this extent, McCosh's perspective, with its outline of a grand progressive design in nature, somewhat resembled Robert Chambers'. But McCosh marked his interpretation off from his fellow Scotsman's. "It is not that one species has run into another," he wrote, "but that the higher species is constructed after the same type as the lower." Here McCosh stood in the years before Darwin's revolutionary thesis of 1859.

In 1868 Princeton College (still formally the College of New Jersey) made McCosh its new president. His writings had won him wide respect in Presbyterian circles in the United States, and he now followed the path of the Scotsman Witherspoon exactly one hundred years before. Just two years previously the two northern divisions of the Presbyterians—the Calvinist Old School and the more evangelical New School—had held separate general assembly meetings in St. Louis. McCosh, touring the country, visited both meetings and won warm receptions at each. The separate meetings agreed to reunite the two branches and McCosh arrived to Princeton as a reconciling force among American Presbyterians (although the southern churches remained separate). However, McCosh's real challenge, he was soon to discover, lay in the area of academics, and academic politics. The college, like the seminary, was staunchly Calvinist, and closely connected to its next-door neighbor. Four of the seminary faculty sat on the college's board of trustees and Charles Hodge served as president of that board. McCosh, in taking up his new office, judged its physical plant and its curriculum badly in need of modernizing. And he would later write that as he traveled the ocean to his new home, he wondered how, at conservative Princeton, he might address the subject of evolution.

He had reason for pause. Princeton's faculty, too, was stocked with solid Calvinists. Thomas Duffield was one of them. He taught Greek and mathematics and served the Old School Presbyterians as a prominent leader. Duffield opposed wholesale the new theories of evolution. He believed they all derived from the "old Greek athe-ists." For Christians, Duffield said, the matter came down to one question: "Is evolution, as it respects man, consistent with the Bible?" Duffield said no. When God breathed into the dust and cre-ated the soul of man, he stated, he acted in a wholly supernatural way; no germ theory of evolution could square with that fact. Duffield also warned that any questioning of Genesis could open the door to a full-blown skepticism in all matters of religious truth. Not all of Princeton was so rigid in its views, but when McCosh prepared to deliver his inaugural address in October 1868, in which he would urge for the venerable school a new and more liberal curriculum, he heard Charles Hodge speak first. Hodge made himself perfectly clear. "We desire that the spirit of true religion should be dominant in this College, that a pure gospel should live here." "Unsanctified learning is a curse," he said. "Nothing is more evident than that knowledge uncontrolled by religion becomes Satanic."

AN EVANGELICAL READING

McCosh, of course, did not want to preside over a college declining in its religious identity. And he shared with Duffield and Hodge a conviction that God presides in the world as Creator and sustainer of life and that a Christian understanding of all things shows the path of truth. But McCosh brought to evolution a different spirit and temperament. He had less a stake in defending the exact authority of scripture than had Hodge and Duffield. Thus, he wrote, when ex-pert study of fossils expands the age of earth even into the "millions of years," it was fruitless to be calculating the generations from Adam as a reliable guide to this essentially scientific question. For religion, he added, could be only the loser if it resisted the record documented by science. In one of the many talks McCosh gave on this subject, he summarized as follows: "Religious people are fright-ened unnecessarily at the idea of development, for the reason that radical evolutionists leave out God in accounting for evolution. . . . The idea exists that evolution is destined to overthrow religion. . . .

I say, do not be captivated by theories, but accept the truths of science." The college especially, McCosh urged, must advance modern learning, doing its best to show its consistency with religion. He was prepared to go a long way with the contemporary views. "My first position," McCosh avowed, "is the certainty of evolution. Evolution is but the continuing of one thing out of another. No scientific man under 30 years of age in any country denies it, to my knowledge. I am at the head of a college where to declare against it would perplex my best students. They would ask me which to give up, science or the Bible." And finally: "Let me warn you, the defenders of religion should be cautious in assailing evolution. . . . The legitimate evolution supports Christianity."

McCosh, however, did not have an easy time explaining just how this fact was true. Several issues divided him from others in the religious camp, but one in particular proved troublesome. For those particularly defensive about scriptural truth, Darwin's idea that one species could evolve from another raised the red flag. McCosh was untroubled by this idea. He had a greater concern for showing that derivation of species could accommodate final causes, thus preserving design in evolution. "I am not sure," he stated, "that religion has any interest in holding, absolutely by the one side or other of this question, which is for scientific men to settle." And ultimately: "I am not sure that religion is entitled to insist that every species of insect has been created by a special fiat of God, with no secondary agent employed."

So then, how might the theist, conceding much to Darwinian science, yet salvage evolution for religion? McCosh made his major suggestion when he delivered a paper to the Evangelical Alliance meeting in 1873. Some historians have even speculated that upon hearing that address Charles Hodge returned from New York City and plunged into the writing of *What Is Darwinism?* as if to head off the impact of McCosh's reconciliation effort. (McCosh provided his full statement in *The Religious Aspect of Evolution*, in 1888.) McCosh intended to show the continuing validity of the argument from design. As he had first argued in *Typical Forms*, he wanted to move beyond the reigning static view of design that shows the simple function and coordination of one organ with the entire complex of the organism. In evolution, McCosh now urged, with one species changing into another, one sees a far greater intricacy, one that impresses more than the technical integration of parts in the static view of life. The evolutionary process, McCosh believed, "impels the concurrence of an immense number of agents, mechanical, chemical, electric, galvanic." Here was collocation on a grand scale, merging blind and indifferent processes to effect the most careful and minute transformations in the countless forms of life. One may legitimately conclude, McCosh avowed, that "the union and conspiracy of forces involved in Evolution furnish new proof, as it certainly supplies new illustrations, of purposes and ends." To that extent, Darwinism supported religion.

To that extent. But neither McCosh, nor any theist generally speaking, could accept Darwin whole. McCosh also had some problems. The gap between man and monkey, for example, seemed to be so clear that one could not posit an unbroken succession of species evolution in this instance. "There is no evidence, then," McCosh wrote, "of a gradual rise by natural law, from the brute to the lowest form of man." McCosh did concede much to Darwin, however, in acknowledging the environment as an agent of evolution and he accepted with ease its extended impact, "over millions of years." For McCosh it was enough that all proceeded in an orderly way, that evolution took place gradually and unnoticeably over much time, and that "there are no violent or revolutionary changes involved. Nature is kept steadfast and theism is satisfied."

McCosh thus tried to give evolution a theistic reading, but he also wanted to read it within the Judaic-Christian tradition. In *Christianity and Positivism* (1871) McCosh read the long history in terms of different stages, or dispensations, and in a way that appropriated a Darwinian framework. Thus, he said, we see in evolution before the emergence of man the dominance of brute strength and force as the determinants of survival. Here the skillful arrangement of physiological forms program the natural selection process. Speed and power, or specific features like a thick skin or sharp teeth, furnish the survival assets and those that lack lose in the struggle. Under

these conditions man should have been the early victim. But Mc-
Cosh, citing Wallace, notes that the thin-skinned and hairless man
thrives the world over, transcending environmental constraints.
Here, he suggested, we have entered the second dispensation, that
of intellect. It is marked by technological innovation and creative
mastery of nature. "The giants disappear and the civilized peoples
take their place," McCosh wrote. Out of the forbidding terrain and
forests cities emerge; the earth, reshaped by tools and machines,
yields new means of sustenance, the result of intellectual advancement.

However, the dispensation of intellect does not perfect the
species. It does not overcome the savage drives residual from the
lower forms of life; beastly passions reign. Intellect builds bridges
but greater vehicles of war and destruction as well. The intellectual
era culminates, McCosh says, in Greece. But then there arrives the
dispensation of the spirit, introduced by Christ. Grace triumphs over
strength (Christ even pronounces that the meek shall inherit the
earth) and it gives new direction to intellect, science, and the arts.
With Christ, McCosh believed, a new level of the evolutionary plane
is possible. "This is the era in which our lot is cast." It challenges humanity to realize the promise of Jesus. Here especially McCosh's
background in evangelical Protestantism reveals itself.

At Princeton McCosh arrived rather quickly to an acceptance of
evolution as Darwin described it. A series of lectures led to his book
Christianity and Positivism. "Depend upon it," he wrote, "when the
process is explored, there will be found an immense number and variety of adaptations to secure that the peculiarity of the individual,
found to be useful, will not perish with the individual, but go down
to future ages." A few years later he acknowledged that the forms of
life do succeed each other in unbroken procession. He employed
Darwinian terminology: "As new and trying circumstances arise
there is a struggle for existence; the unfit disappear and the fit survive, and there is a progress upon the whole through the long ages."
McCosh, reviewing recent addresses by Thomas Huxley, abandoned
the earlier language of his typical forms and ceased to employ
Owen's homologies to describe the continuities in nature's forms. He

simply accepted the "tendency on the part of the reptile to rise to the bird, and the bird to retain the properties of the reptile; and natural selection and development can alone explain this."

At this point, we should make a point of differentiation. The evolutionary hypothesis, as the next chapter will explore, fostered a new era of Protestant theology in the United States. Despite different formulations, liberals generally gave a spiritual reading to evolution by positing a progressive merging of the natural and supernatural, the increasing manifestation of God in his creation. "Imminence" became a key term for the liberal Protestants. The growth of the human race in intellect, the arts, science, and spiritual awareness, along with the moral perfection of the world, suggested God's merging with human history in a progressive record of evolutionary change and advance. Liberals saw at work the certain redemption of the world in a temporal arrangement that preserved a meaningful teleology.

Both Hodge and McCosh saw this tendency and dissociated themselves from it. McCosh could not view the evolutionary pattern in so blatantly optimistic terms. Here McCosh's position reflected his background in Calvinism, albeit a moderate Calvinism, and his activity in the gospel ministry amid the harsh realities of life he witnessed in his pastoral career. McCosh always spoke of religious experience in terms of a powerful inner transformation. As president of Princeton he encouraged and sponsored campus revivals, as he had done in his work for the Free Church of Scotland. McCosh saw in theological liberalism a likeness to the rationalist voices in the Moderate party in the Church of Scotland from which he separated. Nothing, in his view, assured a benevolent progression in human history. He warned in *Christianity and Positivism* that religious optimism too easily obscures the dark side of human nature and human history. It gives "far too fair a picture of the state of our world." McCosh employed the words "contest" and "struggle" to describe the necessities of action in the last dispensation. Liberal theologians might see the progressive merging of the natural and the spiritual; McCosh saw a continuing contest of the one with the other; and it seethes in every human breast, he said, "between the passions raging like the sea and the conscience that would restrain them." Mc-Cosh, the evangelical Calvinist, saw the world much like the naturalist Darwin—an arena of strife, and no easy win in sight. He had more confidence than Darwin that good would triumph, and less confidence than the liberal Protestants. For McCosh believed that victory required much more the work of the gospel ministry than the comfortable assurances of a progressive evolution. McCosh thus contained evolution within the Reformed tradition and its long history going back to John Calvin.

BIBLIOGRAPHY

Bozeman, Theodore Dwight. *Protestants in the Age of Science: The Baconian Ideal and American Antebellum Religious Thought.* Chapel Hill: University of North Carolina Press, 1977.

Conkin, Paul. *The Uneasy Center: Reformed Christianity in Antebellum America.* Chapel Hill: University of North Carolina Press, 1995.

Gregory, Frederick. "The Impact of Darwinian Evolution on Protestant Theology in the Nineteenth Century." In *God and Nature: Historical Essays on the Encounter between Christianity and Science,* ed. David C. Lindberg and Ronald L. Numbers, 369–90. Berkeley: University of California Press, 1986.

Gundlach, Bradley J. "McCosh and Hodge on Evolution: A Combined Legacy." *Journal of Presbyterian History* 75 (1997): 85–102.

Hodge, Charles. *What Is Darwinism?* Ed. Mark A. Noll and David N. Livingston. 1874. Grand Rapids, MI: Baker, 1994.

Hoeveler, J. David. Introduction in *Natural Selection and Divine Election.* Vol. 1, *Darwinism and Theology in America: 1850–1930.* Ed. Frank X. Ryan. Bristol, England: Thoemmes Press, 2002.

——. *James McCosh and the Scottish Intellectual Tradition: From Glasgow to Princeton.* Princeton: Princeton University Press, 1981.

Illick, Joseph E. "The Reception of Darwinism at the Theological Seminary and the College at Princeton, New Jersey." *Journal of the Presbyterian Historical Society* 38 (1960): 152–65, 234–43.

Livingston, David N. *Darwin's Forgotten Defenders: The Encounter between Evangelical Theology and Evolutionary Thought.* Grand Rapids, MI: Eerdmans, 1987.

———. "The Idea of Design: The Vicissitudes of a Key Concept in the Princeton Response to Darwin." *Scottish Journal of Theology* 37 (1984): 329–57.

Moore, James R. *The Post-Darwinian Controversies: A Study of the Protestant Struggle to Come to Terms with Darwin in Great Britain and America, 1870–1900.* Cambridge: Cambridge University Press, 1979.

Noll, Mark. *The Princeton Theology, 1812–1921: Scripture, Science and Theological Method. From Archibald Alexander to Benjamin Breckenridge Warfield.* Grand Rapids, MI: Baker Nook House, 2001.

Roberts, Jon H. *Darwinism and the Divine in America: Protestant Intellectuals and Organic Evolution, 1859–1900.* Madison: University of Wisconsin Press, 1988.

Stewart, John W., and James H. Moorhead, eds. *Charles Hodge Revisited: A Critical Appraisal of His Life and Work.* Grand Rapids, MI: Eerdmans, 2000. [Contains several authors' quotations in this chapter.]

Welch, Claude. *Protestant Thought in the Nineteenth Century: Vol. I, 1799–1870.* New Haven: Yale University Press, 1974.

PROTESTANT LIBERALISM

Henry Ward Beecher and John Bascom

THE NEW THEOLOGY

While Charles Hodge, James McCosh, and others sought to fortify an orthodox Christianity against and with evolutionary ideas, another group of religious thinkers took on a different challenge. Collectively, these individuals recognized the need for a thoroughgoing alteration in Christian thought. A crisis of both intellectual and social proportions brought on this perceived necessity. Christian understanding must change to save the religion, they believed. This concern, and the bold effort that ensued, produced a major body of Protestant thought, dominant from the late nineteenth century and well into the twentieth. Historian Sydney Ahlstrom labeled this era "the golden age of liberal theology." But other names applied: "the new theology," "Progressive orthodoxy," "modernism," "romantic Christianity," "evangelical liberalism." Evolutionary concepts influenced and sustained the movement throughout; they gave it its supreme and often naive confidence. Hence, we have such books as Minot J. Savage's *The Religion of Evolution* (1876), Lyman Abbott's *The Evolution of Christianity* (1892) as well as his *The Theology of an Evolutionist* (1897), and George Harris's *Moral Evolution* (1896). We have already noted McCosh's *The Religious Aspect of Evolution*, and in this chapter we shall have a look at Henry Ward Beecher's *Evolution and Religion* and John Bascom's *The New Theology* and his *Religion and Evolution*.

Protestant Liberalism drew on many sources, some antedating Darwin's book. Romantic philosophy, with roots in Immanuel Kant's transcendental metaphysics, and Hegelian teleology gave European religious thinking a new orientation. We noticed earlier the historicism of David Strauss and its implications for the study of scripture. In England, Frederick D. Maurice and the Broad Church movement influenced American churchmen, especially Episcopalians. In the United States the new liberalism had an early expression in Unitarianism and its more "heretical" offshoot, transcendentalism. In 1847, Horace Bushnell published his path-breaking book *Christian Nurture*. Bushnell, and his congregation at Hartford, Connecticut, could no longer look to the revival as the vehicle of religious transformation and sought less dramatic and less harsh modes of religious experience. These new directions meant for Bushnell a nurture in the Christian milieu of home and church and the progressive growth of the individual into greater spirituality. Bushnell also influenced Protestant Liberalism with his 1858 publication, *Nature and the Supernatural*, in which his dissolution of these traditional dichotomies anticipated a critical thematic shift in the modernists.

The emergence of Protestant Liberalism produced tensions. Among Presbyterians, Baptists, and Congregationalists, the intellectual shifts led to highly publicized heresy trials—David Swing in 1874 and Asa Briggs in 1893, among others—that showed in bold relief how modernism challenged orthodoxy and induced retaliation in turn. Nonetheless, the liberals gained major institutional strongholds in the divinity schools and they produced a new generation of pulpit preachers. Harvard, Yale, and Andover brought the Congregationalists most completely into the new theology. Princeton remained the citadel of Calvinism, but Presbyterianism had many liberal voices. Boston University reflected the new directions among Methodists. Colgate Theological Seminary did the same for the Baptists. And after the turn of the century, the new academic colossus, the University of Chicago, became "the country's most powerful center of Protestant liberalism."

Protestant Liberalism had several themes. First, from evolution's vantage, it saw all things historically. Some influence in that direction had already come from Strauss and the higher criticism, but American religious liberalism signified no mere chronology of events or some prosaic historical narrative. The modernists assigned history an emphatic teleology; they described a history full of meaning and a progression marked by cosmic purpose. Here, especially, the liberals located the means of their ambitious rescue mission, their attempts to discredit in Darwinism its methodology of chance and its blind mechanical operations. They would embrace evolution, and embrace it enthusiastically, to the extent that it brought an active God back into the universe and made him the vehicle of a redemptive history. The liberals' zeal for their cause, and their overreaching hopes, owed much to their confidence that herein lay the real truths of evolution. Lyman Abbott defined the goal of theology in his time: "to restate the principles of the Christian faith in terms of an evolutionary philosophy."

Other opportunities lay in store. The Progressives' reading of change enabled them to attack stale and rigid creeds, obstacles to intellectual advance in all ages. Religious dogma and creedal formulations, even much of the Bible itself, they asserted, always carried the historical stamp of its age. Increasingly they carried the historical baggage of past time, too. Briggs thus wrote that "experience shows that no body of divinity can answer more than its generation." For each age has its own "providential problems" to solve and they become for that time its means of adaptation. Swing wrote that creeds try to contain God's wisdom "in the phrases of a few men at some given time and place." But fixity brings stagnation and religions lose their useful connections to their environments, he warned. For most of the religious modernists the impediments in question signified such notions as original sin, human depravity, and predestination. Indeed, among many liberals the purification that evolutionary understanding would bring applied also to the sacraments and any preoccupation with the forms of worship. Protagonists of liberalism looked to a liberation of mind and a resulting purer Christianity informed by reason, moral good, and modern science. Here is Lyman Abbott effectively conveying the spirit of liberalism:

> The belief that the Bible is a revelation from God is not inconsistent with the belief that the Christian religion is an evolution; for revelation is not a final statement of truth, crystallized into dogma, but a gradual and progressive unveiling of the mind that it may see truth clearly and receive it vitally. The Bible is not fossilized truth in an amber Book; it is a seed which vitalizes the soil into which it is cast; a window through which the light of dawning day enters the quickened mind; a voice commanding humanity to look forward and go forward; a prophet who bids men seek the golden age in the future, not in the past.

Finally, the evolutionary viewpoint created a theology of imminence. History became the progressive presence of God in the world. The old distinctions of natural and supernatural, sacred and secular, broke down. That turn had been apparent for some time, but now the liberals dissolved these distinctions and proclaimed a progressive manifestation of God in human history, working with humanity purposefully toward specific ends. In the new theology, God lost his awesome transcendence and remoteness. A god so worshiped, the liberals believed, turned Christians' attention from the world. As Theodore Munger, a major voice of the liberal pulpit, urged: "The New Theology does indeed regard with question the line often drawn between the sacred and the secular . . . a line that, by its distinction, ignores the very process by which the kingdoms of the world are becoming the kingdom of the Lord Jesus Christ."

Munger's words suggest how Protestant Liberalism would engage the world. In fact, the movement derived from both an intellectual and social crisis that arose in midcentury. It sprang from a sense that the old verities no longer maintained. What D. H. Meyer calls the "Victorian Crisis of Faith" had already set in before Darwin. Alfred Lord Tennyson used his phrase "nature red in tooth and claw" in the 1850s and marked the increasing doubt that nature gave any assurances of a benevolent universe. Darwin deepened the fears. Boston University professor Borden P. Bowne in 1878 summarized Darwin's stark message: "Life without meaning; death without meaning; and the universe without meaning. A race tortured to no purpose, and with no hope but annihilation. The dead only blessed; the living standing like beasts at bay, and shrieking half in defiance and half in fright." Where did God fit into such a picture? What viability remained to venerable moral truths long taught by church, school, and family? Here was the challenge for Protestant Liberalism, that it might restore unity and meaning to things and purpose to history. Protestant Liberalism thus became a "quest for cosmic comfort" amid a fear that human beings confronted only an indifferent universe. A new assurance might emerge, but it could be achieved only, as Meyer wrote, "by dint of intellectual effort."

However, help was soon on the way. By a peculiar twist the British philosopher Herbert Spencer, mentioned previously, attained heroic status in the United States. Indeed, it rather amazes that this thinker, as much reviled in his own country as he was honored in the other, could win for his vast edifice of turgid, speculative writing so enthusiastic a reception among Americans. But Spencer spoke to the Victorian crisis, both in the social messages of his *Social Statics* (1851) and perhaps more superficially in the ten volumes of his *System of Synthetic Philosophy* (1862–1893). His strict empiricism seemed to set well with the greater materialism in America's new industrial civilization, but in upholding an "unknown" God, Spencer made some room for a meaningful cosmos. Spencerian philosophy was emphatically evolutionary and that fact gave it greater plausibility under the standards of the modern intellect. However harsh the world appeared in Spencer's affirmation of a "struggle for existence" pervasive in the human and natural world, he came almost as a prophet. He assured that individual competition underwrote an inevitable progress in human affairs. Indeed, as James R. Moore says, Spencer's philosophy, "though not in every detail, yet in its fundamental assumptions and affirmations, provided a thoroughgoing rationale for the American way of life." With a careful reconfiguring, liberal Protestants could use Spencer as a point of departure from his philosophical agnosticism to their Christian evolutionism.

Finally, this chapter will supply another context for Protestant Liberalism. However much it might have owed to some earlier bold

departures from orthodoxy, Protestant Liberalism found its immediate background in evangelical Christianity. The earlier decades of
the nineteenth century constituted the great era of Evangelicalism
in American religious history. And yes, the liberals broke self-
consciously from Calvinism and from the revivals. But they owed
more to their forebears than they often allowed. They drew from
Evangelicalism a commitment to social reform. Evangelicals found
their causes in temperance, Sabbatarianism, and antislavery. Liberals found other causes, but they embraced as well a theology of the
kingdom and looked to a world improved in all quarters. For the liberals as for the Evangelicals, the United States remained the hope of
the world, the repository of the old Puritan promise, a redeemer nation. To that extent we shall find a recurring language in both
groups. Evolutionary ideas significantly helped moderns craft a new
theology, but it often reverberated with the familiar refrains of the
old camp meeting.

AN EVANGELICAL YOUTH

The two individuals discussed in this chapter well reflect evangelical youth. The remarkable Henry Ward Beecher came from one of
America's most remarkable families. His sisters included Charlotte,
a best-selling writer in her work for American women, and Harriet,
a prolific novelist who electrified the world with her tale of slavery,
Uncle Tom's Cabin, in 1852. In the family patriarch, Lyman Beecher,
evangelical Christianity had one of its major voices. Henry could not
have received a more thorough education in the religious politics of
the day, for Lyman took on all of it. And Henry would experience
the best and worst of Evangelicalism. He fought, with personal an-
guish, to lift himself from the religion his father represented. He
wanted to redefine Christianity for a new America. In doing so he
made a major contribution to Protestant Liberalism. Evolution underscored his efforts.

Lyman Beecher had his church and raised his family in Litchfield,
Connecticut. Born in New Haven in 1775, Beecher graduated from

Yale in 1797, where he had come under the influence of President Timothy Dwight. Dwight had led Yale students in revivals and his work helped inaugurate the "second great awakening." Yale students spread Christianity to the Far East and to the American hinterlands. Dwight also influenced another student, Nathaniel William Taylor, who with Beecher promoted a liberal Calvinism that spread with the new generation of Evangelicals. "Taylorism," or the "New Haven Theology," or the "New Divinity," insisted that the certainty of sin did not preclude a "power to the contrary," and thus allowed for freedom of the will in human action. These ideas stood condemned as heresy among orthodox Calvinists.

Lyman Beecher's career reflected salient features of evangelical Christianity. Beecher promoted revivals in New England and sought to energize the churches in fighting social evils. He championed temperance and crusaded against dueling. In 1826 he went to Boston to lead the fight against Unitarianism, the main institutional and theological expression of liberalism in New England. Beecher feared the threat to religion as the country moved westward, and in 1832 accepted a call to become president of Lane Theological Seminary in Cincinnati, where he also served the Second Presbyterian Church. Beecher's famous essay, "A Plea for the West," written in 1834, constituted a major document of anti-Catholicism during these years when such hatred proliferated in the United States. Despite Beecher's strong service in defense of the standing order in Connecticut and of Trinitarianism in theology, his long association with Taylor made him suspect among the strictly orthodox. In 1835 Lyman Beecher underwent a much publicized heresy trial. The meanness of it all made a lasting and frightening impression on his son Henry.

None of the Beecher children, it seemed, had an easy time with their father. Neither Charlotte nor Harriet experienced the critical religious conversion that would bring them assuredly into the covenant of grace. Henry struggled, too. He was born in Litchfield in 1813, the "baby" of the family, as he was the youngest of the children by Lyman's first wife. He remained in New England to study at Amherst College while the family went to Cincinnati, and he graduated in 1834. But Lyman, despairing, had not gained assurance of Henry's conversion. Nonetheless, an apparent rebirth, which Henry later doubted, led him into the ministry and to his appointment at the Presbyterian Church in Lawrenceburg, Indiana. He now began an extraordinary pulpit career. It would take him next to Indianapolis, the state's largest city, in 1839, and then east to Brooklyn Heights and Plymouth Church in 1847. Several thousand heard him preach on Sundays and thousands more on his many, expansive lecture tours. He spoke on religion and he spoke on political issues. He edited a popular religious periodical and he wrote a widely read novel. Not even a scandalous adultery trial in the early 1870s, followed by the whole nation, seemed to impair his reputation. Edward Godkin, editor of the *Nation*, called Henry Ward Beecher "the most remarkable preacher of his time, the most popular, the most influential." Indeed, Beecher remains a key historical figure. As biographer William McLaughlin wrote: Beecher's career helps us "to explain how Americans made the great shift from Calvinism to Liberal Protestantism, from rural to suburban living, from transcendentalism to Social Darwinism, . . . from an age of reform to an age of complacency, from an age of egalitarian simplicity to an age of conspicuous consumption and the leisure class." As Beecher himself negotiated these shifts, his evolutionary perspective helped him see the way.

Not until 1886, a year before he died, did Beecher formalize his views on evolution. But he was no late arrival to the concept. Along the way he had said and written much, and in the preface to his book *Evolution and Religion* he made a clarifying statement: "Slowly, and through a whole fifty years, I have been under the influence, first obscurely, imperfectly, of the great doctrine of Evolution." Herbert Spencer clearly had the greatest impact. Beecher referred to Spencer as "the ablest thinker of them all, and the ablest man that has appeared for centuries." Breaking from the Calvinist gloom of his father's New England, Beecher seized on Spencer's cosmology, its assurance of progress and advancement, its optimistic teleology. He welcomed in Spencer a recourse to the natural sciences, which Beecher made the vehicle of God's revelation and a doctrine of divine imminence. When Spencer made his triumphant visit to the United States in 1882, wined and dined by an adoring American public in New York City, it was Beecher who gave the great banquet address. Nor could Darwin make Beecher any less the enthusiast for evolution. He could salvage even him for a Christian reading of the idea. In a letter of 1867, Beecher wrote: "I do not think Science, as it will be, is without its Calvary. But, *as it now is*, in the hands of [John Stuart] Mill, Spencer, John Tyndall and I may add, Charles Darwin, it has gone only so far as to have lost the cross, and not far enough to have found it again." Therein Beecher saw a role for himself.

That role he took on not long after his arrival in Brooklyn. He came in from the West and brought with him the evangelical pietism of that region, and of his own rearing. One can glimpse something of the great change that Beecher would now make in his religious practices by noting briefly a publication that had given him his national reputation before the move to the East. Some talks that Beecher gave in Indianapolis became published as a book titled *Lectures to Young Men*, in 1844. They reverberate with evangelical moralism as Beecher addressed the many threats to American male youth at mid-century. They addressed the evil of prostitution, but also sounded warnings against idleness; drinking; and attending the theater, the horse races, and the circus. They alerted to the snares of luxurious living and popular fashions in the marketplace. They cautioned against frivolities, like reading French novels. The antidote to all these evils, Beecher believed, could come only from profound spiritual rebirth. That experience, he assured, will cast away all worldly temptations and focus young men on the real business of the day—application of one's God-given talents in a regime of industry, thrift, and frugality.

But in 1847, Beecher wasn't in Indianapolis anymore. He was in New York City, or at least right across the East River in Brooklyn Heights, sometimes called "America's first suburb." Now he found in his congregants men and women of upper middle-class status—white, professional. They built tasteful brownstone houses, sought out clothes of fashion at city department stores, lusted for culture—art, music, and theater. They read what they thought they should read to be modern, current, informed. Much of it troubled them, these churchgoing people of faith. Science threatened old beliefs, cast out God, raised levels of skepticism. They had confidence in their growing nation, but here, too, doubt intervened. Immigrants were arriving in vast numbers—Irish Catholics, Chinese. In the 1870s the country entered a period of intense class warfare. Labor violence and strikes raised the awful specter of social division, instability, and the wholesale rending of the social fabric. (After novelist William Dean Howells sent his manuscript for *The Rise of Silas Lapham* to his publisher, he was instructed to take the word "dynamite" out of it. Such was the fear of social radicalism and violence.)

Beecher's biographers have found a moment of greatest interest in the arrival of this young minister, only thirty-four years old, and fresh from the West, to this place of affluence and sophistication. How might he address his new congregants? How to allay their fears and doubts? How to describe for them a social and religious role in a nation so rapidly transforming? Beecher at first wanted to promote revivals; he had only moderate success. He soon realized that he could not preach the old doctrines of original sin and predestination, not to *these* people. Nor did he wish to. Beecher's accommodation to Brooklyn coincided perfectly with his own personal liberation from his father's ways. The more adjusted to Brooklyn he became, the more he realized how happily he was leaving the old Calvinism behind. His Protestant Liberalism spoke to his own needs and to the social realities of his congregation. It offered Plymouth Church the portrait of a loving God; it made religion at one with modern science; it celebrated evolution as advance through culture and civilization, with crucial roles to be played by those who flocked to his Sunday sermons. And how eagerly these parishioners listened and how lavishly they rewarded him! Beecher would later draw a salary in the staggering amount of twenty thousand dollars a year (and he took the summers off). In fact, though, the whole country became his congregation. He would give about fifty public lectures annually, at one thousand dollars a pop. He was easily the highest paid clergyman in the United States. The 2006 biography of Henry Ward Beecher bears the title *The Most Famous Man in America*.

Neither in religious ideas or current politics did Beecher shy from controversy. He followed his father to that extent. It is important to know Beecher's political activities because they played significantly in his Protestant Liberalism. At Amherst, Beecher had joined the student Colonization Society, which promoted programs to return slaves to Africa, but he broke from it to form an antislavery group with other students. For a short while after graduation, he studied at Lane in Cincinnati and with sister Harriet (he was closest to her of all his siblings) and others, worked with the free Negro population in that city, promoting civil rights for blacks. Lane's trustees censored this activism and the student body left for more radical Oberlin College in northern Ohio. Beecher carried his commitments into his young ministry. In Lawrenceburg he joined the New Side wing of American Presbyterianism, a significant decision. This denomination underwent a schism in 1837 as Old Side and New Side divided on three issues. Beecher's wing supported revivalism, spoke for a liberal Calvinism, and conjoined politics and religion, especially on the issue of slavery. The success of his *Lectures* encouraged Beecher to speak out against slavery from his Indianapolis pulpit, and his following grew as he did. On the subject of the Mexican War, Beecher condemned America's aggression and material greed, disguised, he accused, in the bogus idealism of "Manifest Destiny." He saw in the conflict a bully nation taking advantage of a weaker neighbor.

Of course, slavery remained the issue of the day. The Compromise of 1850 included the notorious Fugitive Slave Law and Beecher condemned it outright. With other northern ministers he pledged to defy it, denouncing the moral evil of the law and its imposition of the slave owners' values on northern public officials. Moral outrage in Beecher rose the more four years later when Stephen Douglas secured passage of the Kansas-Nebraska Act. With "popular sovereignty" now to determine the situation of slavery in Kansas, that territory became a war zone. Beecher wanted to throw his whole church into the effort to keep Kansas free of slavery. No less prominent an abolitionist than businessman Lewis Tappan had joined Beecher's congregation. The minister now campaigned to raise money and to

purchase the new Sharp's rifles to send to Kansas with the antislavery emigrant groups heading there from New England. The weapons
in question acquired the label "Beecher's Bibles" and Plymouth the
nickname "Church of the Holy Rifles." As did Abraham Lincoln,
Beecher joined the Republican Party immediately on its formation in
the summer of 1854. And when war came in 1861, Beecher welcomed
it. He saw an opportunity for a new idealism and sacrifice amid the
ascendant materialism of the country and at long last an end to the
despised institution of slavery. Beecher would have much to say on
the great social questions of the Gilded Age as well.

EVOLUTIONARY MODERNISM

Beecher had arrived, certainly by the early 1860s, at an understanding of social issues within the larger scheme of evolutionary purpose. And to encourage his readers and listeners toward that perspective, he urged them first to see nature, not as a materialist
alternative to the spiritual, but as the very embodiment of it. Certainly it was fitting that Beecher chose to express such notions
through the vehicle of a novel, one addressed to his highly cultured
audience. *Norwood*, published in 1867, had the subtitle, *Or, Village
Life in New England*. It appeared serialized in the *Ledger* magazine
and then went through four editions in the next twenty years. Ostensibly a story about love relationships and the Civil War, *Norwood*
is also a novel of ideas, with protagonists of rival points of view con-
tending for influence. Beecher used as his own spokesman the wise
Reuben Wentworth. Cast, quite strategically, as a doctor, Beecher
made the character who is the most informed of modern science
also the soundest religious mind in the story. Here are three passages from Wentworth's reflections on nature:

> I have no theory. I have an irregular and fitful conviction that there
> are great truths of the affections seeking an inlet upon men, which
> flow from God, and which reach men, rightly sensitive, through the
> doings and appearances of what we call Nature.

And when God created light and flowers, did he not know what power it was possible that they could exert upon human souls, and design that they should do it? They have a moral function, even if they have no moral *nature*!

God made the soul to be played upon by its fellows, by the whole round of visible nature, by invisible things, and more than all, by Himself. If shaking leaves stir up the soul, there was power in them to do it, as much as in the soul to be agitated. I insist on a living, divine power in physical things. Why should men be so anxious to degrade nature? Is it unsafe to believe that God's eye follows every sparrow, and his taste unrolls every flower, and that his feelings have an alphabetic expression in all natural forms, harmonies, colors, contrasts and affinities?

"All things preach to us," Emerson had written in 1836. In Beecher's Wentworth, Emersonian transcendentalism thrived.

Norwood did not make a plea for evolution as such. But all along Beecher was trying to show that if nature was indeed emblematic of God, then evolution, rightly understood, gave a large and dynamic dimension to that truth. It could break through the "chill mist of doubt" in which modern science seemed to have trapped so many of the kind of people to whom Beecher preached at Plymouth Church. He wanted them to see that science was illuminating the Kingdom of God as a growth, the work of ages. Here was "a great cosmic doctrine" that showed God's work "in the whole development of human society and human thought." Beecher urged especially that the great thinkers of the day, at the best academic institutions, were those who saw religious meaning in evolution; he named specifically James McCosh at Princeton, James Dwight Dana at Yale, and Asa Gray at Harvard.

So how did Beecher understand evolution? Modern science, he said, teaches us that man was born a mean creature, prone to animal instincts but struggling, here and there, to rise above them. None should be troubled by such a view, he insisted. And Christians especially should recognize the approximate teachings of their faith in such a view. For evolution is about the human struggle to break out of low life into a higher level of existence. And the potential in humans, Beecher believed, knew no limits; evolution posed no compromise to the moral grandeur of man. "Born an animal, he shall be delivered from animalism into the glorious liberty of the children of God," Beecher wrote. Humans, if they have a right mind, progress from animalism and subservience to the flesh to an exercise of the divine element that has always existed within us. Beecher summarized: "That is the teaching of Christianity; is it not also that of Evolution?"

Beecher was never one to miss opportunities, but one should not doubt his sincerity in seizing on the new directions in science. They represented not only his personal delivery from the dark and dreadful world of the old Calvinism, so painful to him as the memory of his youth, but the surest way for Christian America. From a letter he wrote in 1867: "It seems to me that I discern, arising in studies of natural science, a surer foothold for these [evangelical] views than they have ever had. In so far as theology is concerned, if I have one purpose or aim, it is to secure for the truths now developing in the sphere of Natural Science, a religious spirit and harmonization with all the cardinal truths of religion which have thus far characterized the Christian system." Beecher wanted that message to reach beyond Plymouth to all America, which was indeed his larger audience. Touring the West Coast in 1883, and perceiving that evolution still troubled American churchgoers, Beecher spoke to his listeners assuredly. "I hold that the foundations of God stand sure, and in the near future this very doctrine of evolution that so alarms many of the churches and many ministers will prove to be a soil down into which the roots of Christian doctrines will grow, and they will be no longer controvertible."

Beecher has struck many as widely optimistic and naive, and these critics have often faulted Protestant Liberalism for these generic characteristics. The charges have some merit, but Beecher did not champion a teleology of inevitable progress, an automatic triumph of good over evil. In fact, Beecher's progressive orthodoxy coexisted with a social elitism, a conservative sociology, and a very judgmental view of the American scene in his days. For the theory of evolution, he wrote, "is as much a theory of destruction and degradation as of development and building up." In all ages of history, including even the wondrous era in which Beecher believed he lived, he saw the failed wreckage of humanity. Most individuals, he lamented, abandoned or never even took up the struggle to attain the higher level of living. They have little sensibility for the finer things of life, he believed. They do not join the march of the moral, esthetic, and spiritual progress of the race. Alas, even in his old New England, these stubborn facts maintained. Thus the narrator in *Norwood* says in the opening chapter: "The lower class of a New England village is chiefly composed of the hangers on—those who are ignorant and imbecile, and especially those who, for want of moral health, have sunk, like sediment, to the bottom." Beecher's natural aristocracy never constituted a social majority, and mass American society he saw as a missionary field.

Human evolution signified to Beecher the sustained advance of civilization, and civilization suggested especially culture, very liberally understood. Here, to be sure, Beecher's optimism had lyrical qualities. It started in his own backyard. New York City opened his eyes; he marveled at all the signs of new technology; he bought books with abandon. He also traveled to Europe and aped its cultural monuments. He joined his new tastes to the cosmopolitan ones of his own congregation. And he wished for religion to embrace art, too. Reflecting back on his upbringing in Litchfield, Beecher said, "I can remember no single thing in my young history inside of that church that ever touched either my imagination or my heart." In *Norwood*, Dr. Wentworth describes himself as an enthusiast of John Ruskin, the great apostle of Gothic architecture in mid-century England. The good doctor gives personal testament to the beauty of the cathedrals. He recalls for his daughter Rose his first encounter with one, "the mystery and awe" that it evoked in him, the "elaborate ornaments" that held him spellbound. "The cathedral is really a symbol of Christianity," he tells Rose, "complex, multitudinous, sublime!" In Gilded Age United States it was the era of the great urban churches, Gothic eminences magnificently visible in the new urban space. Beecher applauded.

Beecher wanted, moreover, to make the message of civilization's progress meaningful to his parishioners and relevant to their social class. Herein lay his great success and his immense appeal. To begin with, he himself also viewed with "mystery and awe" all the new devices of modern living. "Beecher was enamored of every gadget which modern technology had devised to make the labor of housekeeping easier," McLaughlin wrote. Technology frees us from drudgery and liberates us for a wider usefulness in society, Beecher proclaimed. He celebrated leisure when properly used for self-cultivation; it hastened the evolution of the human race, the more so as it reached the farmers and mechanics. Beecher, though, meant his message for the upper classes. It was they whom he saw as the agents of human progress, they who imposed the standards of an advancing civilization.

Beecher made his case in applauding what some have called "the new consumerism" of the Gilded Age, although his own message emerged in the early years of his Brooklyn ministry. For what do the wealthy do with their money? They build beautiful mansions and create landscapes and gardens that frame them. They spend money in art galleries, and give money for public parks and statues. All these activities serve to elevate taste among the larger public, and Beecher encouraged them. Biographer Clifford Clark sees in Beecher's celebrations a "paternalistic and elitist outlook" that made the congregants of Plymouth Church and their like the agents of civilization and progress. But technology, Beecher saw, was also creating a new democracy of taste. Here we see Beecher in one of his many euphoric moods:

> Look at the fabrics sold for a price within the reach of the poor. The finest forms in glass, china, wedgewood, or clay, put classical models within the reach of every table. The cheapness of lithographs, mezzotints, etchings, and photographs, is bringing to every cottage-door portfolios in which the great pictures, scenes, buildings and memorials of the past and triumphs of modern Art are represented. That which only twenty years ago, could be found only among the rich, today may be had by the day-laborer.

Here again Beecher spoke to the doubt of his parishioners, those nouveau riches uncertain of their social legitimacy and anxious for justification, those who enjoyed affluence when workers around them toiled long and hard for a bare subsistence. Beecher's novel *Norwood* again sets the facts in order. In this instance, Mr. Brett and his wife fret about spending money on luxuries. It troubles their Christian conscience when workers struggle, when schools need money, when public needs go unmet. Brett discusses the issue with his neighbors, and then the all-wise Dr. Wentworth joins the conversation and settles the matter. Brett and his wife are wrong to see their family interests as separate from the larger society's, Wentworth tells him. "Nothing is more remote from selfishness," he urges, "than generous expenditure in building a home and enriching it with all that shall make it beautiful without and lovely within. A man who builds a noble house does it for the whole neighborhood, not for himself alone." He goes on: Fine dress is not only a pleasure, it is a duty; fine grounds convey beauty and inspire others as well. Luxury, rightly pursued, Wentworth assures, becomes an aspect of public beneficence.

Beecher found a further application of his evolutionary views in the "social question" of the day. In the common parlance that term meant the issue of labor—strikes, violence, anarchism, and the union movement. Here Beecher showed himself to be most judgmental. He had little good to say for the laboring classes. He did endorse workers' rights to organize for their protection and, just to that extent, eventually supported the Knights of Labor. Beyond these allowances, Beecher was the voice of Herbert Spencer. Evolutionary progress depended on efficiency and efficiency required a sober, disciplined workforce. But Beecher did not see one in the America of the 1870s. And he spoke with callousness: "It is said that a dollar a day is not enough for a wife and five or six children. No, not if a man smokes and drinks beer. . . . Is not a dollar a day enough to buy bread with? Water costs nothing and a man who cannot live on bread and water is not fit to live."

To be sure, Beecher's views softened in the 1880s and his normatively organic view of society reasserted itself. His sermon of 1883,

"Poverty and the Gospel," nonetheless, still elevated individual character above social forces as the prevailing factors affecting the poorer classes. "The men who represent animalism are as a general fact at the bottom," he asserted. "It is their misfortune as well as their fault."

Certainly many Americans shared these views, and applied them to issues of race and immigration in the United States. For the poor of the day were not only poor; they were also Irish or Slavic or Chinese. The Gilded Age saw a high tide of nativism that also embraced anti-Catholicism. Here, too, Beecher addressed the fears of his congregation and issued an optimistic message. He gave an important address in 1871 titled "The Tendency of American Progress." In his talk he acknowledged the "vast masses" arriving to America, "poured upon us by the millions." He recognized, he said, that many people feared that these hordes will "change the color of the nation" and undermine its laws. Beecher, though, was prepared to throw out a large welcome mat. He feared not even the Chinaman, he said. And in a manner that seems contradictory to other pronunciations, Beecher encouraged the labor movement's goal to enhance the purchasing power of the workers. Because wealth, he said, is the great vehicle of assimilation. It is by wealth that the impoverished European workers, after arriving here, find their way into American society. Wealth breaks down their provincial and ancient ways as they buy American commodities and American clothing. The marvels of technology place these new purchases within reach of the worker. The rest of us, and especially the churches, Beecher urged, must teach the new classes the pathway to wealth—work, thrift, and temperance, the classic "Protestant ethic." Beecher thus saw a great opportunity, one perhaps never before realizable in human evolution— to bring the masses of society into the advancing progress created by the social and cultured elite.

Finally, religion itself, Beecher believed, gained from an understanding of evolution. Beecher was not a systematic thinker and did not call himself a theologian. He was a religious thinker and though his thought did not have a comprehensive totality, it did have a lynchpin. Indeed, the idea of evolution in its religious meaning,

Beecher had no doubt, would save the churches, make them useful to society, and in turn advance evolutionary progress itself. So in the preface to *Evolution and Religion*, Beecher proclaimed that the great truth of evolution is a help, not a hindrance to evangelical Christianity. Evolution, he said, takes us beyond the static God of the Enlightenment and presents us with an active God at work in the universe over ages of time. Evolution therefore improves our understanding of design. "Design by wholesale is grander than design by retail," he said. We have through evolution, Beecher attested, design on a higher plane, "more sublime than it ever was contemplated to be under the old reasonings." And those old reasonings also included ones calculated from scripture. Beecher urged his readers to recognize, for example, that the ages of man are much greater than religion has taught. "The six or eight thousand years dwindles into insignificance," he wrote. God, he said, has been at work over "a well nigh incomprehensible stretch of time." A million years are but the seconds on a clock.

So a modern, progressive, useful religion had more to fear from hardened religious orthodoxy than from modern science. Beecher reviled the dogmatists and the heresy hunters. He called them "vaguely bigoted theologians, ignorant pietists, jealous churchmen, whose very existence seems like a sarcasm upon creative wisdom." Beecher resented their efforts to discourage or prevent teaching of evolution from the American pulpits. He liked to quote from Matthew 16:3: "O ye hypocrites, ye can discern the face of the sky but can you not discern the signs of the times?"

Beecher remained confidant in this issue. For church doctrines, too, must adapt or die. An age that has seen the end of slavery, the striking advancement of intellect in all quarters, technology applied to daily living and the resulting marvels of the modern age, he believed, will pay no heed to Calvinism's monstrous God or those literal-minded readers of scripture. Beecher's Protestant Liberalism furnished a loving God. God and man seemed now equally at home in the world, partners in progress, agents of modernity.

So Beecher gave a construction to evolution that he believed helped bring the churches into a modern era. In many respects he had moved far from his father and the Evangelicals. But he had not made a clean break, by no means. He remained an ardent advocate of temperance. *Norwood* has an appealing, evocative depiction of the Sabbath tradition in New England. And Beecher always defended revivals. He described them as the "paroxysms," the fits and starts by which the world advances in its evolutionary progress. "Liberal Evangelicalism" describes Beecher quite well.

THE NEW THEOLOGY

John Bascom shared the cosmic optimism of Beecher and others who shaped Protestant Liberalism. He brought to it a confirmed faith in evolution and a confidence that lessons of all kinds came from a true understanding of the process. His appropriation of evolutionary ideas enabled him to combine with his philosophy, the field in which he spent the most important part of his career, a social and political agenda that made him a man of very radical opinion.

Bascom was born in Genoa, Cayuga County, New York, in 1827. His father, John, a Congregationalist minister, had married Laura Woodbridge; both families traced their ancestors back to the early New England Puritans. John, the only son, was the youngest of four children. He lost his father in 1828 and would have no live recollection of him. The family knew only severe economic circumstances thereafter. Bascom remembered a mother of great piety and strict religious observation but lacking in great affection. He formed a greater bond with the second sister, Mary, and attended the school she conducted at Homer. Afterward, he went on to the alma mater of his father, Williams College in Massachusetts, and graduated in 1849. He engaged for a while in legal studies and practice and found the experience unsatisfactory. He then renewed higher studies at Auburn Theological Seminary. He married Abby Burt after a brief stay there, in 1852; she died but two years later. Bascom then entered Andover Theological Seminary, but returned to teach rhetoric at Williams the next year. He married Emma Eustis in 1856. Rhetoric, too, had little interest for Bascom, though he had a great love for writing. The attention he gained led to his call to the presidency of the University of Wisconsin at Madison in 1874. He remained until 1887, whereupon he returned to Williams, looking forward to a peaceful retirement. Economic exigency, however, required that he resume teaching, until 1903. He died ten years later.

Bascom wrote prolifically. Before he went to Wisconsin, he had published books on aesthetics and English literature, and he addressed current issues in philosophy and religious thought, through the medium of the denominational religious press. During his Wisconsin presidency, Bascom wrote *A Philosophy of Religion* (1876); *Ethics, or Science of Duty* (1879); *Natural Theology* (1880); and *Sociology* (1887). He formulated much of his thought into two books that appeared after he left Wisconsin: *The New Theology* (1892) and *Evolution and Religion* (1897). Bascom most certainly suffered in influence from his often turgid and abstract writing, but he produced some lively and pointed essays and pamphlets. One learns much about this remarkable thinker, for example, in his *The Seat of Sin* (1876), *The Philosophy of Prohibition* (1884), *A Christian State* (1887), *Woman Suffrage* (about 1883), and the collection *Sermons and Addresses* (1913).

A few observations will set a framework for discussing Bascom's intellectual career. He grew up in one of the most intensely revivalistic sections of the United States. Genoa and the Seneca Lake area lay within the "Burned-Over District" of New York state, so named for the fires of camp meetings where Charles Grandison Finney and others were fostering the "second great awakening" in the 1820s and 1830s. Partisans of the revivals, the "New Light" Congregationalists and "New School" Presbyterians, had founded Auburn Theological Seminary in 1819 under the Plan of Union that produced cooperative work between the two denominations. Andover Theological Seminary, founded by Calvinists, had opened in 1808, three years after Harvard College had come under domination by the Unitarians. Until after the Civil War, it remained a stronghold of Calvinism even if not to the degree that Princeton men would have preferred.

All of the above would have suggested for Bascom a training in the old religious ways. But liberal ideas were plentiful and accessible, and

Bascom met one expounder of them directly at Auburn. In his autobiography, *Things Learned by Living* (1913), Bascom singled out for
influence on him the professor Laurens Perseus Hickok. Bascom took
his course in systematic theology. Here, most likely, began Bascom's
exposure and lasting addiction to the German "bug." "Dr. Hickok,"
Bascom wrote, "was strongly influenced by German philosophy, having made an intellectual gymnasium of the works of Fichte,
Schelling, and Hegel. [Bascom should have included Kant, especially.] The boldness and freedom, which belong to these upper
ranges of speculation, were very native to him. In theology, his opinions bore a sober, liberal cast and rendered him a very desirable instructor." And at Andover, Bascom encountered William G. T. Shedd,
also singled out in the autobiography. Shedd had recently edited the
works of Samuel Coleridge.

In his philosophical writings, Bascom addressed the issue of mind
and matter. He refused to assign them sharp, separate spheres and
thus circumvented the Scottish Common Sense dualism that generally prevailed in American college teaching. Instead, Bascom posited
a dynamic interrelationship between mind and matter. Here, he
would seem to reflect the influence of Hickok's appropriation of
Kant. Bascom rendered his expressions in the less technical language of the American transcendentalists, but the Kantian format is
clear. In his book *Natural Theology*, Bascom explains to his readers
that the mind orders the world for us, that it imposes on raw empirical data the structures of time, space, and causation by which we
fashion the world we daily confront. Bascom saw the supremacy of
mind both in individuals' shaping and organizing matter for their
own ends ("it is mind that shapes matter, that uses it as an instrument for its own ends") and in God's creation of the world. "Mind,"
Bascom wrote, "presents itself with a sovereignty over the physical
world. Hence the easy, natural, inevitable inference of one Supreme
Mind, when human thought strives to rise beyond its immediate experience and explain the phenomena of the world on a broader
field."

For Bascom, though, this understanding had greater applicability
and relevance from the perspective of evolution. It gave mind a

more active role in the universe and it rendered Bascom's philosophy emphatically teleological. A vast, unfolding system that illustrates such precision of parts and movements, recurring designs and their subtle modifications, can derive, he said, only from a thinking subject that gives inert matter an extended place in a cosmic whole. Divine plan, as evolution showed, prescribed a progressive improvement in the physiology of species, but among humans it also prescribed the progressive unfolding of the rational, moral, and spiritual powers. This process, Bascom believed, also indicated God's increasing presence in the world. Evolution signified the dissolving boundaries of the natural and supernatural.

From this perspective, Bascom also drew implications for his entire educational and social philosophy. Evolution, he believed, gave a new scope to the human intellect. The mind, Bascom said, correlated with the universe itself, so that its constant expansion alone assured humans' grasp of God's progressive manifestation in the world, his revelation of himself in the evolutionary scheme of things. Evolution thus also, Bascom rejoiced to report, sounded the death knell of stale creeds, church rituals, and rigid formulations of divine truth. God's revelation, he said, could never be a completed fact or past event; we grasp it as our intellects perceive God's expanding presence in the world. Thus, Bascom wrote: "What we may call the movement of evolution is also the movement of reason. . . . The world is thus laid open to us as a dynamic, living spiritual product." Moreover, Bascom, who celebrated every aspect of scientific advancement in his time, saw religious truth as now, more than ever previously, united with secular truth; one could no longer sequester that truth as sacred dogma, the privileged preserve of a priestly class.

To an extent, Bascom saw the world as the Evangelicals did, in terms of its pervasive moral and spiritual character. But he made an important alteration. Both he and the Evangelicals held the model Christian society, the Kingdom of God on earth, as their objectives, but the latter saw the obstacles to it in terms of individual sin. For them, the path to salvation lay mostly along the lines of the special and separate conversions of individual souls, as by use of the "anxious bench" at revival meetings. Bascom wanted to revise the meaning of

CHAPTER 5

sin. For as evolution illuminated the oneness of things, and as it demonstrated the complicated matrix in which all things found themselves, it greatly enlarged, in Bascom's view, the area, or the social nexus, in which the moral sense must operate. We must now view the world, Bascom wrote, in terms of the "ever growing tissue of moral relations" that embraced it and complicated it. Moral reformers, he urged, could no longer rely on the isolated individual as the vehicle for the perfection of community; they must instead have mastery of all the social laws affecting society. Bascom wrote allegorically about the new situation in religion: "Pietism must break camp, dismiss its camp followers, and carry the glad tidings of a salvation that waits to sweep through every kingdom, physical, economic, social." Bascom thus wrote that "a theology which seeks the regeneration of society in ignorance of social laws is doomed to failure."

Here emerged Bascom's interest in sociology. In discussing "sociology," however, he continued to use the language of the Evangelicals. He wrote of "conversion," "redemption," and the "Kingdom of God." Evolution gave these terms new meanings for Bascom. Thus "conversion" now signified not a sudden or convulsive change in an individual, but slow, constant improvement wrought in the world's social material. And the objective also acquired new means. For conversion in this sense required not so much the skill of a preacher (as in Charles Grandison Finney's "getting up" revivals by established methodologies) as it did the expertise of the social scientist. Thus, as the race advanced, Bascom believed, intellectual and rational powers would continually supplant emotional ones as the critical vehicles of human progress. Bascom used the terms "reason" and "spiritual power" often interchangeably and employed both as surrogates for the Evangelicals' "grace." They supplied for him the source of social energy and power that the other group found in the revival, and Bascom even asserted that the full application of intellectual power to the unfolding spiritual laws of the universe described the certain means for the "redemption" of the world. "We are brought by these universal facts of law, unfolding themselves progressively in evolution, in contact with the world in a new way," he wrote. "It is not only capable of redemption, it is being redeemed." So also did evolutionary ideas, as Bascom understood the concept, apply to the Evangelicals' quest for the Kingdom of God. Bascom had a ready definition of that notion. "The Kingdom of heaven," he said, "is a physical, intellectual, social, and spiritual product. It adjusts all things and persons to each other."

John Bascom brought together many of the ideas he had developed at Wisconsin, and he published them during his last year at Madison in his book *Sociology*. This academic discipline was just emerging, along with economics and political science, from their common home in moral and mental philosophy. In fact, Bascom had participated in a longstanding academic tradition in America in which the college president instructed the senior class in these subjects, the capstone of their undergraduate educations. Bascom's book reflects the transition taking place; it is very much a moral treatise and not much like a contemporary sociology textbook. Bascom thus defined sociology as the study of social, civic, economic, religious, and ethical forces in their various operations. The last aspect, however, the ethical, Bascom labeled the most important. For with the evolutionary advance of the race, he believed, ethical forces emerge in more pronounced forms. Sociology, therefore, constitutes a quest for the just society, and it utilizes the spiritual as well as the empirical faculties as its tools of analysis and perception. How may society discover and use spiritual power most fully? That question summarized for Bascom the central concern of the new science he now explored. Evolution, with its norms of oneness, harmony, and integration, supplied him the proper focus. "The widest and most inclusive diffusion of power," issuing in the largest aggregate of power, he wrote, "is the aim of society."

These reflections led Bascom to one of his most important ideas, the doctrine of state power, which he developed and pressed forcefully upon the minds of students at Wisconsin. Bascom became thoroughly preoccupied with the problem of organizing social power, as his *Sociology* shows. But many things troubled him. He described for his students an age he judged destructive in its distribution of power—a ruthlessly competitive society with aggregated wealth and control in the hands of a few individuals. Such an arrangement of forces, he stated, created a society unethical and un-Christian in nature. When Bascom therefore called for "harmonious power" and "beneficent power," he turned directly to the state, the agency of public power, for its exercise. The state, Bascom wrote in *Sociology*, must create social power. Furthermore, the state must assure power to the weaker elements in its midst, a concern that suffused some of the reform measures that Bascom advocated. Bascom was of course making an important modification of the evangelical format. He turned more to the state as a surrogate for the churches and voluntary societies, the key agencies, along with the state, to be sure, of the Evangelicals' Benevolent Empire. Modern America, Bascom asserted, could no longer rely on these institutions for the perfection of the nation and must look instead directly to the state for moral leadership and action.

Three social issues in particular illustrate how Bascom applied these ideas. One (and this one most directly shows the connection back to the evangelical program) was temperance. John Bascom believed strongly in the prohibition movement and contributed to it. In Wisconsin he became one of the prominent members of the national party organization in that state, to the extent even that it created enemies to his university presidency. He paid much attention to the subject in his sociology text and wrote a pamphlet, for public distribution, called *The Philosophy of Prohibition*. Here was a large moral issue, he stated, one that affected the whole power of society to function at its maximum strength. It was by definition, then, a matter of the state. Bascom could not entrust reform on this front to the voluntary societies and he urged government controls by legislation. For nothing, he believed, more seriously blighted the spiritual powers of contemporary America than the destructive abuse of drink. On this matter, he insisted, the public interest must outweigh private privilege. Indeed, Bascom wrote, "to affirm the personal rights of an individual in a case like this is to enable him to stand across the path of public progress, to check the organic movement of society." "Society," Bascom insisted, "is under no obligation to subject . . . its own high fortunes to those morally ignorant and repellant." It must "overrule unreason with reason, unrighteousness with righteousness."

Bascom's *Sociology* announced that no social issue had more significance to the views he expounded than the rights of women. Here also Bascom played an activist role. He supported coeducation at the University of Wisconsin, at a time of much public opposition. He advocated women's suffrage and other feminist causes. Bascom's stance derived directly from his new theology, with evolutionary props. He did not pose the women's issue in terms of natural rights or personal freedom. In Bascom's appropriation of evolutionary ideas, the social organism had priority over the individual parts. He appealed instead to the advancing spiritual powers of society in the evolution of the human race as a whole. Rights may take on a higher prominence in this evolution, but Bascom upheld the collective needs above all. Evolution signified for him progress toward the full integration of society's parts into a harmonious whole. Women must now gain admission, in full standing, Bascom wrote, to the ongoing spiritual and social progress of the world. And in this matter, too, because of its great moral consequence, the state must assume an active role. It must provide the proper conditions "to make ready for the free exercise of [the] intelligence and virtue" of women. Bascom defended his position by calling even for the end of certain social customs. Old habits of chivalry, he believed, actually concealed a contempt for women and conspired against the exercise of their greater strengths.

Finally, on the issue of the rights of labor and unionization, Bascom took a stand uncommon for the college presidents of his day. In fact, he was one of the first to break the stranglehold of laissez-faire ideology in academic economics in the nineteenth century. Bascom endorsed labor organizations because he saw them as vehicles of power that could redress the unfair balance of power in an age of industrial and financial corporations. That imbalance, Bascom believed, constituted a grave danger to the nation. It represented a spiritual and physical deprivation, rendering much of the nation powerless and alienated. The imbalance, he stated, thus violated the organic ideals of modern society that evolution sought to achieve. On this matter, too, the state must act. For if society was still "The Seat of Sin" (the title of Bascom's 1876 baccalaureate address at Wisconsin), then the state must be "the seat of righteousness."

Bascom, like Beecher, was an evolutionary optimist. Both individuals believed that human history was moving on a teleological course. God had his intentions; they were clear to any who read the signs of the times and the teachings of modern science, enhanced by religious insight. But their confidence in an improving course of evolution never dissuaded Beecher or Bascom from speaking out angrily when they saw where society lagged behind God's direction. And thus stood the United States in the 1870s, Bascom believed. He had in mind the economic question. "We are in the full swing of individual assertion," he said. "Unbridled enterprise is our controlling temper." He also wrote: "The money-power vigorously asserts itself, and it easily overawes the moral and social forces which should work with it." Of the major college presidents of his day, Bascom certainly expressed the most socially radical sentiments. And he often did so bluntly. Thus, in addressing the "new economic tyranny" that he believed threatened the nation, Bascom went after John D. Rockefeller, the major object of his moral wrath. "He has turned business into unceasing and unflinching warfare," Bascom wrote. "[And] he has done this with an open profession of Christian faith. . . . Herein lies the guilt of this man, and of others of the same ilk, and of all who put themselves in fellowship with them, that they confound ethical distinctions and make the world one medley of wrong-doing." Against this immoral order there existed no recourse but for society to assert its own collective interests, Bascom urged. The state must not be indifferent. It has as much right and need to defend itself against the millionaire's raw personal power as it does to thwart the drunkard in his reckless individualism, Bascom asserted. Both defy the organic ideals inscribed in evolutionary progress.

In these ways, Bascom's intellectual career conjoins evolution to other movements of ideas that shaped American history in the late nineteenth and early twentieth centuries. He formed his own version of Protestant Liberalism. He helped lay the foundations of the Social Gospel movement. And he anticipated the political ideologies of Progressivism. Bascom made his major impact in Wisconsin, where his ideas about religion, society, and politics gave the first outline of "the Wisconsin Idea," an emblematic expression of the Progressive movement. One of Bascom's students was Robert La Follette, an 1879 graduate. La Follette led an insurgent movement in the Republican Party in Wisconsin that won him the governorship in 1900 and helped him make Wisconsin a state leader in the reforms of the Progressive Era. La Follette always acknowledged a debt to Bascom, especially respecting the role of government. "He was forever telling us," La Follette said of Bascom, "what the state was doing for us and urging our return obligation not . . . for our own selfish benefit, but to return some service to the state." "The Wisconsin Idea" represented a close partnership of the university and the state government. Another Bascom student helped bring it into being. Charles Van Hise graduated with La Follette in 1879 and later served as president of the university from 1903 to 1918. In these years the university developed the Legislative Reference Bureau and saw university faculty assume significant roles in shaping state legislation. Bascom had anticipated as much: "The time will come," he said, "in which educational men will gather influence within their own field, and become the servants of the State to counsel action as well as to carry it out." The next chapter, however, will show that not all evolutionists believed that evolutionary ideas led in the direction of the positive state.

BIBLIOGRAPHY

Applegate, Debbie. *The Most Famous Man in America: The Biography of Henry Ward Beecher.* New York: Doubleday, 2006.

Bascom, John. *Things Learned by Living.* New York: Putnam, 1913.

Clark, Clifford E. Jr. *Henry Ward Beecher: Spokesman for a Middle-Class America.* Urbana: University of Illinois Press, 1978.

Hibben, Paxton. *Henry Ward Beecher: An American Portrait.* New York: George H. Doran, 1927.

Hoevcler, J. David, Jr. "The University and the Social Gospel: The Intellectual Origins of the 'Wisconsin Idea,'" *Wisconsin Magazine of History* 59 (1976): 282–96.

Hutchison, William R. *The Modernist Impulse in American Protestantism.* Cambridge, MA: Harvard University Press, 1976.

McLaughlin, William C. *The Meaning of Henry Ward Beecher: An Essay on the Shifting Values of Mid-Victorian America, 1840–1870.* New York: Knopf, 1970.

Meyer, D. H. "American Intellectuals and the Victorian Crisis of Faith," *American Quarterly* 27 (1975): 585–603.

Moore, James R. *The Post-Darwinian Controversies: A Study of the Protestant Struggle to Come to Terms with Darwin in Great Britain and America, 1870–1900.* Cambridge: Cambridge University Press, 1979.

Roberts, Jon H. *Darwin and the Divine in America: Protestant Intellectuals and Organic Evolution, 1859–1900.* Madison: University of Wisconsin Press, 1988.

Ryan, Frank X., ed. *The Benevolent Hand.* Vol 2, *Darwinism and Theology in America, 1850–1930.* Bristol, England: Thoemmes Press, 2002.

Werkmeister, W. H. *A History of Philosophical Ideas in America.* New York: Ronald Press, 1948.

SOCIOLOGY

William Graham Sumner and Lester Frank Ward

When John Bascom wrote his book on sociology, he drew from German philosophical idealism and Protestant religious liberalism. They provided an evolutionary framework for his discussions on that subject. The work in the same field by William Graham Sumner and Lester Frank Ward takes us into a much different intellectual realm. Sociology now aspires to be strictly "scientific." It appeals to raw nature–physical, animal, human–and nothing else. The world loses design and purpose, to be shaped only by the intelligence of those organisms known as human beings. The evolutionary structure of the new sociology derives from a Darwinian understanding of life. The two principals of this chapter both embraced these new norms. But they differed dramatically in interpretation and application. Thus, these two Darwinians exemplify two divergent strands. One will speak for "social Darwinism," the other for "reform Darwinism." (To be sure, these terms have caused confusion and elicited the judgment of stark ambiguity by historians employing them or otherwise trying to give them precision. A shorthand of convenience employs these categories in this chapter. But see the Bannister and Bellomy citations in the bibliography for clarifications.)

William Graham Sumner became, in the ontological sense, one of America's purest Darwinian thinkers. There were not many of this kind because most American intellectuals who espoused evolution nonetheless shunned a strict naturalism. Sumner's intellectual career, in fact, displays an evolution from religion to naturalism. He would surpass other thinkers like Herbert Spencer or Andrew Carnegie, who, for all their harsh portraits of the raw competitive struggle that life dictates, clung to an assuring teleology of progress and advancement in human society. Sumner would offer no such assurances and little comfort. He knew there was no certain way out for humans; he offered a possibility, not a promise.

FROM MINISTER TO PROFESSOR

William Graham Sumner was born in Paterson, New Jersey, in 1840. His father, Thomas, from humble circumstances in England, had recently come to the United States at the age of twenty-eight. He settled in Hartford, Connecticut, and worked as a railroad shop mechanic. He married Sarah Graham, who also had migrated from Lancashire. Young Bill began his long association with Yale College when he entered as a freshman in 1859. He excelled as a debater and did quite well academically; "Graeme" graduated eighth in his class of 122 students. Study in Europe followed (his father bought his son's exemption from Civil War service) and the intellectual experience there began a long and influential shift in Sumner's thinking. He felt a growing estrangement from Anglo-American theology, once commenting that Göttingen had left him "thoroughly Teutonized." But while other Americans who caught the German bug acquired an idealistic strain of thinking, Sumner's education moved him more toward naturalism. Sumner now saw humanity as having only its own end, removed from any supernatural direction and charged with finding self-realization, by individuals or by groups, apart from any supernatural assistance. Moreover, as Sumner now embraced "scientific" standards, he judged religion an impediment to intellectual progress and the wellspring of debilitating sectarian warfare.

We may be surprised then to find Sumner, after a brief span as a tutor at Yale, taking on a ministry at Morristown, New Jersey. Sumner still valued religion. He had abandoned the Calvinism of his family and become an Anglican, seeing in that tradition a history of religion and reason. He received ordination in 1869. Meanwhile, he had become editor of a publication named *The Living Church*, established previously for the purpose of effecting a harmony "between revelation and science." Sumner valued in the broad church religious habits he judged "scholarly and intellectual." Above all, he valued religion greatly for its moral influence. And for all his naturalism, now becoming stronger, Sumner remained forever a moralist. Tensions between religion and science, though, now became acute in Sumner. He could no longer continue in the church. So in 1872, Sumner, aged thirty-two, left the ministry. He would later write: "I never consciously gave up religious belief. It was as if I had put my religious beliefs into a drawer, and when I opened it there was nothing there at all."

The same year Sumner accepted a chair in political and social science at his alma mater. The year before he had married Jeannie Elliott. Sumner's academic affiliation with Yale would last until his retirement in 1909. As professor, and indeed an immensely popular professor at Yale, he did not shy from partisan opinion, neither in his scholarship nor among his colleagues. He had "strong friends and strong enemies," his biographer tells us. Sometime around 1875 Sumner became fully "converted" to evolution. And while he did not consider Darwinism a perfect theory, and while he often had recourse to the theory to give rhetorical flourish to his classical liberalism, Sumner did pronounce it "the best yet." He employed writings of Herbert Spencer in his courses and provoked the intervention against them by Yale president Noah Porter. Sumner stuck to his principles, strongly pleading for academic freedom to the College Corporation, and prevailed. He wrote extensively and much of his important work appeared in academic essays collected into larger volumes. He remains best known today for his two books, *What Social Classes Owe to Each Other* (1883) and *Folkways* (1906).

Sumner did not fall suddenly into Darwinian mode. Previous reading prepared him to move there. Thomas Malthus, considered with Adam Smith and David Ricardo as the early British formulators of classical economics, raised for Sumner the compelling questions that troubled him most. In 1798 Malthus offered his famous trajectory in which population growth inevitably surpasses the world's ability to sustain it. Add to this dilemma the other problem of the law of diminishing returns and we have, Sumner believed, the enduring crisis that threatens the human race. It faces starvation unless it finds some way of circumventing these grim laws of numbers. Sumner, who marveled at the age's proliferation of new machinery and new efficient business methods, knew that man could beat the odds only by such creative means. Human societies must attain a greater control over nature, wrench from it more production by better methods of extraction, or devise other ways to force from it a greater yield.

Ultimately, for Sumner, this situation necessitated capital formation. A society could escape the impeding crisis only by producing capital, which means wealth not used in consumption of goods but directed to machinery or technology that promises in the future to increase productivity. For Sumner, however, that answer was no easy proposition. He held a low estimate of human nature, viewing most people as inherently hedonistic and given to immediate gratifications. Capital, however, signifies delayed enjoyments, abstaining from the available marketplace of goods to place time and money in hopes of a later, more abundant availability. But how to induce anyone to make such a present sacrifice? How, for example, to persuade anyone to forego planting and harvesting this year's crop for this fall's sale at the market and persuading him instead to give all his time to inventing a harvester that next year will enable him to triple his acreage and his income? In short, how does one induce capital creation?

Sumner drew two points of instruction from this crude model. First, one who creates capital, "the capitalist," has to exercise a certain discipline, and he must have a certain character to be able to exercise that discipline. For such an individual must prepare himself to live with less for now in order to realize more later. And Sumner, secular Calvinist that he was, doubted that many such people existed. Few could bring upon themselves such sacrifices of the moment, such delayed gratification. Thrift and frugality did not govern the norms of humanity, in Sumner's judgment. People go where their lusts take them; they thrill to whatever attractions and pleasures present themselves and spend their money accordingly. So Sumner came to see the capitalist, the one who resists the allure, as a person of superior virtue and superior intelligence—self-disciplined, self-controlled.

Second, however, the capitalist must know that his actions will earn their eventual and full reward. She otherwise has no reason not to join the throng of profligates that most others join. The capitalist must have the certain knowledge that her later, higher gains will not succumb to the state's taxation, that they will not fall victim to schemes of income redistribution. "If it were not so capital would not be formed. Capital is only formed by self-denial," Sumner instructed, "and if the possession of it did not secure advantages and superiorities of a high order men would never submit to what is necessary to get it." To Sumner, the capitalist was hero; he alone helps the human race avoid the awful dilemma of the numbers that it confronts. He alone outwits nature's harsh dictates. His creativity takes what nature supplies and compels nature to supply more. And everyone gains from the effort. The capitalist performs a huge social service. He must, however, have incentives and rewards. Society deprives him of them only to its own disadvantage, only in its own folly.

SOCIAL DARWINISM

All of these insights made sense to Sumner from the perspective of Darwinian evolution. Nature compels adaptation by all species, leaving death and extinction as the only alternatives. In humans, adaptation demands mental skills and moral habits. Any society must summon among its population such habits as will enable it to confront a stingy nature. When Sumner described these habits, he celebrated the proverbial Protestant ethic—hard work, thrift and frugality, entrepreneurial skills, and organizational genius. The terms "strong" and "weak," Sumner insisted, "are terms which admit of no definition unless they are made equivalent to the industrious and the idle, the frugal and the extravagant." The world's sages had always known that these virtues prepared the way to wealth. Sumner gave the message a contemporary urgency, however. He considered the capitalist virtues as ideals, to be sure, but also necessities. When nature prescribed the "survival of the fittest," Sumner described the millionaire as "a product of natural selection." And many lessons followed from that understanding.

If matters proceeded in the best way, Sumner described, human society could, and just might, stay one step ahead of a begrudging nature. Society, however, must avoid a host of temptations that could wreck it. The public and its government must realize what a bargain are the wealthy, Sumner urged. Instead, however, this group may generate resentment and inspire retaliation against it. The public could also fire resolves to diminish disparities of rich and poor. Governments can hardly resist such well-meaning policies, Sumner knew. Wise counsel, however, he believed, will avert such action. As wealth indicated a superior virtue, creativity, or executive talent, society had best arrange itself so that its holders can pass on that virtue to later generations. In no other way, Sumner believed, could it avoid the Malthusian dilemma.

In this matter, Sumner rendered his harshest pronouncements, ones that have shocked his readers, past and present, and left him an unloved figure in American history. For he spoke vehemently against any interference with the natural law, the survival of the fittest. He cited many threats to it—Christianity, socialism, humanitarian good will, and democracy. But "if we do not have the survival of the fittest," he wrote, "we can have only one possible alternative, and that is the survival of the unfittest." Sumner opposed poor laws, minimum wage legislation, maximum hour mandates, and public beneficence of just about any kind. To be sure, he both validated and encouraged private charity and did acknowledge society's obligations to care for the insane, the mentally incompetent, and the disabled. He drew the line, though, at people who constituted the class of the morally unfit. Toward them, nature looks with indifference, eliminating them without pity. So seeing, Sumner rendered his oft-quoted ruling, "a drunkard in the gutter is just where he ought to be." He believed it a vain and hopeless task to save this individual, and very dangerous to society besides. His character has determined his fate.

A surviving society will always display marked signs of inequality, Sumner believed. It is the price it pays for being a surviving community. Sumner warned that the state can only dangerously seek to redistribute wealth or scheme to protect the weak. It always does so at great cost, diverting money and energy from the necessity of creating wealth for the social pool. Sumner considered socialism the most offending of ideologies. And the most ruinous of political systems. He categorized three types of people who embrace this foolish doctrine. One—the lazy; they simply want to gain from the sacrifice of others. Two—the envious; they simply want what others have earned. Three—the sentimental; their emotions rule their intellects. Sumner knew that equality was a powerful sentiment. But we must resist it. For when all humans are equal, they will be equally poor . . . or equally dead.

This summary describes the raw outline of Sumner's thought. Over his career we find some shifts and we find some qualifications. Toward its end, for example, he came to see more legitimate roles for the state to play. We do need to note some other concerns of Sumner, however, because they give a larger meaning to his social Darwinism.

At first glance, Sumner seems preoccupied with individuals and part of an American tradition of individualism. His moving away from religion possibly deprived Sumner of a large social ethic. He no longer joined humans to large cosmic purposes. "The end of life is [simply] to live," he wrote. Self-fulfillment became a major preoccupation with Sumner, and the major obligation of each individual in Sumner's hierarchy of values. But Sumner was a sociologist. He studied people in groups and their group culture. Many consider *Folkways*, his book of 1906, Sumner's major scholarly work. Here too, however, sociology reinforced Sumner's laissez-faire system. He saw humans shaped by a long history, by social institutions, habits, customs, and beliefs. These forces gave a certain stubborn logic to the way things are, to the world as found. Long entrenched ways, products of a formidable evolution, made societies immune to social engineering, to the fine-tuning that emboldened politicians and savants to believe that they can reconfigure the social system. Sumner came to see the world as the way it is because that is the way it has been. "The great stream of time and earthly things will sweep on just the same in spite of us," he wrote. "The tide will not be changed by us and our experiments. . . . That is why it is the greatest folly of which a man can be capable, to sit down with a slate and pencil and plan out a new social world."

Another consideration: Sumner was not trying to defend wealth of any kind or the wealthy classes as a special group. In the tradition of Andrew Jackson, of whom he wrote a biography, Sumner railed against wealth gained by privileged connection to government. Natural selection may have produced America's captains of industry, Sumner said, but they inherited no right to invoke the federal government's assistance, neither in beginning their businesses nor in protecting them later. Tariffs headed Sumner's list of government abuses. In 1885 he published a book that bore the title *Protectionism: The -Ism Which Teaches That Waste Makes Wealth*. This practice, "legalized robbery," he called it, "seems to me to deserve only contempt and scorn." He added that "protectionism arouses my moral indignation." It supplied an issue in which Sumner, to his chagrin, found himself joined to a cause of populist indignation and democratic reform.

Special connection to government unfairly, and unwisely, privileged some and always made victims of others, Sumner insisted. None so suffered, in his view, as much as the middle classes. Here Sumner found the moral virtues he cherished displayed most visibly, among the hard-working and tax-riddled people of America, who themselves made no demands on the state. They had attained "comfort without luxury" through their talents and skills, but now see their modest savings devoured by taxation. Their enterprising efforts, Sumner lamented, pay for the indolence of others, at the upper and lower ranks of society. Sumner celebrated this middle-class individual as "the Forgotten Man." This person found himself caught between a "proud and powerful plutocracy" and a "hungry proletariat."

Sumner's Darwinism, therefore, did not make him an unreflecting champion of Gilded Age America. Not only did an emerging plutocracy—the rich connected to the state—threaten to place the nation under a heavy stranglehold, Sumner warned, it was already corroding its moral health. Sumner feared materialism as the most dangerous side effects of industrialism. He warned against "Mammonism," as he called again on the religious language of his days in the church. Love of luxury, he warned, dissolved the old habits of self-discipline; it softened the national fiber and elevated self-indulgence. Late in his life, Sumner grew pessimistic. He saw the plutocracy ever stronger and his ideal, the Forgotten Man, ever more overwhelmed. He doubted that liberty could thrive where the struggle among equals had given way to a society of stark unequals.

Sumner, however, had never been optimistic. His system did not allow it. Here one may observe again how Sumner and social Darwinism signified a significant shift in American thought. However similar Sumner and Herbert Spencer seemed in their social prescriptions and their ardent defense of laissez-faire economics, the British philosopher represented older metaphysical habits. He affirmed a teleology, a cosmic plan, such that if humans allowed the natural system, the unhampered course of evolution, to go its own way, it would assure and hasten human progress. The better would survive. Interference by the state, fine-tuning in the name of social benevolence and protection of the weak, however, only gums up the machinery and confounds its functions. Sumner, though, could offer no such assurances about the directions of human history. Nature did not disclose design; it revealed only indifference. Sumner thought he knew how humans might win out, but he could offer only a "might" not a "will." He could assure only that by sheer hard work, by frugal plan, by delayed enjoyments, by the restraints of the state and all those envious and rapacious individuals who commandeered its offices, humans might just get by; they might endure in a system of nature that made too real the prospects of starvation.

Sumner's Darwinism moves far from the eighteenth-century world of Thomas Jefferson and the Enlightenment. How confidently Jefferson and other Americans of his generation had asserted, and justified, their independence from Great Britain by citing certain truths, truths built into nature itself. Their nature, or "nature and Nature's God," as Jefferson said, posited inalienable rights and held them out to all human beings. They did not have to explain the how and why of them; they were "self-evident" to all thinking people. Sumner looked to nature and saw no such truths and no such god. From any notion of "natural rights" Sumner stood wholly estranged—"the purest falsehood in dogma that was ever put into human language," he asserted. The only right nature gives us, he believed, is the right to die.

Historian Richard Hofstadter once suggested that the social Darwinism that Sumner espoused had a particular resonance with the new world of post–Civil War America. The nation now entered into a raw industrial age. Iron and steel, coal and oil defined the new economy. Factory, office, warehouse, and skyscraper came to define the American landscape. Inhabitants might think they had entered a new age marked by the supremacy of material fact, a world quite removed from an earlier and more pristine natural environment that registered a spiritual presence. We should not, however, dismiss Sumner's own religious past, for he carried the shell of religion into the contents of the Gilded Age. As Hofstadter wrote of the social Darwinists: "Theirs is a kind of naturalistic Calvinism in which man's relation to nature is as hard and demanding as man's relation to God under the Calvinistic system." Calvin's God gave humankind no more promise of a better future than Sumner's nature gave of its ultimate survival.

A MIDWESTERNER COMES TO WASHINGTON

In some respects, William Graham Sumner and Lester Frank Ward have much in common. Both pioneered in American sociology, helping forge the intellectual parameters of an academic discipline. Both fortified their systems through evolution. Each brought to that subject a social philosophy already in bold outline: Sumner drew from classical liberalism, Ward from progressive Whig principles. Neither gave any place to religion or the supernatural in his explanation of history or evolutionary processes. They projected no providential design or teleology onto human affairs, no overriding cosmic scheme of things. So when Ward put Sumner's system to a thoroughgoing critique, the attack did not represent a religious dissent from naturalism or the specter of a godless universe. It represented one evolutionary outlook, rooted in science, rivaling another purporting to have the same foundation.

Lester Frank Ward enjoys today a wide recognition. He rightly ranks as one of the most important contributors to the intellectual foundations of American liberalism, modern liberalism. None in his day did more than Ward to provide a logic for the active state, for positive government. Ward saw the need early on in his life; evolution would provide him the perfecting rationale for his program. Similar efforts succeeded his and in the example of John Dewey we will see another extension of liberalism, also rooted in Darwinism. Ward also formed personal and intellectual connections to the major reform thinkers of late nineteenth- and early twentieth-century America—Richard T. Ely and Edward A. Ross in economics and sociology, Simon Patten and Franklin Giddings, Charlotte Perkins Gilman also. His legacy lasted through the New Deal and beyond. Historian Henry Stele Commager once wrote: "Though Europe first created the welfare state—Germany and Scandinavia and Britain—it is no exaggeration to say that Americans were the first to develop the philosophy of the welfare state." Ward led in that effort.

Lester Frank Ward never celebrated his family roots, but they went back far in American history. Andrewe Ward of Sheffield, England, came to Massachusetts with the earliest New England settlers. He moved to Connecticut later, where a high school in Fairfield now bears his name. Lester's father Justus fought in the War of 1812. He had various trades—millwright, mechanic, farmer—and attained a modest living. He married Silence Rolph, daughter of an itinerant minister, in 1816 and they settled in the "burned-over-district" of

New York, an area quite suitable to his pious wife. The couple already had nine children when they relocated to Illinois in 1840. "Frank," their tenth and last child, was born in Joliet the next year. Subsequent moves took the family to St. Charles, Illinois, and to Buchanan, Iowa, in 1855. Ward recalled: "Two summers and two winters were spent in the new home. They were years of work, of course, but, as I look back on them, it seems that most of my time was spent in roaming over those boundless prairies, always with a gun, killing the game for both sport and the table, and admiring nature. I believe I was a born naturalist, but the opportunity to be scientific was meager—no teacher, no books."

When their father died in 1857, Frank and a brother accompanied their mother back to Illinois. Shortly thereafter, Frank joined brother Cyrenus in a business undertaking in Pennsylvania. It failed and Ward worked on a farm and taught school. About this time he took up his ambitious program of self-education. It concentrated first in languages. "I had read *Ollendorf's Greek Grammar*, and went through it while about my work. I could then conjugate all the irregular Greek verbs!" He also took up French, German, and Latin.

The Civil War broke out in 1861. All the influences in Ward's life to date made him an enthusiast for the Union cause. The Ward family was Methodist. As such, it stressed free will over Calvinist determinism. It also embraced a moral regime for individuals and moral reform for the larger society. Ward's father and mother supported temperance and opposed slavery. They mistrusted Roman Catholicism. The son inherited these rather standard evangelical prejudices but would merge them into a more secular, Whig social outlook. Ward supported regimes of moral virtue and character construction, he defended free labor, and championed education. He had a contempt both for slavery and for the southern aristocracy, decrying the wide and pervasive ill effects of the southern system generally. Ward eagerly wished the destruction of the rebel states, and at the very time he married his beloved Lizzie (Elizabeth Vought), he joined a regiment of Pennsylvania volunteers and went off to war. He saw in Abraham Lincoln the best model of the Whig-to–Republican Party transformation and he hailed Lincoln's Emancipation Proclamation when issued in September 1862. Ward fought at Fredericksburg and Chancellorsville. He incurred two battle wounds and sat in a Confederate prison.

After personally petitioning President Lincoln, Ward obtained a job with the Bureau of Statistics in the nation's capital. While resuming his education at Columbia College (now George Washington University), Ward continued to learn on his own. He began reading John Stuart Mill and other English liberals and in the late 1860s added Darwin to the list. He also discovered a particular liking for Thomas Paine's writings and those of the outspoken agnostic Robert Ingersoll. Ward organized the publication of a new journal, the short-lived *Iconoclast*, designed to appeal, as it enumerated, to "Liberals, Skeptics, Infidels, Secularists, Utilitarians, Socialists, Positivists, Spiritualists, Deists, Theists, Pantheists, Freethinkers"—in short, to "all who desire emancipation of mankind from the trammels of superstition, and the dominion of priestcraft." All the while, Frank and Lizzie gave much time and energy to promoting women's suffrage and temperance.

Through his work with the U.S. Geological Survey, Ward became part of an important group of Washington intellectuals that included most actively Ward's close friend John Wesley Powell. They shared republican ideals of service to the state by an informed citizenry. That vision pointed to an expansive role for government at all levels, but above all the federal government in the city where this group lived. The program called for an intellectual alliance of the national government with data-gathering agencies—bureaus of statistics, labor, weights and measurers—and knowledge organizations like the Geological Survey, the National Museum, the Anthropological Society of Washington, and the Smithsonian Institution. These goals and activities gave Ward a driving purpose and enthusiasm. But he did not escape personal tragedy. He and Lizzie lost their son Roy Fontaine, less than a year old; then Lizzie died from an acute appendicitis in March 1872.

Ward found himself restless and intellectually frustrated in the decade after the Civil War. Writing in 1870, he commented that the old metaphysical systems were dead, as were the "rotten timbers of theological error and popular superstition" allied to them. Waiting in the wing and ready to burst into new influence he sited all varieties of what he called "the Positive" way of thinking, or, more familiarly, positivism. Enlisted in these ranks Ward found Bacon, Galileo, Franklin, Humboldt, and August Comte. He also named a new avant-garde of this thinking: Mill, Spencer, Darwin, Thomas Henry Buckle, and John Tyndall. Ward prepared to champion their cause enthusiastically: "from each and all of the recognized lights of the Positive Philosophy the cry has gone up for more knowledge, better knowledge! Education, and of the true sort, is what they demand, and that for all mankind."

This new passion made Ward an eager follower of the debates about evolution in the 1870s. The spark came first from Louis Agassiz, whom Ward read before he took up Darwin. Ward heard Agassiz speak in Washington and then immersed himself in his writings. He did not endorse all of the Harvard scientist's idealism, but adhered to Agassiz's affirmation of the fixity of species and to the reality of a "grand universal intelligence" governing change in nature. Agassiz furnished Ward a kind of halfway house in his movement from a family religiosity to a thoroughgoing naturalism. He did not long dwell in that house, however. By 1876 Ward had taken up Darwin again and quickly moved over from Agassiz and into Darwin's camp. Biographer Edward Rafferty writes: "Ward now accepted the Darwinian idea that nature was a sea of change and development haphazard and without direction."

So judging, Ward soon arrived at the conviction that would underscore all of his sociological principles and the prodigious literary output that he gave to expressing them. The idea underwent refinement and reinforcement, but by the early 1880s it stood in his mind boldly outlined. In essence it was this: If nature is chaotic, purposeless, sporadic, and directionless, it is a bad model for humans to use for their own societies. Ward had no illusions about the obstacle he faced in getting an American reading audience to recognize this fact. For almost everywhere, but in the United States especially, the appeal of the "natural way" of things, or the "natural system," flourished as virtually axiomatic truth and ideal. For the natural way was in essence God's way. Thus, human progress depended on the free operation of natural laws. Economic growth derived from free trade. Genius and invention must be spontaneous. And so on. This worship of nature, this faith in the natural way, Ward wrote, culminated in an overriding public credo, which he succinctly summarized: "Every attempt on the part of Government to interfere with these great processes of nature only recoiled upon the agent and imperiled the safety of the State. Government must protect—it must not control; it may forbid—it may not command."

But this faith, Ward believed, had left only a legacy of misery in human history. Ward spent the rest of his life so demonstrating, but at this time he faced the challenge of simply disabusing people of the notion that nature has a wisdom superior to human intelligence. How to go to the root of the matter and demonstrate that nature in fact does not do things very well, that the natural system exhibits serious flaws? Ward offered a primal fact: nature is wasteful; it is profligate; it squanders its own resources, and it everywhere exhibits inefficiency. A single octopus lays fifty thousand eggs; a single sturgeon emits almost a million ova at one spawning; the codfish hatches a million young fish each year that two of them may survive and spare the species extinction. Ward cited recent studies and supplied more examples: the eel may contain at one time nine million eggs and a tapeworm more than a billion ova.

Ward presented these facts in a Darwinian light. He understood that the struggle for existence determines nature's processes, the steps it takes to protect the species. It must overproduce, in huge numbers, so that but a few may live. Ward wrote: "In the animal kingdom the struggle is desperate and unceasing. . . . [And] not only is the waste of reproductive power enormous in proportion to the amount of life brought forth, but of the latter by far the greater part meets with premature destruction." So why then, Ward asked, is nature so worthy a model for humans? Why should human societies pattern themselves after the animal kingdom? If the competitive system, the struggle for existence, yields such waste, such suffering, should not humans work to mitigate or overcome this struggle? Should not human beings devise systems that direct work into productive channels and away from the mere ordeal of simply staying alive? "Animals," Ward wrote, "prey upon each other, producing universal and indescribable suffering, and placing every living thing in a state of chronic terror in the midst of its countless enemies." If our human society also illustrates this description, Ward urged, is it not time for a wholesale reconsideration of it?

Ward thus made a pitch for the priority of the artificial over the natural. By the artificial Ward meant every human interference in or against the natural way. He always liked to point out to his readers how such intervention, as, for example, in cross-fertilization of plants and animals, showed how humans improved nature itself. "How long," he asked, "under nature alone, would it require to develop the wheat, the maize, and the apple, that human agency has brought forth? How long to produce the Ayreshire, the Devon, the Cheviot breeds of animals?" But man, who has so successfully applied the artificial to nature, has done too little in applying it to his society, Ward believed. The human species, however, alone among all of them, has the one organ that assures its own survival—its brain. All that distinguishes man from animal inheres in that critical differentiation. For all human progress derives from it. Referring to the example of cross-fertilization, Ward wrote, "It gives us a faint idea of the enormous acceleration which we may imagine human progress to acquire if it could be made the subject of artificial instead of natural selection."

These points became a major burden of persuasion in Ward's first book, *Dynamic Sociology*, in 1883. The massive, two-volume work resulted from years of research and the struggle to find a publisher to take it on. Ward announced at the outset that he wanted his book to combat "the essential sterility" of the social sciences and bring them out of their mode of passivity into a new, "dynamic" era. Ward faulted Mill, Spencer, and John Fisk, indeed all who spoke for the iron laws of economic competition and celebrated laissez-faire standards. Ward intended sociology to be a science and a program (which he would later call "sociocracy"), rooted in a conviction that the artificial, not the natural, alone assures human progress. That prescription signified for Ward a view of all social phenomena as requiring intelligent control by society itself, the collective intelligence acting in the larger interest. Ward would reinforce this underlying principle many times over and draw from it modern liberalism's understanding of the positive state.

REFORM DARWINISM

Now that laissez-faire capitalism had struck a partnership with evolutionary ideas, Ward would use evolution to attack it. He became the foremost critic of "social Darwinism" in America and set against it his own "reform Darwinism." He prepared to bring the whole notion of "survival of the fittest" under scrutiny. Nothing had more misled peoples' thinking, he believed, than this idea that unrestricted competition guaranteed that the best survive and thus assured the thriving of the species. That assertion, Ward conceded, might have some validity in the animal world, but it had little in the human world. Competition, left to operate with no state intervention, works only to the advantage of the *actually* fit, those who have a head start on others by virtue of social privilege. Among the highly touted "self-made men" of his age Ward assured that only a small fraction emerged from mean circumstances. Worse, such circumstances assign millions to no chance of improvement and thus deprive the whole society of great potential gain from their unrealized talents. "Poverty and monotonous toil," Ward wrote in *Dynamic Sociology*, "crush out millions of potential luminaries in society."

Even more than the great millionaires of the day, Ward had in mind great thinkers, like Newton and Darwin, who escaped oppressive toil and who would have otherwise obscured their talents in grinding labor. For society gains as much from the leisure that enables intellectual work as it does from manual labor. The brute struggle merely to stay alive, Ward emphasized, actually lowers the standard of the so-called "fittest" themselves. "Those who have succeeded in bursting these bonds [of poverty] have usually done so at such an immense cost in energy, that their future work is rendered crude and well-nigh valueless." They too often acquire a coarse and rough character, Ward believed, and, contrary to the myth, emerge narrow in mind, bitter partisans given over to self-interest. Ward held up the counter example of great, creative thinkers, scientists, and artists. To them society owes the greatest debt, and Ward assured that "without exception they have been in possession of rare opportunities that have somehow exempted them from the necessity of toil." Herein the challenge to society: to maximize opportunity for all.

This goal turned Ward to government and an expanded role for the state in all aspects of modern life. Here also he knew the prevailing prejudices he had to overcome, but he believed strongly that the artificial intervention against nature mandated an enhanced role of government as the agent of an improving evolution for human beings. Europeans did not have the antistatist prejudices Americans did, Ward knew. And European nations had made major gains from government regulations. He cited control of the railroads in England and actual ownership in Germany and France. Other states had greater regulations of banks and financial institutions. Ward hailed these achievements as signs of advancing democracy, "the will of society" exercised against powerful interests. He could be euphoric and even glib on the matter of state power. "There is not one [enterprise] that the state has not managed better and more wisely than it had been managed before by private parties," he postulated.

Ward's declaration of independence from laissez-faire economics put him in company with a generation of reformers in the late nineteenth- and early twentieth-century United States. Many, like the Social Gospel leaders and like Richard T. Ely in the American Economic Association, wanted to instill Christian principles into American life. But Ward's liberalism differed from theirs. They turned to the state as an ethical and humanitarian force that would help reshape America along those lines. A brutally competitive system that exploited labor and rationalized the triumph of the powerful over the weaker elements in society, did not, they asserted, reflect the moral imperatives of Jesus. But Ward did not wish to set modern liberalism on any religious footing. He had himself gone through a slow but steady detachment from the religiosity of his early family and moved into an intellectual distancing from religion. His dissent had focused first on the churches. In a lyceum address around 1866, he spoke angrily: "The impudence of the church is only equaled by its hypocrisy." He considered it socially reactionary, responsible even for slavery. Ward indulged in free thought and spiritualism (as indeed did many American intellectuals), but early in the next decade went over entirely to science. It represented for him a kind of "conversion." Science assured Ward of an order in a natural universe not dependent on dogmatic authority. It gave him the confidence he needed in human progress. For Ward now prepared to champion a new American liberalism, differentiated from "Christian" reform, and rooted in a new authority—evolutionary naturalism.

What Ward needed specifically was an understanding of evolution that dissolved its appropriation by the social Darwinists and made it useful for social reform. To that extent he made a distinction between what he called "genetic evolution" and "telic evolution." By the former he meant the strictly physiological changes by which successful species adapt to environmental change or gain advantages against others in the struggle for existence. He concurred with Darwin that these changes spring from pure chance in an unplanned and undirected process of evolution. But this kind of chance could not at all explain the dramatic triumph of *Homo sapiens* in the hierarchy of nature. For strictly in terms of physiology, Ward pointed out, humans are ill adapted to survive. In comparison to many other species, they lack strength and speed. Their hairless skin makes them vulnerable to climates all over the world. Yet they alone among the species have relocated to inhabit all areas of the earth. They have done so because of telic evolution.

"In the development of mind," Ward wrote, "a virtually *new power* was introduced into the world." "Mind" signified the power to intervene against nature, to transform and reshape it for survival purposes. It signified an evolutionary shift of momentous importance, like the development of the cell or the origin of vertebrate life. "Mind," Ward said, "is a natural product of evolution." But it is the gift to only one species. It reverses the pattern of evolution that heretofore prevails because man is not changed by the environment but instead applies intelligence to change the environment for his protection and well-being. "The great truth to which I allude," wrote Ward, "is that . . . [man] *has*, from the very dawn of his intelligence, been transforming the entire surface of the planet he inhabits. No other animal performs anything comparable to what man performs. This is solely because no other possesses the developed psychic faculty." What, though, was telic evolution but the use of the artificial as opposed to the natural? "If nature's process is rightly named natural selection," Ward declared, "man's process is artificial selection."

Of course, as Ward knew, people understood this process on an individual basis. We all engage in problem solving for our well-being and success. Social Darwinists took this fact and turned it into a reward system for the strong and virtuous. Ward, however, insisted that telic evolution had its most meaningful application at the social level. Civilization, he believed, albeit by fits and starts, had progressed to the degree that social intelligence, or the collective intelligence of a people, could address collective needs. Ward had no doubt that this practice would gain as people recognized that a society is itself an organism, a collection of parts that must work together to assure its survival, as with any individual organism in the animal kingdom. Herein lies the role of the state and the established offices of government.

Ward employed the term "sociocracy" to describe the role of collective intelligence in solving social problems. It is the planned control of society by society as a whole. If the American people comprehended the full dimensions of telic evolution, Ward believed, they would see the logic of the positive state. For as mind is to the individual, government is to society. Government is the adaptive agency of the social organization, its mind. And both mind and government have the same necessities. As the individual needs information to make intelligent decisions, government needs social and scientific data to plan for the collective good. The positive state, Ward urged, had its roots in nature itself, specifically in that turn in evolution where mind emerged to its powerful presence among humans. With this recognition, he stressed, we should give no priority to ideals of the negative state and the so-called natural system in hu-

SOCIOLOGY

man affairs. In short, evolution, grasped and considered in its widest meaning, should abuse us of laissez-faire ideals and the cult of the negative state long dominant in classical economics and now triumphant in social Darwinism.

Several corollaries followed from Ward's brief for the positive state. To function well the state needed knowledge. Ward spoke for the creation of a national university. To be located in the nation's capital, it would have scientists and social experts of all kinds. They would make extensive studies of natural resources, the environment, and demographics. They would become indispensable to legislators in their law-making functions. They would also disseminate information to businessmen and farmers. Government must be the brain center of the social organism, and a national university would help supply critical data to it.

The term "social organism" also had much significance for Ward's new liberalism. He wanted it to inspire a view of society not as constituted by autonomous individuals at war with one another, but a creature of integrated and cooperating parts. Here Ward modified Darwin, for he believed that Darwin wrongly made competition a vehicle of improvement among the species. Perhaps, for lower forms, Ward acknowledged, but not for humans. Telic evolution again demonstrated a great reversal. Ward now reinforced his earlier prejudice against unrestrained competition and its destructive effects. A healthy and improving society, he urged, looks to the well-being of all its people and government devises the means by which to do so. "If nature progresses through the destruction of the weak," Ward wrote, "man progresses through the preservation of the weak."

Ward provided many of his thoughts on this subject in his 1892 book *The Psychic Factors of Civilization*. With Darwin he recognized the critical role of the environment in evolution, but he countered that people, with human intelligence, shape the environment in which they live. Ward explained the evolution of mind as a gradual transformation from a subjective, emotional response to the world to one of reasoned intellect. Humans passed on these acquired traits and civilization advanced. This perspective, along with other considerations, made Ward a strenuous advocate for education. Although he looked to the role of intellectual experts in bringing about social reform, he knew that democracy required that legislative leaders also know the science of society and that they must also have the endorsement of an informed electorate to put them into effect. Against the social Darwinists' focus on the competitive forces of biological change, Ward accentuated those distinguishing psychic factors that make humans reasoning animals, capable, by applied intelligence, of directing their societies on a purposive and ameliorating course.

In 1900, Ward gave a major address to the Institut International de Sociologie (IIS) in Paris. His audience seems to have appreciated Ward's efforts. He won election to the presidency of the IIS after presenting his talk. Ward had earned this recognition. By this time, he had gained a world following among social scientists, and, as Rafferty points out, he appealed to liberal thinkers from France to Russia, everywhere liberal democracy needed encouragement and intellectual reinforcement. In the United States he gained wide recognition and appreciation. Dorothy Ross writes: "His brief for the application of intelligent reform to the problems of modern society was the first major statement in American social science of the new liberalism." If critics did not always endorse all of Ward's program, they did recognize the immense erudition of this sociologist. Commager calls him "perhaps the most variously learned man in the country." Here was an intellectual who, as late as 1906, was confident enough to offer a university course labeled "An Outline of All Knowledge"! In 1912, a year before his death, Ward received a letter from the noted Progressive Frederick Howe. It offered effusive praise for Ward, crediting him with reorienting the thinking of a whole generation of American reformers. "You have done that for all of us," he wrote, "whether we are able to trace the parenthood of our thoughts or not. Certainly the whole social philosophy of the present day is the formative expression of what you have said to be true."

Ward merged three intellectual traditions in his thinking: an Enlightenment confidence in reason and intellectual inquiry, an American Whig endorsement of the positive state, and a scientific naturalism that underscored his idea of telic evolution. He had perhaps too much confidence in government. The rest of the twentieth century would reveal the horror of the totalitarian state. But Ward is also the corrective to the prolific government bashing that thrives in the America of the early twenty-first century. Ward, in fact, intended his prescriptions to establish a middle way. Certainly, as we have seen, he recoiled from laissez-faire ideas. But he was no extremist. He endorsed neither the Marxism embraced by his brother Cyrenus nor the socialist alternative to the capitalist system. Workers, he said, "need no revolutionary schemas of socialism, communism, or anarchy," he assured. He prepared no assault on wealth; none should begrudge the millionaire his due, he affirmed. The manufacturers and merchants, the railroad "kings," all help organize production in a useful way. But too much of their wealth, Ward warned, fell into the hands of "idle persons" who offer nothing to society. Ward demanded more reward for laborers and more recognition of the dignity of labor. In a truly inclusive democracy, Ward believed, workers would find their surest course for improvement. "The problem of today," he said in 1892, "is how to help on a certain evolution by averting an equally certain revolution." Thus did Ward summarize his reform Darwinism. He hoped fervently that Americans would heed that instruction.

BIBLIOGRAPHY

Bannister, Robert C. *Social Darwinism: Science and Myth in Anglo-American Thought*. Philadelphia: Temple University Press, 1979.

Bellomy, Donald. "Social Darwinism Revisited." *Perspectives in American History*. New Series 1 (1984): 1–129.

——, ed. *The Essential Essays of William Graham Sumner*. Indianapolis: Liberty Fund, 1992.

Boller, Paul F., Jr. *American Thought in Transition: The Impact of Evolutionary Naturalism, 1865–1900*. Chicago: Rand McNally, 1969.

Commager, Henry Steele, ed. *Lester Frank Ward and the Welfare State*. Indianapolis: Bobbs-Merrill, 1967.

Curtis, Bruce. *William Graham Sumner*. Boston: Twayne, 1981.

Fine, Sidney. *Laissez-Faire and the General Welfare State: A Study of Conflict in American Thought, 1865–1901*. Ann Arbor: University of Michigan Press, 1956.

Haskell, Thomas. *The Emergence of Professional Social Science: The American Social Science Association and the Nineteenth-Century Crisis of Authority*. Urbana: University of Illinois Press, 1977.

Hofstadter, Richard. *Social Darwinism in American Thought*. 1944. Boston: Beacon, 1963.

Rafferty, Edward C. *Apostle of Human Progress: Lester Frank Ward and American Political Thought, 1841–1913*. Lanham, MD: Rowman & Littlefield, 2003.

Ross, Dorothy. *The Origins of American Social Science*. Cambridge: Cambridge University Press, 1991.

Russett, Cynthia Eagle. *Darwin in America, the Intellectual Response: 1865–1912*. San Francisco: Freeman, 1976.

Sumner, William Graham. *Earth Hunger and Other Essays*. New Haven: Yale University Press, 1913.

FEMINISM

Charlotte Perkins Gilman and Eliza Burt Gamble

In a half century of extraordinary developments for American women, evolution found an important relevance to the subject of feminism. Two women who contributed significantly to that subject constitute the focus for this chapter. Each seized on new materials from modern science to interrogate the gender culture of the United States in the Gilded Age and Progressive Era. They questioned the structure of family and sex roles and joined their Darwinian feminism to an expansive literature of political and social radicalism in these years.

A TURBULENT LIFE

Charlotte Perkins Gilman had close connections to the Beecher family, to great-uncle Henry Ward, Charlotte, and "Aunt" Harriet. She was born in 1860, in Hartford, Connecticut, and had an early life that was anything but stable. Her father Frederick had attended Yale College but did not graduate. He engaged in teaching and edited newspapers but had little financial success. On many occasions he left the family for extended periods of time, and then finally for good. Charlotte, however, always liked her father; she admired his independent spirit and valued his social conscience. She later reflected: "What a sad dark life the poor man led. So able a man—and so little to show for it."

Charlotte also saw, poignantly, the severe toll taken on her mother, Mary Westcott Perkins. On several occasions she had to relocate the family, nineteen times in eighteen years, in fact. Mary Perkins imposed a perverse kind of protection on her daughter. In a famous segment of Gilman's autobiography we learn how Mary deprived Charlotte of her affection, refusing to hug her at bedtime until after she had fallen asleep. So Charlotte pricked herself with needles to stay awake, awaiting her mother's embrace as she pretended to be asleep. Mary Perkins did not follow routine paths. In 1874 she moved, with Charlotte, into a Swedenborgian cooperative, the two living there for a year and a half.

Charlotte went on to study art at the Rhode Island School of Design, but her life continued to be rooted in unusual relationships. Her mother's coldness led her to win her father's love and respect. Confidant now of her intellectual powers, she strove to impress Frederick with them. In 1877, determined to advance her education by herself, she asked Frederick to specify some books that would launch her onto a broad path of learning. Her father responded with a list of nine, "the beginning of my real education," Charlotte later called it. Several of the books reflected Frederick's own interest in Darwinism, especially as it was influencing scholarship in anthropology. He also included recent issues of *Popular Science*, which was playing a key role in informing American readers of new directions in evolutionary thinking. Collectively, Charlotte's new reading immersed her in ideas about race. The anthropologists traced the emergence of civilization from its primitive base and celebrated the Anglo-Saxon role in those achievements. Gail Bederman summarized this critical turn in Charlotte's intellectual career: "In short, Frederick's reading list depicted 'the white man' as the cutting edge of civilization's advancement and the 'primitive' races as evolutionary losers. All human history was a cosmic process of racial evolution, which was now thrusting the white races ever higher, toward a perfected civilization."

Charlotte soon took up the challenge to redefine this scheme in terms of gender. In the years before the publication of her famous book, though, she engaged in radical politics and in one intense personal relationship. In 1881 she became passionately connected to Martha Luther. Their intimacy showed much fervor, even if we acknowledge the culture of sentiments that bound many women of this era affectionately to each other. Charlotte wrote to Martha: "As for you I could spend hours in cuddling if I had you here . . . and I'd be willing to bet five cents, if I was in the habit of tellin', that you will make up to me for husband and children and all that I shall miss." Charlotte did get married, though, to artist Charles Walter Stetson, in 1883. Within two years the marriage was dissolving. Charlotte knew things were not right in her life, and later in her autobiography she wrote: "Here was a charming home; a loving and devoted husband; an exquisite baby, healthy, intelligent and good; a highly competent mother to run things; a wholly satisfactory servant—and I lay all day on the lounge and cried."

Charlotte left her husband some years later in 1894 and sent their daughter Katherine away to live with him, now remarried; she had no relation reflecting any closeness with Katherine thereafter. In the meantime, Charlotte lived with Adeline Knapp, and, immediately after Katherine's departure, with Helen Campbell, a famous writer of children's fiction. In 1900 she married her cousin George Houghton Gilman.

All along during these years, Gilman moved in various directions of American radical politics. She attended her first women's suffrage convention in 1886. She championed the cause of labor and in 1887 contributed a suffrage column for the *People*, a Rhode Island journal, sponsored by the Knights of Labor. The publication supported both feminism and workers' rights. Now Gilman herself self-consciously conjoined these two causes. She urged women to take up work outside the home. She wanted women to break from a social scheme that geared all their lives toward marriage and motherhood. "Let girls learn a trade or a profession, as well as boys," she wrote, "and have an independent life of their own; they will not have to spin webs for a living." Gilman took inspiration from her Aunt Harriet's own radical notions and liked to quote them in her column. She accepted enthusiastically the Nationalist program of Edward Bellamy, whose Utopian novel *Looking Backward* enhanced the cause of socialism after its publication in 1888.

Gilman was now centering her life on these reform issues. She wrote extensively, contributing also to the *Impress*, which supported the Populist movement and vigorously assaulted the powers and privileges of wealth in the United States. In 1896 she met Lester Frank Ward, at a woman's suffrage conference. Ward almost immediately became her mentor, even as Ward acknowledged Gilman's writings and cited them himself. One can see why Gilman thrilled to Ward's ideas. In 1888 he had written, in an article titled "Our Better Halves," that women made the links in genealogy. "Woman is the unchanging trunk in the great genealogic tree," Ward wrote, "while man, with all his vaunted superiority, is but a branch, a grafted scion, as it were." Ward acknowledged, though, that various hereditary and environmental forces had deprived women of a just exercise of their talents and positive influence. Human society stood to gain, however, by opening up to women's participation, Ward urged. One could almost say that Charlotte Perkins Gilman took that position and ran with it.

Years of energetic writing, derived from her prolific readings from the wide range of reform literature, prepared Gilman for her great book of 1898. The evolutionary perspective, so powerfully conveyed in Ward and others, put the last piece in place for her. She had observed the American family and had experienced it, and she knew how profoundly out of sorts it was with the best course of human evolution. She had studied American women and judged how badly skewed were their lives; they, too, did not square with evolutionary progress. Nor did America's economic arrangement. Gilman continued to call herself a socialist, and she believed that the socialist state would triumph in evolution's course. It would emerge naturally, without class warfare, because evolution, Gilman insisted, would always be pushing, "upward and onward through a world of changing conditions. You can count on it." For now Gilman understood that "life means progress."

DARWINIAN FEMINISM

The subject of women became Gilman's major preoccupation in the 1890s. Here above all, she believed, the lessons of evolution could shed light on the modern situation and in application could produce major reforms. *Women and Economics* (1898) was an intellectual tour de force, one of the most creative and suggestive contributions to evolutionary thinking. Translated into languages and seeing nine editions by 1920, it would outsell all Gilman's other books and set her on expanded lectures tours around the country. For all her arguments in the book, she looked for examples from evolution, for patterns of behavior in other species that made the gender pattern among humans seem perverse and abnormal. Gilman never abandoned her faith in progress nor her faith that human society would aright, must aright, the distortions and contradictions that beset the modern human condition. But to obtain this end, she insisted, one needed a right understanding of things.

For her to take the lead, Gilman had to confront the conventional wisdom and the academic scholarship of the day. The effort involved her in both sex and race considerations. She believed emphatically in human advancement through evolution; it was the race's purpose and her own. But American culture defined women's contribution to race progress through her role as wife, mother, and child-rearer. More challenging to her enterprise, many evolutionists defined race progress as measured by gender differentiation. That is, the more human society advanced in evolution, the more accentuated became gender distinctions. No less a figure than the prominent psychologist G. Stanley Hall warned against gender approximations, a "degenerative influence," he labeled it, adding the alarm that such a trend "would inaugurate regressive evolution."

Gilman, to be sure, lived in an era where the separate "spheres" of male and female were accentuated everywhere. All the more reason, then, for evolutionists to describe in self-congratulatory manner the advance of Western civilization beyond its savage roots. For Gilman, though, the domestic role was little better than a prison sentence. Here lies her challenge. She had to show that race function had nothing to do with sex function. She would seek to erode prevailing notions of sex differentiations; however, she would not abandon the prevailing views of race distinctions among the human species. All the accounts in her extensive writings on gender roles applied only to the "advanced races." Thus, when asked specifically if the evolutionary interpretations applied to Negroes, Gilman responded emphatically, no they did not. That race had not reached the level at which the male and female roles demanded the reconfigurations that she urged so strenuously for whites.

Here evolution would lead the way. Gilman begins her *Woman and Economics* with these words: "Since we have learned to study the development of human life as we study the evolution of species throughout the animal kingdom, some peculiar phenomena which have puzzled the philosopher and moralist for so long, begin to show themselves in a new light." The anomalies were many, Gilman believed, and they amounted, collectively, to a wholesale distortion of nature's norms. They assumed the form of an unwonted economic dependence of the human female on the male of the species. For in no other species "does she depend on him absolutely." Whereas Gilman's friend Ward went to nature to cite examples of how humans ought not to live, Gilman sought examples that provided much instruction for humans. Consider how the male bird often helps the female feed the young and how the lioness presses her quarry with frightening effect. Gilman then made the contrast to humans: "Whereas, in other species of animals, male and female alike graze and browse, hunt and kill, climb, swim, dig, run, and fly for their livings, in our species the female does not seek her own living in the specific activities of our race, but is fed by the male."

In all the other species, Gilman wrote, females have survival skills that enhance their livelihood; these skills they pass on to their offspring. They derive from the female animals' interactions with their natural environment. But human evolution has effected dramatic changes, and they have intensified with the onset of the Industrial Revolution. For as humans advanced, they moved beyond a direct relation to nature and progressed toward one based on social interactions. And especially with the onset of industrialism, Gilman explained, when women remained at home while their husbands left home to be "breadwinners," a peculiar economic dependency emerged. An "abnormal sexuo-economic relation," she maintained, now described men and women; in short, the male became the women's immediate environment. To it she would now have to adapt. In the process, woman's "work" became peculiarly detached from economic functions. Now it bears relation only to the man she marries, who is now the basis of her sustenance. As Gilman put it: "Her living, all that she gets—food, clothing, ornaments, amusements, luxuries—these bear no relation to her power to produce wealth, to her services in the house, or to her motherhood. These things bear relation only to the man she marries." "Successful" women, "whose splendid extravagance dazzles the world," Gilman asserted, have gained their status neither by skills in working in the home or mothering, but by connecting to men of means, by application of their sex characteristic.

This perversion made sense to Gilman when she saw it from an evolutionary perspective. For again, the comparison to other species informed the human situation. The issue was sex differentiation. In all species, she wrote, primary sex characteristics describe those physiological features that govern reproduction. Secondary sex features assist this function without being essential to it. Thus, we distinguish the male and female in the species, by, for example, the mane of the male lion, or the horns of the elk, or the colorful plumage of the peacock. These features, secondary ones, enhance sex attraction and thus encourage reproduction; they serve the survival of the species in question, without, however, having any value for the functioning or the self-preservation of the individual organism. That is, the male peacock's glorious feathers do not help him gain his food; the lion's imposing mane does not make him a better predator. But neither do they impair these survival activities.

See the facts with humans, though. "We, as a race," Gilman wrote, "manifest an excessive sex-attraction." We flaunt and exaggerate sex differences, and to the point that they obstruct our progress; they serve the needs of neither the individual nor the race. In all categories of human life today, Gilman said, we differentiate men from women. This stark dualism increases sex attraction but to a morbid degree. Our culture compels us to see individuals in terms of sex types—male or female. The exaggerated differentiations obscure our vision of the species as a whole and the needs of the race collectively. This effect Gilman labeled "our inordinate sexual indulgence," and she judged it "the distinctive feature of humanity."

Gilman reinforced her point by suggesting that if the lion's mane was too big, it would reduce his speed and impair his hunting. Were the elk's antlers twice their size, he would be nearly immobile. In other words, nature, in the animal species, puts a check on sex differentiation. It will not permit it to obstruct race survival. But human beings, Gilman argued, have allowed this danger to occur. "Our excessive sex-distinction," she wrote, "manifesting the characteristics of sex to an abnormal degree, has given rise to a degree of indulgence that injures motherhood and fatherhood." Human sex differentiation, Gilman argued, has thwarted the survival functions of the race.

The critical manifestations of this danger appear in the human female. Again, Gilman had recourse to comparison. Among animals, she observed, male and female differ with respect to individual organisms but remain similar in race development. When both sexes of a species gain their food from the same exertions and from the same sources, they confront like environments and evolve together. They adapt and evolve with the same environment and survive accordingly. They do so, Gilman stated, because natural selection acts as a check on sexual selection. As sexes, animals perform different functions and evidence physiological differences to that extent, but as species, they perform the same functions and evolve together. Witness again the female lion, the huntress extraordinaire. Sex difference has not injured her progress and she could survive independently.

Among humans we have a unique situation: The balance of forces is altered. "Natural selection no longer checks the action of sexual selection," Gilman wrote, "but co-operates with it." Now among humans the male has become the environment of the woman. He becomes the strong, modifying force in her life and her economic necessity. Sex distinction intensifies under these conditions. Woman cultivates and displays any and all manner of appearance and behavior to attract and hold what sustains her, the male in her life. Here is the human exception; we find this pattern in "no other creature under heaven," Gilman asserted.

Gilman addressed this human peculiarity often with amusement but more frequently in frustration. Only among humans do we celebrate the "weaker sex," she observed. We refer to a "feminine foot" but never to a "feminine paw." Only in the human species, she remarked, are hands and feet secondary sexual characteristics. In female humans they suggest delicacy and even frailty. But where else in nature do we perceive a weaker sex? Not in the powerful motions of birds in flight; not in the arduous treks of migrating herds; not in the resolve of breeding salmon swimming upstream. The human female, however, looks clumsy when she runs or jumps or performs other normative race functions. Advancing "civilization," Gilman observed, has made these shortcomings more pronounced. Contrast the "fair, fainting vessel" of the Victorian parlor with the sturdy peasant woman working in the field.

Modern sex differentiation (i.e., human) reverses the norms of nature, according to Gilman. Whereas elsewhere the male displays color and ornamentation, among humans the female does, and much to excess. The habits begin early in childhood, visible in female dress and adornments, which become obstructive of physical activity. Gilman, of course, could see the full, bizarre effects of this sex differentiation in Gilded Age America. The fashions of the day, the corset and the bustle, seemed to render women almost immobile.

Always Gilman made her observations with reference to evolution. For her major point in *Women and Economics* centered on the devastating effects that sex differentiation had on human evolution. They had rendered one half the species remote from its gains and made it an impediment to the advance of the race. For human evolution, Gilman assured, placed a unique emphasis on reason, intelligence, and accumulated wisdom. These now overtook and surpassed the mere animal instinct, the survival agency, of the other species. The human race expressed these gains in industry, science and technology, the arts, religion, and government. Man had rendered no greater disservice to woman, Gilman believed, than to deprive her of participation in these race-advancing activities. When he began to feed and defend her, she ceased to feed and defend herself. Gilman wrote: "When he stood between her and her physical environment, she ceased proportionately to feel the influence of that environment and respond to it. When he became her immediate and all-important environment, she began proportionately to respond to this new influence, and to be modified accordingly." Thus women became cut off from the working of natural selection, the powerful force that acted alike on the sexes of other species. Speed, prowess, dexterity now became irrelevant to the human female. Other devices now prevailed as she adapted to her new environment.

But this new environment, one of "mere passive surroundings," is, Gilman insisted, "counter-evolutionary." Here woman is restricted, confronting a uniform world of little change. But an environment that does not change does not demand new thought or new knowledge; it does not induce creativity. The male has always had the wider environment in human history, Gilman said, but now, in advanced civilization, the difference has become acute, and very dangerous to all humans. It impairs race development. For in her "confinement to the four walls of the home," Gilman wrote, woman does not develop ideas, gain information, sharpen her powers of judgment, or test her survival skills in the manner of virtually all the females of their species. And if she cannot advance and hone those skills, Gilman warned, she cannot pass them on to her children.

To the subject of motherhood Gilman addressed some of her most trenchant commentary. To her, motherhood had become an object of sentimentality, and with terrible consequences. No contemporary institution, she argued, commanded such reverence, none stood more above reproach, more removed from any interrogation, any skepticism. As a practice "more sacred than religion, more binding than law," motherhood operated now as the reserve of a woman's unique and special intuition, the peculiar gift of her sex, her nature. The world assumes, said Gilman, that, as in the animal kingdoms, instinct fully serves the purpose of motherhood. That model, however, serves us very badly, she believed. For human advancement, Gilman reminds her readers again, proceeds by reason and intellect, applied to the shifting circumstances and challenges of our environment. But "in no other field," Gilman asserted, "are we so blinded by our emotions." And the results fall little short of disaster.

Motherhood, Gilman wrote, like any other human activity, should come under scientific investigation. It should undergo empirical studies to measure its effectiveness and we must judge it by its results. Of course, she said, it would all boil down to one question: Does it serve the young of the species? Left as it is to "female instinct," however, motherhood cannot pass this test. It would never occur to us, Gilman stated, to send soldiers into battle relying on their "male instincts," but we subject women to these very disadvantages. But, think of it: "The most important and wonderful of human functions is left from age to age in the hands of absolutely untaught women." And here, too, Gilman perceived a decline as humans advanced in civilization. For the mother fashioned by modern gender roles and gender culture has no preparation, no training for motherhood. Segregated to sex functions only, cut off from the trial and error of the economic world, dependant on the male, she brings to motherhood virtually nothing that equips her children for race survival. She does not obtain food for them, does not provide other aspects of their livelihood. She can educate them only for the social relations of the confined environment of family. Human mothers, Gilman believed, do less for their young than females in the other species. Gilman wrote in Lamarckian mode, assuming that acquired characteristics in the parent pass to the progeny. She pressed the consequences forcefully: "The record of untrained instinct as a maternal faculty in the human race is to be read on the rows and rows of little gravestones which crowd our cemeteries."

By such stark statements Gilman hoped to prepare her readers for a full reconsideration of the modern family. Traditional marriage she supported; the family she questioned. Clearly the family had become antiquated, no longer able to function as a vehicle of evolutionary adaptation, crippling especially to that half of humanity trapped in its sterile environment, Gilman wrote. The restructuring she envisioned looked for women to escape that environment altogether. The household, under Gilman's reconstruction, would acquire a new management team—experts trained in hygiene and diet and in the advanced technology of household maintenance and improvements. While women would join the outside world, acquiring the key survival techniques useful to their offspring, the outside world, the arena of modern science—from biology to chemistry to electricity—would enter the home.

Women and Economics, fortified by Gilman's other works such as *The Home* (1903) and *Human Work* (1906), established Gilman as the leading intellectual feminist of her time. In a sense, she described what later feminists would label "the problem that has no name." In 1910 novelist Margaret Deland wrote that everywhere one found "a prevailing discontent among women" in America, and especially among the women of privilege in their safe and sheltered domains. She wrote: "One meets wives, young or mature, apparently happy, gay; suddenly they confide in you that they are bored to death. . . . Many fall into a state of depression, develop nerves, lose the taste of life." Gilman tried to sound the depth of this "problem" and drew on evolutionary theory with great effect in doing so. Through her own personal depression she never lost the taste of life. But in 1935, after learning that she had breast cancer, she took her life by chloroform.

THE FEMALE PRINCIPLE IN EVOLUTION

Eliza Burt Gamble was born in Concord, Michigan, in 1841. Her parents, Luther and Florinda, had come from upstate New York three years earlier. Eliza lost her father when she was two and her mother died when she was nineteen. Left to her own resources she became a teacher and advanced to the position of assistant superintendent in the East Saginaw school system. Her progressive politics took her into the women's suffrage movement, and she quickly became a major officer in the state organization dedicated to that cause. She also did considerable writing for it, with pieces published in newspapers throughout the Middle West. Gamble believed, however, that women's suffrage addressed only the surface issues of sexual equality, and she wanted to know the deeper roots of the female condition in contemporary societies. She undertook extensive reading, with a year in Washington, DC, consulting the many collections in the Library of Congress. Her efforts led to the publication of her book *The Evolution of Woman: An Inquiry into the Dogma of Her Inferiority to Man*, in 1894. The book had a reprint, expanded with updates, in 1916 under the title *The Sexes in Science and History*. She married James Gamble, an attorney, in 1867. They had three children, including a daughter who died in infancy. Eliza Gamble died in 1920.

Gamble acknowledged a decisive debt to Darwin. But not until 1886 did she read *The Descent of Man* and gain the insights that fostered her theory. She wrote in her preface to *Evolution of Woman*: "I first became impressed with the belief that the theory of evolution, as enunciated by scientists, furnishes much evidence going to show that the female among all the orders of life, represents a higher stage of development than the male." She observed that scientists had by then widely accepted Darwin's thesis but had ignored facts that would have led them to conclusions that she now offered as an alternative reading of evolution. Gamble further asserted that a long record of metaphysical speculation and theological dogmatism, entrenched in Western culture, had conspired to obscure an objective reading of evolution. Prominent among the misreaders was Darwin himself.

That Darwin had correctly described human beings as evolved from the lower forms of life, however, Gamble had no doubt. She explains to her readers that naturalists now derive from complicated particles "all the forms, both animal and vegetable, which have ever existed upon the earth." She also confirms that Darwin's explanation by way of natural selection adequately accounted for the changes that advanced species into higher forms of life. Gamble and Gilman would differ in their respective appropriation of evolutionary ideas for feminist platforms in Gamble's greater willingness to recognize clear, innate differentiations among male and female in the human species. She would affirm a maternal instinct and celebrate its diffusion into social patterns as the most progressive factor in human evolution. But like Gilman, she, too, saw the evolutionary process distorted by male ascendancy and decried its baneful effects on human civilization.

Her study of evolution led Gamble to posit two foundational points for understanding sexual and gender evolution. The lowest forms of species, she affirmed, disclose little sexual differentiation, and females in these groups are generally indifferent to courtship. They would have to be led into it by male persuasion. In higher species, then, we find males taking on those aspects of coloration, charm, and grandeur that more sharply distinguish them from females. Darwin had written that females know and come to favor these features. The female bird will favor a male for his alluring warble. Combs, multicolored feathers, a love dance—these, too, enhance attractiveness. They also, it is to be noted, make the female the selective agent in evolution.

Furthermore, for Gamble, this situation also makes the female the agent of an advancing civilization and an improving society. A nurturing female instinct evident in the lower forms yields an acute sensitivity to the preserving qualities of things and a discriminating power with respect to taste and beauty. As sex differentiation advances through the males, however, they acquire a greater aggressiveness in competition with rivals for female favors. They develop, in contrast to females, a greater disposition to individual self-preservation and a greater habit of sexual gratification. Gamble, unlike Gilman, noted Darwin's acknowledgment that male sex characteristics often veer to excess, as in the large horns of the antelope, to the point that they could disadvantage the male. But Darwin assured that natural selection will prevent any excess dangerous to the species itself. Gamble concluded, though, that sex differentiation deprived males of a progressive role in evolution. She wrote with regard to the advantage that some males will gain over others that "it is plain, however, that this advantage, although it enables them to gratify their desires, and at the same time to perpetuate their species, does not imply higher development for the male organization." The sexual adjustments in question do not imply any successful adaptation to the physical environment and are thus "not within the true line of development" and may in fact be "useless or worse than useless" for evolutionary advance.

The female, in contrast, bears those traits that do advance evolution. From the instinct of nurture and protection for her young come the social instincts writ larger and from these habits the origin of the moral sense, or conscience. This derivation was crucial, Gamble believed, for this faculty "constitutes the fundamental difference between the human species and the lower orders of life." Here Darwin helped Gamble for he had written that "parental and filial affection lies at the base of the social instincts." He also derived those instincts from natural selection; those individuals who showed the strongest nurturing activities toward their offspring would survive and multiply, outdistancing others. Gamble readily gathered the evidence to show that females, among birds, for example, show far greater protective behavior toward their young than males. She cited Charles Letourneau's book *The Evolution of Marriage and the Family* (1892) to illustrate this fact, exemplified by the extreme cases where fathers injure or kill their own offspring.

Gamble had recourse to studies of earliest human society and her book references many recent works in history and anthropology. She marshaled that evidence to advance her point that primitive human societies had inherited from the lower species from which humans evolved the salient sex qualities previously described. Specifically, the ascendancy of the female traits, precisely their moral high-level and altruistic inclination, gave to tribal, or gentile, collectives a pronounced egalitarianism. It also assured a cooperative structure that overrode the destructive competition rooted in the male ethic of individualism. Lewis Henry Morgan's studies of the Iroquois Indians contributed to this thesis. His description of female roles among them particularly interested Gamble. Morgan wrote: "The women were the great power among the clans, as everywhere else. They did not hesitate to 'knock off the horns,' as it was technically called, from the head of a chief, and send him back to the ranks of the warriors. The original nominations of the chiefs also rested with them." In Alfred Russel Wallace's book *The Malay Archipelago*, also cited by Gamble, the description of "small uncivilized societies" speaks generally for humans in the lower status of barbarism. He found a pervasive social equality—no great disparities of wealth and poverty, no servile class, no great divisions of labor. And "there is not," he wrote, "that sever competition and struggle for existence or for wealth which the dense population of civilized societies inevitably creates." Gamble thus posited a romantic and idyllic situation as the normative state of human society in its precivilized condition. In government, "liberty, fraternity, and equality were the original and natural inheritance of the human family." Female characteristics and womanly authority laid this foundation.

THE GREAT REVERSAL

Like many grand narratives of human history and evolution, Gamble's locates a kind of ur-point into which enters an alien or satanic agent that becomes a corrupting presence and vehicle of a downward trek. Sexual differentiation, according to Gamble, did have a progressive effect in the form of female selectivity, but it yielded an errant direction as well. Gamble believed that as females placed premiums on certain physiological qualities in males that appealed to females' esthetic sense, they forced on males a competition for their favor. But that competition reinforced the dominant male traits. Speed, dexterity, strength, and, above all, aggressiveness became survival assets that grew more accentuated in the superior males. As humans inherited from the lower forms the selective role of females, they also inherited, and their societies reflected, a sex differentiation that gave males controlling powers based on the original competition with one another. The most crucial application of that brute strength, Gamble believed, appeared in the males' new role as hunters and warriors. Women then acquired an economic dependency on men that has ordered and distorted sex roles down to the present. "Through the processes involved in the differentiation of sex and the consequent divisions of functions," Gamble asserted, "it has been possible during the past six thousand or seven thousand years . . . for women to become enslaved, or subjected to the lower impulses of the male nature."

Gamble saw a long process unraveling here. She judged the change from female to male supremacy "among the most important in the evolutionary processes." In her book she gave much attention to the origins of marriage and traced its beginnings to the practice of wife-capture, which she located in Rome, Arabia, and Israel. It succeeded to wife-trading and then, over time, settled into the contractual arrangements for marriage that have long prevailed in human societies. The institution of marriage sealed women in their inferiority to men. "Marriage," Gamble wrote, "still retains its original meaning, namely, the ownership and control of women." Thus, women are "given" to men in marriage; the woman promises to "obey" her master, and accepts a ring "as a badge of her dependence upon him." She surrenders her own name and assumes his; then she follows him to his home where "she is subject to his will and pleasure." Gamble, after tracing the long history of marriage back to key evolutionary shifts in the species, came down severely on its ultimate effects. "Of all the forms of human slavery which have ever been devised," she wrote, "there has probably never been one so degrading as is that which has been practiced within the marital relation, nor one in which the extrication of the enslaved has been a matter of such hopelessness."

The *Evolution of Woman* goes deeply into anthropology and history, referencing many contemporary works. From early human societies it moves into some examinations of ancient Greece and Rome and the place of women, as social players and cultural objects, in those civilizations. Gamble attributes to Rome some significant advances from the Greeks, but then describes a devastating turn for women in Christianity. That religion, she believed, had much potential for female equality, especially as it grew from a cultural connection to Greek philosophy. But it picked up notions of male supremacy from Judaism and from Greek mythology.

The great reversal in the Judaeo-Christian nexus occurred with Paul, Gamble maintained. He had early on, she claimed, embraced a vital role for women, even acknowledging them as prophets. As Paul gained in power and influence in the new Christian community, however, "his strong masculine" nature asserted itself. It could no longer coexist with a religion that embraced feminist themes. Under the Pauline aegis, Christianity reverted to pagan themes and skillfully appropriated them. Jesus now became the Solar Deity; he was born at the winter solstice; he died and was buried at the vernal equinox (Easter) and rose from the dead as the Savior of mankind. "Every page in the history of the Pauline religion," Gamble insisted, "reseals its masculine origin." Christianity worships a father and a son. All the angels and archangels are men. Males also wrote all the extant Gospels and Epistles. Only much later did a popular movement yield a female principle in this religion, "an afterthought," the Virgin Mary. Her invocation, though, did nothing to redefine the sexual priorities in Christianity; she was human, said Gamble, while the Father and Son were divine. "She was matter. They were spirit."

Gamble took the historical measure of Christianity and could see only a great regression. What began in the Periclean age of democratic Athens had passed to Rome where, at the time of the Christian advent, lawyers had just completed their work of establishing legal equality between the sexes. The reforms, however, died with pagan Rome. "When Christianity, in the person of Constantine, ascended the throne," Gamble wrote, "the results of four centuries of civilization were destroyed, or for more than six hundred years were practically annulled." Women, she charged, would now be let out to dry on the edifice of the canon law. Citing the work of W. E. H. Lecky, Thomas Henry Buckle, and Sir Henry Maine on ancient law and morals, Gamble argued that daughters and wives all fell to inferior status under the new ecclesiastical jurisprudence, and females altogether assumed "the most stringent subordination." From the Genesis depiction of Eve forward, Gamble believed, "the entire Christian superstructure rests on the dogma of female weakness and female depravity."

This female subordination, Gamble maintained, represented one cultural construction that took place within the larger framework of the critical evolutionary shift that occurred in early human society.

This paradigm, she wrote, registered in all sorts of ways, even to the minutiae of daily life. Like Gilman, for example, Gamble cited woman's clothing. What else but a perverse sexual selection could explain "the incongruities and absurdities" evidenced in the woman's fashions of the day? So long as woman was the selecting agent in evolution, sexual differentiation had manifested itself in the male. After the reversal, woman, in her subjection to the male, has assumed the burden of pleasing him through the senses, the visual claiming the highest priority. Woman, Gamble asserted, must marry to gain her support, and she accepts the dictates of dress imposed on her. As Darwin also noted, women all over the world adorn themselves with the feathers of male birds. In doing so they take on painful restraints, injurious to their health, immobilizing, confining them to their "sphere," and further removing themselves from the competitive arena that advances the species. Consequently, the evolution occurs now only along male lines, but hardly in the way of the species' improvement.

As we find in Gilman, we find also in Gamble both a despairing tone and expressions of optimism. For Gamble, the accumulated record of human society, denoted by "all the ignoble and degrading uses to which womanhood has been subjected," makes one wonder that they have attained any successes at all. And it might make them wonder about the idea of progress itself. Gamble could find little herself and offered the summary observation that "so far as her sex relations are concerned the position of civilized woman is lower than that of the female animal." Human society had become a debilitating arena of the "survival of the fittest," Gamble lamented. Under that regime, the moral sense atrophies. Only the most exploitative people gain, always those who operate from an inherited superior advantage at the beginning. This situation, Gamble believed, derived from the emergence to dominance of the male traits. However, she could envision it going no further. An anomaly could not forever check the natural course of things. "The old regime has run its course," she wrote. "The useless elements in evolution are wearing themselves out." Male energy is becoming irrelevant. Unfortunately, Gamble offered more of hope here than of evidence.

Gamble believed that the female condition always offers the best measure of a society's true status. It is clear why. "Society," she wrote, "advances just in proportion as women are able to convey to their offspring the progressive tendencies, transmissible only through the female organism." It follows that mankind will never advance to a higher plane of existence until women recover their original liberties, until, that is, they bring their "natural instincts" to every department of human activity. If the contemporary world but understood the evolutionary scheme, that day of liberation, and of human improvement, she believed, would arrive all the sooner.

Charlotte Perkins Gilman and Eliza Burt Gamble surveyed the situation of women in the United States and found it wanting. Their critical assessments concurred with trends and developments of great significance in women's history. Women in the last decade of the nineteenth century, for example, entered into higher education in unprecedented numbers, at rates not to be equaled until much later, in the 1970s, in fact. They were also assuming more visible public roles. Movements such as the temperance crusade, rooted in the antebellum years, took them into other activities. Not the least of these efforts was the struggle to win the right of suffrage for themselves. The nation's largest women's organization, the Women's Christian Temperance Union, exemplified the transition. The movement made its gains first in the western states and ultimately in ratification of the Nineteenth Amendment to the Constitution in 1920. At least the promise and prospects of these reforms may have supplied Gilman and Gamble with the optimistic voice in their writings. But those writings also resounded with harsh judgments. For both women found the sexual arrangements of modern civilization profoundly unnatural. Certainly the long view of things that they took through evolution and history prompted that judgment. Gilman made her arguments recurringly through references to other species, Gamble by the same, but also through analysis of earliest human society. The evolutionary view governed the rhetoric of their feminism and thereby marks a significant shift in American feminism. An earlier formulation in that movement, for example, the famous Seneca Falls "Declaration of Sentiments," in 1848, flourished with the Jeffersonian language of natural rights and equality. Gilman and Gamble, however, judged modern society from the vantage of evolution. Their feminism did not resound rhetorically with the sentiments of Seneca Falls, but flourished instead with the language of the natural sciences. From that perspective, modern society stood condemned as a disruption and distortion of evolutionary progress. Evolution, however, also pointed to the corrections needed.

BIBLIOGRAPHY

Bederman, Gail. *Manliness and Civilization: A Cultural History of Gender and Race in the United States, 1880–1917*. Chicago: University of Chicago Press, 1995.

Degler, Carl N. *In Search of Human Nature: The Decline and Revival of Darwinism in American Social Thought*. New York: Oxford University Press, 1991.

Hausman, Bernice. "Sex before Gender: Charlotte Perkins Gilman and the Evolutionary Paradigm of Utopia." *Feminist Studies* 24 (1998): 488–510.

Hill, Mary A. *Charlotte Perkins Gilman: The Making of a Radical Feminist, 1860–1896*. Philadelphia: Temple University Press, 1980.

Lane, Ann J. *To Herland and Beyond: The Life and Work of Charlotte Perkins Gilman*. New York: Pantheon, 1990.

Rosenberg, Rosalind. *Beyond Separate Spheres: Intellectual Roots of Modern Feminism*. New Haven: Yale University Press, 1982.

Russett, Cynthia Eagle. *Sexual Science: The Victorian Construction of Womanhood*. Cambridge, MA: Harvard University Press, 1989.

Seitler, Dana. "Unnatural Selection: Mothers, Eugenic Feminism, and Charlotte Perkins Gilman's Regeneration Narratives." *American Quarterly* 55 (2003): 61–88.

METHODOLOGIES

Thorstein Veblen and Oliver Wendell Holmes Jr.

When thinkers like Sumner and Ward, or Gilman and Gamble, read Darwin, they saw opportunities. Evolution provided them with insights which, with appropriate applications, led to social improvement. Darwinism could write programs for social reform and the perfection of human institutions, such as the family or the state. For others, like Beecher or Bascom or McCosh, evolution, rightly understood, clarified God's ways in the world, outlined a cosmic understanding of events and human history, or confirmed a teleological scheme at work in the world. And these insights, too, could have melioristic social applications.

For others, Darwinism provided different tools; they saw different opportunities. They did not have an interest in making evolution a vehicle of reform, but wished instead to make it a way of understanding human behavior. They did not project evolution into any transcendent reality or grand design for human life and world history. In fact, in the two thinkers examined in this chapter, we recover a stricter Darwinism, one that learns from Darwin's own understanding of natural selection. For that process, the key explanation of species creation disclosed only a blind mechanism, a purposeless activity, the ways of chance. To see the world in this way, to understand human behavior apart from any teleological scheme, became for these individuals the essence of modern thinking. It denoted "scientific" habits of mind as opposed to religious, moral, and metaphysical ones. And when intellectuals like Thorstein Veblen and Oliver Wendell Holmes Jr. surveyed their own disciplines, the one in economics, the other in law, they realized how unmodern, indeed archaic, they had become. They thrived, but faltered, in old habits of thinking, pre-Darwinian mentalities, to be precise. Evolution then became for each a methodology, a new and more accurate mode of explanation.

EVOLUTIONARY ECONOMICS

People saw Thorstein Veblen as an eccentric through and through. From his personal habits to his manifold writings he was, well, unorthodox. Born in 1857 to poor Norwegian parents on the Wisconsin frontier, he moved with his family to Minnesota and grew up on a farm. One of twelve children, he did not know English as his original language, though his readers would later discover a formidable vocabulary and an intimidating prose. Thorstein attended Carleton College and then Johns Hopkins University, and Yale, where he studied with William Graham Sumner. Here he wrote his doctoral dissertation in philosophy, on Immanuel Kant. Afterward, he lapsed into his "slow" years, from 1884 to 1891. Jobless, he hung around the family farm. He didn't pitch hay; he preferred instead to indulge himself in reading anthropology and Scandian folklore. He scandalized the neighbors, this "good-for-nothing."

Veblen, it seemed, did nothing by the book. Stories abound: how, looking for a job, he showed up at Cornell University in corduroys and a coonskin cap; how, living in a cottage near Stanford University, he allowed dishes to pile up in the sink, then doused water on them and returned them to the cupboard, to start afresh; how he moved from campus to campus because of the scandals, sexual liaisons, putatively, that he created. Veblen taught at Stanford, Chicago, Harvard, and Missouri and earned dismissal from all of them. He, in turn, scorned the whole academic routine, especially the network of committees and bureaucratic rivulets that bear the burden of his famous book *The Higher Learning in America* (1918), still one of the best ever written on the subject. But his disdain extended even to the classroom. He was known to mutter the words of his lectures; only the most intellectually ambitious of the students stayed through the semester to gain from Veblen's mind. He would announce on the first day of class, we are told, that everyone in the course would get a "C." So, we can now skip the attendance requirement and the exams and, for the professor, the tedium of grading, and get on with our business. So did Veblen behave and so was he perceived in his profession—as an eccentric. One heard then, and hears now from the number-crunching econometrists, that "Veblen is not an economist." He gained no recognition or awards from the academic establishment and only late in his life was he offered the presidency of the American Economic Association. He spurned the honor. Veblen died in 1929, just before the stock market crash of that year.

The association that offered Veblen this honor had, like other social science disciplines in the United States, enjoyed several decades of professional development. These disciplines had all secured places in the modern university. Their appearance coincided with the great transformation of American higher education in the late nineteenth century. After the Civil War, graduates from American colleges found that they had no place in their country to pursue advanced research. Even before the war, these students had gone to Europe, and to Germany above all, to study with the leading scholars there. Inspired by the atmosphere of academic freedom and motivated by universities dedicated to the advancement of new knowledge, a new American generation now redefined the old-time college. Research and scholarship became the watchwords; a college education would now mean much more than the mere passing on of an acquired tradition of learning. Thus, Johns Hopkins University, established in Baltimore in 1876 and modeled after the German institutions, welcomed young scholars like Veblen to its graduate program.

The dramatic expansion of knowledge demanded both curricular and structural changes in the American schools. Under the old regime, the college president typically taught classes in moral and mental philosophy to the seniors. The subject embraced the rudiments of economics, sociology, and politics and reflected the Christian moral understanding of human affairs. Francis Wayland, president of Brown University, included in his best-selling textbook, *The Elements of Moral Science*, (1835, 1856) such subjects as the Sabbath, personal property, oaths, marriage, chastity, the duties of parents, the nature of just government, war, charity, and poor laws. But now new academic disciplines, and their corresponding departments, crystallized out of moral philosophy. They defined new standards of scholarship for themselves and they became professional organizations. The American Historical Association formed in 1884 and the American Economic Association the next year. The American Political Science Association began in 1903, and three years later Lester Frank Ward and William Graham Sumner joined with others to establish the American Sociological Society.

In a series of trenchant essays, Veblen marked the intellectual progress, and mostly the lack of it, in these organizations, focusing on economics. His essay "Why Is Economics Not an Evolutionary Science?" supplies a major document of Darwinism in America. Veblen meant to show that the discipline of economics had not absorbed the Darwinian revolution in thought, although it *should* have. In short, economics was not an evolutionary science, though it must become one. It would remain, otherwise, in the category of "prescientific." Veblen offered his thoughts on this subject in 1898, his essay appearing in the *Quarterly Journal of Economics*. He further advanced his position with two critical essays, one on Adam Smith and one on Karl Marx.

As typically he did, Veblen, in the first essay, gave his analysis a deep historical setting. He intended to initiate no narrow academic dispute, but wanted instead to use this subject to place the course of Western thinking under interrogation. So he approached the matter anthropologically. Early humans, he wrote, sought to understand things, especially mysterious natural phenomenon, by projecting personalities on to them. An assortment of local deities thus sufficed to explain why strange or threatening events occurred. People attributed lightening and thunder to angry gods in the sky. But as humans gained a better understanding of their world, anthropomorphic habits of thought changed, Veblen explained, into explanation by impersonal causes, or natural laws. These verities still held transcendent status; they reflected the design of a single intelligence who has oversight of the creation and the progress of human history. They gave rise, Veblen asserted, to the great ages of theology and metaphysics and those "canons of truth" that acquired certitude.

This habit of thinking correlated to particular modes of explaining things. At that time, Veblen said, fully to understand something required that one look behind the sequence of observable phenomena "and seek higher ground for their ultimate synthesis." Natural behavior makes ultimate sense, then, only when the detached and isolated events under observation are made to relate to some governing pattern or process, some larger superstructure that gives them an expanded significance. True understanding emerges when we know things in terms of a larger synthesis, some abstract or invisible cause, or, usually, "some teleological projection." This larger, cosmic operation bestows meaning on the disparate events and activities we see in nature or know in historical time. The local and singular acquire significance in terms of the extended relations that forge them into a unifying whole. Furthermore, Veblen asserted, this appeal to a transcendent normality or higher truth had turned the study of human behavior into an aspect of moral philosophy, as it judged the incidental as measured against the higher standards of the cosmic plan. For Veblen, and for other Darwinians like John Dewey, this understanding gave Western religions and philosophical systems their motivating purposes.

The truly modern thinker, which means for Veblen the Darwinian, will not, however, look at the world this way. This methodology is "prescientific." And for Veblen the difference between the prescientific and the modern, scientific habit of thought constituted "a difference of spiritual attitude." Darwin's manner of explaining evolution supplied the key differentiation in the two habits of thought. Veblen became one of the few American thinkers to fashion a more or less strict Darwinian explanation of evolution. It did not appeal to grand designs and ulterior, or formal, causes. It saw life as an open and continual process without final causes. Veblen wrote: "The evolutionary point of view . . . leaves no place for a formulation of natural laws in terms of definitive normality, whether in economics or in any other branch of inquiry." Neither does it make science or sociology an aspect of moral judgment. Under the Darwinian mentality, science seeks to explain the sequence of events through mechanical causation, a matter-of-fact accounting that confines itself to observable behavior.

In his extended critique Veblen went after big game—Adam Smith and Karl Marx. Smith, the moral philosopher at Glasgow University, represented classical economics, which he had given a famous construction in his 1776 work, *The Wealth of Nations*. In taking on Smith and Marx, Veblen chose well for laissez-faire economics enjoyed a virtual orthodox hegemony in American colleges and universities in the nineteenth century. It had, to be sure, met recent challenges from several thinkers, including Richard T. Ely (with whom Veblen studied at Johns Hopkins) and his Christian socialism. Ely helped create the American Economic Association and after 1893 taught at the University of Wisconsin. Second, Marx, who had written *Das Kapital* in 1866, did not have a large influence in academe, but inspired some radical movements largely associated with immigrant groups. Veblen recognized his world renown, though, and his genius. But Veblen also wanted all to know that both of these economic theorists had fatal flaws. Both were prescientific.

Smith represented the eighteenth century well. His system described an orderly scheme, which, if set properly into motion, assured maximum benefits and material progress. The arrangement worked through an "invisible hand" that directed the play of perfect competition into the most rational distribution of goods and services at optimal prices. But these gains for the social whole came though the exertion of a strict self-interest on the part of individuals with only minimal interference from the public sector. Thus, as Veblen wrote on behalf of Smith, "the guidance of the invisible hand takes place not by way of interposition, but through a comprehensive scheme of contrivances established from the beginning." Smith assumed all individuals to be self-seeking, rationally calculating, and pursuing their necessities of life. The collective effect of what Veblen labeled "this hedonism" is the enhancement of the larger social welfare. Smith had recourse to a coordinating design in human affairs. It rather resembles the collocation described by James McCosh and others in explaining evolution in nature. Both systems affirmed a careful contrivance, an intelligent design.

Smith's perspectives led him, Veblen charged, to posit certain norms and ideals. The invisible hand worked when free and open competition prevailed. And under these conditions, furthermore, there existed a "real" or "nominal" price for every commodity. That is, the market price would equal that price under free competition, or would approach the nominal, the normative price as the economic system approached free competition. Veblen believed, however, that economic understanding gained nothing from these idealizations. They constituted for him "teleological preoccupations," abstractions that have no causal role in economic behavior. Veblen credited Smith with a "painstaking scrutiny of facts" that gave his writings a superiority to his predecessors, but everywhere he saw in Smith an idealizing habit, one that judges everything against an imagined grand design and its intended effects. Smith employed this strategy in discussing market values. With Smith, said Veblen, "the substantial fact with respect to these market values is their presumed approximation to the real values teleologically imputed to the goods under the guidance of inviolate natural laws. But, Veblen insisted, "the real, or natural, value of articles has no causal relation to the value at which they exchange." Such judgments might be worthy of the moral philosopher in Smith, Veblen allowed, but they impaired his ability to explain behavior in the marketplace.

Karl Marx, too, had devised a grand system. "There is no system of economic theory more logical than that of Marx," Veblen wrote. "No member of the system, no single article of doctrine, is fairly to be understood except as an articulate member of the whole." Veblen's gesture of praise for Marx's holistic thinking, however, prepares the ground for his acute critique. Veblen considered Marx foremostly a Hegelian, one who grounded Hegel's idealist system in a materialist philosophy. Marx's materialism, Veblen recognized, might have assisted him in achieving a truly evolutionary economics. The dialectical logic, for one, pointed to process and change. It broke from the static mechanism of the previous century. Also, the class struggle, for Marx the catalyst of historical change, certainly had a Darwinian resonance.

But Marxism and Darwinism, Veblen averred, represent two very different intellectual systems. For Marx went beyond an explanation by cumulative causation to impose final causes, and thus a teleological projection, onto the class struggle. Onto the hard realities of social competition and the stark realities of economic power, Veblen accused, Marx injected a "pious fancy," a teleological world process. The Darwinian conception of natural selection, Veblen insisted, could never be appropriated for such a scheme. "Neither," Veblen wrote, "could it conceivably be asserted to lead up to a final term, a goal to which all lines of the process should converge and beyond which the process would not go." But Marx took that process toward history's end point—the triumph of the proletariat and the establishment of a classless society. All the contradictions of capitalism overcome, the dialectical system arrives to its final synthesis. Veblen, however, had to insist, "In Darwinism there is no such final or perfect term and no definitive equilibrium."

Furthermore, as Veblen saw it, once one invents a superstructure of ideal or normative "realities," then one invariably makes it the measure of all empirical realities. Moral assessments enter the picture and the social sciences perpetuate a moral-philosophy character. Here, Veblen judged, Marx fell into the same trap as Smith. Veblen saw in Marx's labor theory of value a descriptive ideal that had no causal role in economic behavior. Thus for Marx, the "real" value of a commodity was the cost of the labor to produce it. Ideally, labor would get the full return of its input, but under capitalism, owners of the means of production appropriate shares to themselves in the form of profits. Only under a socialistic state that has eliminated private property, Marx urged, would the workers get the full value of their labor. Marx, of course, saw history moving by its own inviolate logic toward that end, but Veblen dismissed the Marxian explanation as but another project working by its own inner necessity and moving along a teleological trajectory. Furthermore, he charged, this pre-Darwinian thinking made Marx, like Smith, a moralist. The labor theory of value constituted a measure by which to judge any existing price structure, but, like Smith's ideal, it did not explain economic behavior.

Veblen thus undertook to assess the status of economic thinking as represented by two formidable theorists. But he was doing more. Smith and Marx exemplified two great traditions in Western culture—the Enlightenment of the eighteenth century and the romantic movement (in Marx's appropriation of Hegel) of the nineteenth. Veblen measured each thinker by the standards of a new paradigm, the modern scientific habits of thought. These habits connoted for Veblen one particular worldview—that of Darwin. By Darwinism Veblen intended an open-ended system of evolution, one that proceeded by spontaneous change, undirected and uninfluenced by any larger or transcendent reality, any designing intelligence, any cosmic plan, or any occult contrivance. Economic theory, in his judgment, had failed to incorporate or utilize this way of thinking. And Veblen intended to make some corrections.

He began by faulting a staple of classical economics, the notion of "economic man." Veblen believed that Smith viewed all people as rational calculators of their needs—mechanical and hedonistic actors in the marketplace, whose activities for themselves move, by the guidance of the invisible hand, to a higher social good. Human nature thus appeared to Smith as pretty much the same everywhere. Economic man, Veblen found, had an even larger use for Smith's successors in the classical school—the utilitarians. Veblen saw right through the fallacies. "This perfect competitive system," he wrote, "with its untainted 'economic man,' is a feat of the scientific imagination, and it is not intended as a competent expression of fact. It is an expedient of abstract reasoning; and its avowed competency extends only to abstract principles, the fundamental laws of the science, which hold only so far as the abstraction holds."

So, out with "economic man." Needed now, Veblen exhorted, was a different conception of human nature, of the actual individual behaving in the marketplace, an evolutionary understanding. Veblen put it this way: "The economic life history of the individual is a cumulative process of adaptation of means to ends that cumulatively change as the process goes on, both the agent and his environment being at any point the outcome of the last process. His habits of life today are enforced upon him by his habits of life carried over from yesterday." This perspective complicates the matter. We are less creatures of reason than we are creatures of habit, Veblen insisted, and, more precisely, of an inherited instinct of behavior. We must then take account of a larger environment of influence; we enter a vast realm of cultural complexity. Veblen urged that "the economic interest does not lie in isolation," and we cannot describe any activity as strictly "economic."

Economics must become an evolutionary science, Veblen urged. It must explain a long process of cultural impact and race history and promote "a genetic account of an unfolding process." "It is necessarily the aim of such a science," Veblen insisted, "to trace the cumulative working-out of the economic interest in the cultural sequence. It must be a theory of the economic life process of the race or the community." Under this perspective, the researcher will find a less rational human nature. Humans are not simple calculators of pleasure and pain. "The conception of the economic interest which a hedonistic psychology gives does not afford material for a theory of the development of human nature," Veblen wrote. It is too static. It does not see things in terms of growth and cultural shift. It does not see inherited traits and atavistic behavior. It does not fit the evolutionary method.

DECODING THE GILDED AGE

Veblen best exemplifies an evolutionary economics in his brilliant classic *The Theory of the Leisure Class*. Published in 1899, the book also addresses the Gilded Age at its high point. By now visitors to New York City could see the massive domiciles of the Astors and Vanderbilts, the French châteaus on Fifth Avenue. These imposing edifices had luxurious interiors furnished by appointments brought from around the world. Wealthy people traveled the country in private railroad cars, elaborately furnished and displaying the finest craftsmanship. (If you were J. P. Morgan you traveled in your own train.) Elaborate banquets in city restaurants entertained and indulged the American plutocracy. The Gilded Age marked an era of excess. Veblen gave us the term "conspicuous consumption" to describe the purchasing habits of the rich. *Leisure Class* was Veblen's first book. All those "lazy" years of reading anthropology around the farm seemed to have paid off.

How can we explain this extravagant behavior? Veblen did so by recourse to social evolution and began early on in human history. In the period of savage society, Veblen found prevailing peaceful conditions where men and women lived in a cooperative and functional manner. No one class dominated by virtue of property and class distinctions had little form. Here, too, the "instinct of workmanship," (the title of Veblen's book of 1914) directed labor toward production for social use. Under generally poor economic conditions, these early humans shunned waste and ostentation. Women had a proximate equality with men, and a communal ethic, rooted in the necessity of cooperation, forestalled the ravages of individual self-interest and personal gain.

These conditions changed under barbarism, Veblen explained. Technological advance created wealth available more for demonstration than useful application. A warrior class emerged and secured its status by capturing booty or rival tribesmen. Society now honors force, fraud, and prowess, and disparages crude menial work. "Invidious distinctions" (one of the many expressions that recurs in this book) set in. Men kill animals by skill but disdain the menial job of bringing the game home; the women fetch it and prepare if for meals. Under barbaric society, Veblen speculated, the new conditions of primitive industry might have fostered an ethic of practicality and a value system rooted in thrift, frugality, and enterprise. But instead, waste took on an honorific status and an early leisure class, marked by manifest signs of exemption from useful productivity, emerged and fixed itself permanently in Western society, fully in place by the Middle Ages. Thus, a tribal chieftain comports himself in a way that reflects this exemption from useful work. He surrounds himself with slaves and has porters carry him from place to place.

We now see also the phenomenon of "pecuniary emulation." The main economic motive in human behavior, Veblen believed, is not merely to consume for use and enjoyment in the strict sense; it is to display artifacts and mannerisms that reveal one's exemption from useful productive activity. "From this point," Veblen writes, "the characteristic of leisure class life is a conspicuous exemption from all useful employment." Veblen did not say that the leisure class did not work. Quite the contrary. It had arrived to wealth by exploit. Leisure class ways did, however, reflect atavistic behavior—throwbacks to earlier societal norms and cultural values, the honorific status of leisure, that emerged early in humans' social evolution.

In most of the rest of his book Veblen turns his discerning eye to exemplifications of leisure class life in the United States of his day. And with what great effects! He moves from some commonplace observations to many suggestive insights. So first we enter the palatial homes of the leisure class. We find in all of them a library—obligatory. Many volumes line the spacious shelves along the walls. Books suggest leisure time and ample opportunity in which to indulge them. So their owners, it appears, must have sufficient exemption from useful productive activity to enjoy them. But look closely. Many of these books are the great classics, from the Greek and Roman era into the eighteenth century. Some bear their original "dead" languages. So these books are not guides to engineering, investment, or marketing; in fact, they have no "practical" value at all, and no association with menial activities. Hence, their higher honorific status.

Everywhere one finds servants. But these servants are not menial drudges. They, too, must suggest a certain leisureliness, a marked exemption from useful productive activity, the more so to reflect favorably on the master of the house. Some of the servants wear white gloves, unsoiled. The servants must not reflect the habits of a ploughman or a sheepherder, Veblen assures. The most visible of the servants speak French, or, at the very least, a refined and eloquent English. One may find a servant whose only job is to open the door for entering and exiting guests and for the traffic of the master's family. Leisurely ways prevail everywhere as the master's high status is such that he effects an entire personal environment exempt from useful productive activity.

Veblen saw another mark of leisurely habits in drunkenness. For imbibing in drink requires, first of all, a certain amount of unproductive time, and, second, it conveys dysfunction, such that one could not be practically engaged while indulging. (One of J. P. Morgan's cars, in his private train, was lined with wine racks.) Women also enter the complex. Men spend inordinate amounts of money, Veblen observed, to dress their wives elaborately. And the Gilded Age fashions supplied Veblen with plenty of evidence for his case. Women submitted their bodies to bustles, braces, and buckles, to a disabling confinement that shrieked loud of exemption from useful productive activity. For not only the moguls themselves but all that they touch much exude leisurely habits.

In a section labeled "Pecuniary Canons of Taste," Veblen extended his vision to the remotest corners of human behavior and commodity characteristics. He noted the utensils at the dinner table of the leisurely—the Victorian bric-a-brac, the ornamentation, and stylistic excess. What could be more functional than a fork? Why, then, must it be lined with floral patterns, for example, or geometric designs? Veblen here spotted nonfunctional, decorative embellishments that raised the dinnerware above the level of ordinary practicality into a domain of esthetics, or emphatic nonpracticality. Veblen's glance even finds its way to women's underwear. Lace and delicate embroidery embellish these eminently practical garments, which, in fact, are to be obscured from the public eye. Leisure effects, however, extend even to the realms of the inconspicuous. Or consider domestic pets. Why do people prefer not to bring a pig into the household but will provide elaborate quarters therein for a cat or a dog? The answer is simple: The dog and cat have little practical value and the course of their daily routines clearly shows an exemption from useful productive activity. But invidious distinctions go even further in this category of leisurely ways. Anyone will observe that the preferred breed of dog for the wealthy woman is the poodle. Does this foppish canine, who seems to have spent the day at the coiffeur's, not display rather magnificently an exemption from useful productive activity?

Finally, Veblen takes this subject right to the heart of Western civilization with a glimpse at its religion. Here one might begin with the question, what does God do all day? He appears usually to have a sedentary posture, seated on a throne, and surrounded by a retinue of leisurely cherubim and seraphim. He is uncontaminated by any sensual interests. The deity, in short, Veblen says, seems given to "a peculiarly serene and leisurely habit of life." But this exemption from useful productive activity extends also to the rituals of religion. Priestly vestments display a rich ornamentation, not the marks of workaday routine. The worship service proceeds in an unhurried pace. It mandates no display of agility or dexterity on the part of the clergy. The Sabbath, the day that honors the Judaic or Christian God, is a day of rest. Thus God himself, the most honored in the realm of being, thrives in an honorific culture that mandates exemption from useful productive activity.

To the cold eye or the naive observer, all this behavior may seem irrational in the extreme. Veblen meant to describe it that way. But it is irrational only by the rational norms of "economic man." In the long vantage of evolutionary change, a continuity appears. Consumption in the marketplace reflects atavistic behavior, a reversion to primordial habits and values. And what does Veblen make of all this? Does all this elaborate account display the habits of a detached, scholarly observer explaining his age? Or did Veblen execute a stinging satirical rebuke of the capitalist system in the United States? Was the age of the moguls an age of extravagance and waste, worthy of our moral censure and outrage? Were we to understand the captain of industry as the latter-day heirs of that system of exploit whose traits we can find among our primitive ancestors? Historians have debated Veblen's intentions. But clearly foremost in his purposes, Veblen wanted to uphold a methodology for the new economics profession, a model for study. His methodology sought to explain the manners of the marketplace in Gilded-Age America. To do so he had to trace a long evolutionary trek.

LAW AND NATURAL SELECTION

Whereas Thorstein Veblen grew up among plain, immigrant folk in the Midwest, Bostonian Oliver Wendell Holmes Jr. was, almost, to the manor born. "Born into the most traditional of families in the most traditional of American cities," biographer Liva Baker writes. Holmes certainly qualified as "Brahmin" status. If the family lacked great wealth, it did not lack the intellectual and cultural connections that have won the attention of Americans and the interest of scholars for generations since. Holmes's father, physician and popular essayist, had the personal acquaintances of James Russell Lowell, Henry Wadsworth Longfellow, Nathaniel Hawthorne, and Ralph Waldo Emerson. The son would know them all. Later as a young man returning from the Civil War, and a bit uncertain about his future, Holmes made his way directly to Emerson to discuss the subject. From the family summer retreat in Pittsfield, Holmes knew Herman Melville, a summer neighbor there.

New England intellect—intense, introspective, boldly speculative—could not but influence any bright young man or woman. Holmes's biographers always give much attention to weighing that influence. Socially proper, class-conscious, and acutely cognizant of ancestry, New England seems to explain the conservative side of Holmes. But New England was progressive and innovative, too. Harvard College had departed its Calvinist foundations by 1708. The Unitarian takeover in 1805 further identified the school, and the Boston merchant class, with rational religion. The transcendentalists—Emerson, Henry David Thoreau, Theodore Parker, Margaret Fuller—moved New England in directions set by European romanticism and provided the country with fresh thinking. Immersion in these two strains of tradition and innovation could make one profoundly ambivalent. Holmes always revered his ancestry but he also yearned to burst the bounds of New England constraints.

The family reflected both sides. David Holmes, arrived to New England in 1652, gave the family humble beginnings in America. He was an indentured servant. His great-grandson Abiel, paternal grandfather of the later justice, forged the trilogy of Holmeses, Wendells, and Olivers. Abiel graduated from Yale and became a Calvinist clergyman. He married Sally Wendell (her mother was an Oliver) and she would give birth to Oliver Wendell Holmes, one of five children. Abiel Holmes had long, running battles with the religious liberals in his congregation, but in sending son Oliver to Harvard he hastened the family direction away from his own Calvinism. Oliver Wendell Holmes graduated in the class of 1829, and, as the class poet, delivered a commencement address. He attended Harvard Medical School and then went into practice. The literary life, however, also lured him and he wrote novels, essays, and poems. He married Amelia Lee Jackson in 1840, daughter of the noted Judge Charles Jackson. Her mother came from the Cabot line.

Son Wendell, born in 1841, inherited a family and a past. Baker writes: "Wendell, as he was called, was pampered like a colt bred to run the derby. He was groomed, petted, encouraged, tested, carefully surrounded with other boys of his social class, and fed a high-protein intellectual diet." He attended Mr. Dixwell's Latin School and then went on to Harvard, "the next step" for Brahmins like he, as Henry Adams liked to put it. Wendell followed and then extended his father's line in religion, moving from mild Unitarianism into skepticism, and ultimately Darwinian atheism. He also went a different way politically. His father, "autocrat of the breakfast table," as his essay collection of that title would label him, embraced a social and political conservatism. In 1855 he penned an address excoriating the abolitionists. Boston seethed with their sentiments, however, and vigilantes formed to protect escaped slaves from headhunters coming up from the South; violence often ensued. Wendell embraced the cause. Father-son relations, in fact, had long been tense and that fact surely influenced Wendell's commitments to some degree. So also did it influence his decision for soldiering. In 1861, shortly after the outbreak of the Civil War, Wendell quit Harvard to join the Union army. He deemed it his aristocratic duty.

Wendell Holmes experienced the horrors of a horrible war. Thrice-wounded and recurringly sick, Holmes committed three years to the cause. He relished the independence from home; he rejoiced to win recognition for his own accomplishments; and he acquired a taste for "action" that he preserved amid his passion for intellectual pursuits. The war changed Holmes in another way. Louis Menand writes: "The lesson Holmes took from the war can be put in a sentence. It is that certitude leads to violence." Hereafter we will see a Holmes who recoils from absolutes, from hardened ideologies, from utopians and passionate reformers (Holmes later turned against the old abolitionists), from dogmas religious or secular. The war, Menand adds, "made him lose belief in beliefs." The war in fact prepared Holmes for Darwinism and both influences would forge his place within American pragmatism. It also shaped his career in the law.

Now Holmes stood at a crossroads: how to choose between a life of action and a life of intellect? He had told his classmates at Harvard that he wanted to study law, but he had to convince himself of its worthiness as an intellectual vocation; could it accommodate his passion for thinking? He discussed the matter urgently with Emerson, who, as Holmes had told him, "first started the philosophical ferment in my mind." And so he finally convinced himself: The law embraced action, conflict and struggle, and drama, but it also thrived with philosophical notions; it "opens a way to philosophy," Holmes affirmed. Why could he not bring to it an intellectual relish and learn more in doing so? Besides, the good Dr. Holmes had only contempt for the legal profession.

What lay ahead for Holmes was marriage to Fanny Bowditch Dixwell in 1872, brief legal practice, study at Harvard Law School, a twenty-year term on the Massachusetts Supreme Court, and his illustrious career as associate justice of the United States Supreme Court. In a certain sense, however, Holmes had early and permanently set his intellectual parameters for all these activities. The influence came from science. As G. Edward White explains, what the nineteenth century understood by "science" underwent a significant shift in the midde decades. The old science suggested the habit of classification, the organization of natural phenomena into their identifiable categories. This habit coexisted well with religion, suggesting the design aspects of a divine intelligence, as affirmed in the idealistic science of a Louis Agassiz. Science as such did not connote induction and the testing of hypotheses by experiment. Darwin, of course, gave much attention to classification, but he also presented the radical feature of a methodology that moved to ascendancy in Western science in the later century. The reorientation took place while Holmes was studying at Harvard, and Holmes seized on it. Holmes, White writes, "took 'science' as Darwin intended it to be taken: as a concept encompassing two discrete methodological aims, the conventional one of systematic classification and another one that more approximated the empiricist orientation that later generations would assume to be the central feature of 'scientific' inquiry."

Darwin had received a rude unwelcome from Harvard's moral philosophy professor, the Unitarian Francis Bowen. He labeled Darwinism one of the "licentious and infidel speculations which are pouring in upon us from Europe like a flood." Another professor worried that Darwin's ideas would erode student morals. We know what Agassiz thought of Darwin. Holmes, however, took a course on botany with Asa Gray, just a year before Darwin's book appeared. Holmes read Darwin (an 1860 edition of the book Holmes read survives, with pages annotated), but did not read widely in science as such. The methods of scientific inquiry held greater interest for him. Like John Dewey later, Holmes acquired the confidence that application of scientific methodology could solve the major problems faced by human societies.

At Harvard Law School things were changing in the 1870s, but not enough for Holmes. The law school's dean, Christopher Columbus Langdell, introduced the case method study of law in the early 1870s. Langdell meant to be both scientific and empirical. He feigned to be emulating procedures in biology or chemistry—isolate an element in order to know its properties. One could then apply this logic to legal principles, locating their origins and tracing their development to the present. Holmes summarized this approach: "The common law training [here] is to keep a student at the solution of particular cases. Just as Agassiz would give one of his pupils a sea urchin and tell him to find all about it he could." And like Agassiz, Langdell believed that within the pluralities of this judicial history existed an ideal order, not unlike the ideal forms Agassiz posited in the natural world. As Thomas Grey writes: "Langdell thought of legal categories and principles as ideal realities which the legal scientist could discover and describe and which a judge could simply follow." The fundamental principles of the common law, Langdell believed, extracted by induction from the cases studied, supplied the law with axiomatic truths. The methodology signified to Langdell the study of law "as a science."

For Holmes, Langdell's system betrayed conceptions of law he judged too logical, too ideal, too abstract, too self-contained, and old-fashioned in their idea of science. His own reading—Darwin, anthropology, history—set him square against Langdell. Holmes would not say that no logic exists in law; he would insist only that logic did not make the law what it is. Experience did that. Holmes had already arrived at an instrumentalist understanding of ideas; they get us where we need to go and establish themselves as true to the degree that they succeed. The law, like all else, emerges out of the interaction of human organisms with their environment. Societies do not formulate laws by applying abstract truth deductively to particular circumstances. Holmes had learned to see the law as much more dynamically functioning within the vast complexities of an historical situation. Logical reasoning from a priori truths simply does not describe how people make decisions. As Holmes would later say on the Supreme Court: "General propositions do not decide concrete cases." Langdell perpetuated a pre-Darwinian understanding of law, Holmes believed, and he labeled Langdell a "legal theologian." After a year at the law school, Holmes called it quits.

In 1865, Holmes entered private legal practice with the Boston firm of Chandler, Shattuck, and Thayer. He had little relish for this work and gave every minute he could spare to intellectual pursuits— the history and philosophy of law. Holmes's approach to the law— empirical, scientific, eventually experimental—set him against an established tradition. Americans, from the early influence of Sir

William Blackstone in the eighteenth century, through the commentaries of Joseph Kent in the early nineteenth, assumed the law
to have a foundation in higher principles, divine edicts, or truths of
nature derived from supernatural origins. These assumptions established the natural law basis of American jurisprudence. Blackstone
in the eighteenth century stated the matter directly:

> Good and wise men, in all ages . . . have supposed, that the deity, from
> the relations we stand in, to himself and to each other, has consti-
> tuted an eternal and immutable law, which is, indispensably, obliga-
> tory upon all mankind, prior to any human institution whatever. This
> is what is called the law of nature, which, being coeval with mankind,
> and dictated by God himself, is, of course, superior in obligation to
> any other. It is binding over all the globe, in all countries at all times.
> No human laws are of any validity, if contrary to this; and such of
> them as are valid, derive all their authority, mediately or immedi-
> ately, from this original.

Holmes, as he now enthusiastically took up legal scholarship in
the early 1870s, drew quickly away from this natural law bias. Along
with the Darwinian methodology, Holmes's wide readings in history
and anthropology contributed to his dissent. As he studied, similarly
to Veblen, the ways of early human societies, he saw how primitive
marriage customs and other social practices reflected environmental influences. Baker writes: "The law was emerging in Holmes's
mind, more and rapidly now, as an evolutionary body. Darwin's
principle of natural selection was hard at work on the law as well as
on the horse." Later Holmes would refer to law "as a great anthropological document" and followed with interest the works of Edward
B. Tylor and others who were studying law and that discipline.
Holmes in 1870 had become coeditor of the *American Law Review*
and was soon at work in the project to prepare a twelfth edition of
Joseph Kent's *Commentaries on American Law,* with the grandson of
the chancellor as collaborator. The two often found themselves at
odds, Holmes wanting to edit Kent's writings and update them. In
fact, he simply found Kent terribly unmodern. Kent had derived his
legal scholarship from natural law principles and to that extent ig-

nored historical factors in law and instead established the law in biblical authority and moral philosophy.

Furthermore, Holmes reacted skeptically toward a prevailing interest in codifying American law. That effort, he feared, would en-
tail an extensive categorization of the law into logically precise and
rigid distinctions. Critics of the effort, like Holmes, feared that a
brittle formalism would result, a legal stasis. Holmes considered
the common law an ongoing process, dynamic and creative. It
moved too fast for precise formulation, and new cases, coming
from new circumstances, always threatened to undo "the most precise formula." By this time, clearly, Holmes had come to see the
law as a living organism, working less according to rules of logic
than as a component of a historically situated economic and social
milieu.

Much of Holmes's early legal writings constituted a dress re-
hearsal for his famous work of 1881, *The Common Law.* He continued to read widely. Furthermore, he joined a loose inner circle of intellectual friends who sparked his thinking on this subject and
others. With William James and Charles Sanders Peirce, Holmes
formed the Metaphysical Club. He had known James for some time;
they had met regularly before James went to Europe in 1867 and in
serious intellectual discussions they "twisted the tail of the cosmos."
Nicholas St. John Green, an attorney, also joined and became a catalyst for Holmes's developing ideas. Green's student Joseph Bangs
Warner also participated, as did the energetic conversationalist
Chauncey Wright. Almost all had Harvard connections, but what
joined them in common cause was their effort, as Baker writes, "to
make sense of a universe turned upside down by Darwin." The
Metaphysical Club formed in January 1872.

The Common Law began as the Lowell Lecture Series in late 1880.
Holmes took on heady stuff—torts and liability, criminal law, and
contract law. He ranged well beyond the Roman and Anglo-Saxon
sources of law and his listeners heard references to the aborigines of
the Brazilian rain forests, the Kukis of southern Asia, and the ancient
records of Icelandic criminal courts. In the opening paragraph of *The
Common Law*, Holmes set forth the idea he wished most urgently to

convey. And herewith, probably the most quoted lines in the history of American jurisprudence:

> The life of the law has not been logic; it has been experience. The felt necessities of the time, the prevalent moral and political theories, intuitions of public policy, avowed or unconscious, even the prejudices which judges share with their fellow men, have had a good deal more to do than the syllogism in determining the rules by which men should be governed. The law embodies the story of a nation's development through many centuries, and it cannot be dealt with as if it contained only the axioms and corollaries of a book of mathematics. In order to know what it is, we must know what it has been, and what it tends to become.

Here Holmes set himself, if not apart from all other legal scholars, at least at the head of a group that wanted to move the study of law out of the realm of logic and moral philosophy and into history and Darwinian evolution. The work came as a jolt to that set of lawyers and judges who still considered statutory law as rooted in divine edict or natural law. Holmes did not escape formalism altogether and did not wish to, and he valued continuity in the law. But he wished to give it life and breath, to show its vitality to the social complex, to make it a critical organ within the live social organism. In fact, to extend the analogy, Holmes helped people to see the law as an evolving component of an evolving species. By implication, fixity, finality, and permanence meant stagnation, decay, and death. Holmes had earlier written, in a critique of Langdell, that "no one will ever have a truly philosophic mastery over the law who does not habitually consider the forces outside of it which have made it what it is." The law embodies the story of a nation's development over a long past. It reifies its intellectual history. "We have evolution in this sphere of conscious thought and action no less than in lower organic stages," Holmes wrote, "but an evolution that must be studied in its own field." "The law finds its philosophy not in self-consistency . . . but in history and the nature of human needs."

Holmes, in fact, may have gotten a pass on his book. *The Common Law,* as Professor White shows, does not consistently deliver on a promise to show historical change in the various categories that Holmes reviews; he has little to say about the changing content of doctrine and the forces outside the law that allegedly shaped it. Nonetheless, reviewers heralded a breakthrough, seeing in *The Common Law* a triumph of the new philosophy and the scientific methodology. One reviewer wrote: "The entire work is written from the standpoint of the new philosophy, and those hackneyed terms *natural justice* and *equity* are excluded from it." An English reviewer welcomed Holmes's book as "a most valuable—we should almost say an indispensable—companion to the new scientific study of legal history."

The new recognition Holmes won through *The Common Law* helped him gain an appointment as professor in the Harvard Law School. But he stayed less than a year. When an opening on the Massachusetts Supreme Judicial Court appeared in late 1882, the Massachusetts governor offered it to Holmes, and he seized it. He had few regrets about leaving the "half life" of academe. Now he entered the world of action—the judicial bench.

DARWINIAN JURISPRUDENCE

Holmes's judicial career will always be of interest and a challenge to students and scholars. It ranges widely and from the long record of a long life it leaves us with much to ponder. This chapter deals with Darwinism as a methodology. As Thorstein Veblen supplied the example of a Darwinian analysis of economic behavior, he left others to wonder whether he also played the role of moral judge or social critic. Holmes's record has left others to contemplate whether he was liberal or conservative. What is his intellectual legacy, politically considered? The fact is, as Holmes combined evolution with other perspectives, even with his own personality and idiosyncrasies, he made that record ambiguous. Darwinism could serve both causes.

At the risk of being somewhat imprecise in using the labels "liberal" and "conservative" (if indeed these terms permit of any exactitude of meaning), we can nonetheless identify outlooks, attitudes, and prejudices in Holmes that have endeared him to one or the other of these camps. The narrative will follow this summary with Holmes's record on the United States Supreme Court and some of the famous pronunciations he made there.

Most historians identify Holmes as a liberal. They join him to the revolt against hardened ideologies, and especially laissez-faire economics, that motivated reformers in the late nineteenth and early twentieth centuries. If they followed Darwinian leads, these reformers emphasized the need for adaptation, for applied "intelligence" as the key survival technique for human beings. Those convictions made reformers relativists when talking about "truth." That term, they insisted, was situational, never abstract, and never universal. It is around the Progressive Era that the term "liberal" takes on its modern meaning. It looks to government as a kind of collective intelligence for society, its brain center, as, for example, in the prescriptions of Lester Frank Ward and, we shall see, John Dewey. If, at the same time it stood for individual rights and personal liberties—free speech and the right to vote, especially—it did so with the demand that the state embrace all its citizens and with the intention to provide government with the widest input it needed for intelligent planning.

By intellectual experience and temperament, Holmes opposed all ideologies and emphatic truth claims. Holmes once said, "I like to multiply my skepticisms." He almost reviled those who made the claims of universal truth for their particular causes. As Menand says of Holmes: "In his work as a judge, he took delight in exposing prejudices that masqueraded as timeless truths." Holmes acknowledged no such truths anyway. Least of all, he believed, should the law aspire to such status. Law derives from the survival needs of society. It justifies its activity to the extent that it aids society in adaptation; it is orientated to a particular environment and always a changing one. How wrong, then, for judges to uphold a law because it reflects a priori truths or because it holds consistently with previous decisions, because it shows logical cohesion with them. Law must serve the present, existing needs of society, Holmes emphasized. He called it "revolting" to retain dysfunctional laws through "blind imitation of the past." "The present," Holmes wrote, "has a right to govern itself so far as it can" and a right to judge precedent with "scrutiny and revision" and under the priority of "social desires instead of tradition."

The same life outlook, however, could make Holmes sound conservative. As an evolutionist, Holmes had a profound appreciation for life as found, for the way things were. All life is a struggle; if the strong prevail, they do so generally by way of superior survival skills, Holmes believed. Darwin taught as much and Holmes had no complaint. All social arrangements, and the law especially, he believed, reflect the logic of this intractable fact of nature. The certain rightness, then, of things they way they are did not lead Holmes to say they should stay that way. But they did convince him that they could not be easily undone. He had no truck for sentimental reformers; they certainly were not entitled to change the world simply because they held some high moral claim against it. Holmes detested the one-sided thinking of most reformers he knew, their hard-and-fast ideologies, their sentimentality and piousness, and self-righteousness. Holmes wished only to keep the game open. Neither superior force nor abstract moral right should preclude society from making the piecemeal adjustments it needed to make.

This concern made Holmes a defender of judicial restraint. Not the courts, but the legislatures, he argued, constituted the scene of contest where forces contend with one another. To close down this arena of conflict and adjustment, to place arbitrary or narrow minded constraints on it, Holmes believed, conspired against all Darwinian logic. On the bench, Holmes often exercised this allowance even when he thought the legislation in question was downright stupid. But society works by trial and error. In nature, some mutations protect and advance a species; others are detrimental to the organism and are destined not to endure. Holmes, writing in 1897, observed with concern an increasing trend (certainly visible in the recent history of the United States Supreme Court) of people "who no longer hope to control the legislatures to look to the courts as expounders of the Constitution." Social struggle works itself out in contested elections; the winners take their seats in the legislatures and they write new statutes. It all made good Darwinian sense to Holmes. "Wise or not," he wrote, "the proximate test of good government is that the dominant power has its way." Only in cases of clear consti-tutional violation should the court intervene against the majority will.

For the same reason, Holmes bore a deep skepticism toward indi-vidual rights. He thought in terms first of the social organism and its needs. Individual rights found legitimacy insofar as they opened the way for people to be parts of, instead of exclusions from, the politi-cal whole, the commonweal. Holmes gave individual rights no pri-ority as claims against the norms of the majority and the will of the legislature. Libertarianism—whether as liberty of contract or free speech—Holmes rejected. In one of the controversial cases Holmes faced on the Massachusetts high court, he confronted the situation of a police officer dismissed from the force for partaking in political activities. In speaking for the court, Holmes said that the officer "may have a constitutional right to talk politics, but he has no con-stitutional right to be a policeman." No individual, Holmes asserted, can stand athwart society's designs for its own progress, its evolu-tionary course of improvement. And "no society," he wrote, "has ever admitted that it could not sacrifice individual welfare to its own existence." If it needed men for its army, it took them. If it needed property for a new road, it took it. And it should.

Holmes's critics have found him too detached, too impersonal, too "bloodless" in his social views. Methodology and procedure often seemed more important to him in matters of the law and judging than did moral outrage or humanitarian sympathy. This considera-tion suggests comparison of Holmes with other American pragma-tists. Holmes shared with John Dewey, among the American prag-matists, the closest affinity. (The others, Charles Sanders Peirce and William James particularly, Holmes claimed, took philosophy and their constructions of evolution too much toward accommodation with religion.) But Dewey was, nonetheless, too much the political liberal for Holmes. "He talks of exploitation of man by man," Holmes complained, "which rather gets my hair up." Accepting that history has its own impervious logic, Holmes tolerated the new American age of powerful businessmen and giant-size corporations and trusts. He disliked the Sherman Antitrust Act. In private correspondence Holmes wrote: "If [John D.] Rockefeller owned [all the national wealth], and had committed more imperial crimes than Frederick the Great or Napoleon to produce it, still he has made the nation richer by an imperial result—a great coordinated machine—and to destroy the machine because you disapprove the builder is folly." Of all Holmes's decisions, his critics say, the one that most confirms his callousness came in the Supreme Court decision of 1927, *Buck v. Bell*. Here Holmes defended compulsory sterilization: "Three generations of imbeciles are enough," he wrote.

Finally, for all his sangfroid, his Darwinian detachment, and his skepticism, there was something else in Holmes that probably deserves posting on the conservative side of him. It's something akin to a Burkean love of the past, of antiquity, a "romantic antiquarianism," as Grey puts it. "I love the old," he wrote to a friend. "I feel . . . to my fingertips a reverence for venerable traditions." He could apply that sentimentalism even to the common law, growing "for near a thousand years," "one of the vastest products of the human mind." He applied it to his Puritan ancestors, however irrelevant they had become to the modern world, and to the wider New England he loved. He had an acute sense of place and loved "every brick and shingle of the old Massachusetts towns" where his Puritan forebears had worked and prayed. History should serve us vitally, Holmes believed, inducing "reverence and love" and connecting past to present. The evolutionary perspective prescribed change, but sanctioned continuity as well.

ON THE BENCH

Holmes brought all of these convictions to his service on the Supreme Court of the United States. President Theodore Roosevelt appointed him in 1902 and Holmes stayed on the Court until 1932, three years before his death. Roosevelt thought he had placed on the Court a like-minded Progressive, but in the first major case on which Holmes ruled, he delivered a shock to the president. Known as the *Northern Securities Case* of 1904, the issue involved creation of a railroad holding company that combined the financial interests of moguls J. P. Morgan and Edward H. Harriman. The case tested once again the effectiveness of the Sherman Antitrust Act of 1890, which the Court had previously, by fine distinctions, eviscerated. But this one looked easy because it combined huge business powers and Roosevelt wanted federal prosecution to secure his reputation as a "trust buster." And indeed, the Court, albeit by only a 5–4 decision, delivered the goods to Roosevelt. Justice John Marshall Harlan for the majority asserted that the Sherman Act "embraces *all* direct *restraints* imposed by any combination, conspiracy or monopoly upon . . . trade or commerce." The earlier *Knight* case (1895) had construed the federal legislation to apply to commerce, not manufacturing.

Holmes, as noted, did not like the Sherman Act. Agreements in restraint of trade, he said, had long existed in common law, and, in the modern era, enterprises like railroads always monopolize trade, to some degree, in all areas where they operate. Holmes would draw the line only at arrangements designed deliberately to exclude others. Northern Securities had committed no such offense. Holmes believed he ruled in the larger social and national interest in his dissent. Harlan's majority, he said, would project America backward, to the recent era of destructive, small-scale competition that "would disintegrate society as far as it could into individual atoms." Holmes never felt affection for any society so characterized.

Holmes could take from the Progressives and he could also give, and the very next year he rendered a profound intellectual service to their programs in the famous *Lochner* case. It involved a New York state labor law that limited bakers to a maximum of ten hours of work a day or sixty for the week. The Supreme Court had not set itself against such regulations, as it had approved in 1897 a Utah law limiting miners to an eight-hour work day. In that case, it acknowledged health reasons as a valid consideration. The New York statute presented itself under the same concern. Now, however, the Court, speaking through Justice Rufus Peckham in a 5–4 decision, minimized the health factor and then went on to overrule the legislation as a violation of the Fourteenth Amendment. Why? Because, the majority ruled, the law deprived workers of the right of contract as provided in the Bill of Rights of the federal Constitution, and by the amendment now a restraint on the states. The Court's majority believed that the New York state statute took from workers the means to contract for their material advantage if they chose to work more than sixty hours per week. Holmes was livid.

The majority ruling in *Lochner* cut right against the grain of Holmes's Darwinian view of the world. First, it put the Court in regal judgment against local legislatures, that critical locus of adaptation and experimentation that vitalized society's survival strategies. The majority decision, then, represented a blatant violation of judicial restraint. The Court, Holmes admonished, perverted the true meaning of liberty by intervening "to prevent the natural outcome of a dominant opinion." Here Holmes spoke under his long-established understanding that history is the scene of contest and that winners have the right to enact their will into law, short of any manifest constitutional wrong. The New York statue, then, reflected the logic of historical change and had a prima facie legitimacy that the Court must acknowledge.

Second, Holmes protested that the majority opinion in *Lochner* imposed on these important state activities an abstract, ideological constraint, or, as he put it, "an economic theory which a large part of the country does not entertain." Here are Holmes's famous words: "The Fourteenth Amendment does not enact Mr. Herbert Spencer's Social Statics. . . . A constitution is not intended to embody a particular economic theory, whether of paternalism and the organic relation of the citizen to the State or *laissez faire*." His cryptic statement spoke volumes about Holmes's long-standing partiality to the concrete and particular over the abstract and general: "General propositions do not decide concrete cases."

Finally, Holmes's judicial pronouncements on freedom of speech have won him lasting appreciation and enduring quotability. They afford us another glimpse of his Darwinian habits of thought. In its history before World War I, the United States Supreme Court had said little on this subject. Now it confronted some major cases, beginning with the *Schenck* case in 1919. It involved federal prosecution under the Espionage Act of 1917. The United States government indicted socialist Charles Schenck and others for distributing materials that urged conscripts to resist draft induction into the United States Army. A unanimous Court speaking through Holmes had no problem with this case. It clearly had the wartime situation in view, and Holmes allowed that in different circumstances the Court might have considered the matter differently. Thus: "When a nation is at war many things that might be said in time of peace are such a hindrance to its effort that their utterance will not be endured so long as men fight." Holmes, however, also made a larger, general point that characterized how he had always believed the law should work. "The character of every act," he wrote in this case, "depends upon the circumstances in which it is done." No dogmatic statement about free speech can apply usefully, certainly no libertarian formulation. No one has a right to yell "fire" in a crowded theater. So Holmes offered a guideline: "The question in every case is whether the words used are used in circumstances and are of such a nature as to create a clear and present danger that they will bring about the substantive evils that Congress has a right to prevent."

Holmes knew that his guidelines here gave a deference to the state over the individual in the specific situation of the case (i.e., the war). In the next case, however, he became a dissenter. And beginning with *Abrams* later that year, Holmes established himself as a continuing dissenter from his judicial colleagues. Holmes's formulation had in essence stated a "bad tendency" criterion for judging speech. He quickly saw the abuses to which it could lead. In the *Abrams* case, defendants faced prosecution for distributing pamphlets critical of American intervention in Siberia, a protest against the United States' efforts to hinder or undo the Russian Revolution of 1917, which the pamphlets celebrated. This case, too, involved the Espionage Act. The Court's majority cited the "bad tendency" standard and upheld the government.

Holmes believed the Court had gone too far. He could not judge the defendants' activities as at all threatening to America's war efforts. Abrams and his colleagues, "these poor and puny anonimities" as Holmes called them, barely merited the government's attention. Nor did Holmes have any sympathy for their communist ideology, "the creed of ignorance and immaturity." But in these matters, Holmes insisted, all bias should favor free speech. Holmes now reverted to a statement he had made twenty years before on the Massachusetts court. There he had described "the struggle for life among competing ideas, and of the ultimate victory of the strongest." Holmes did not speak of individual rights; he was referencing the gains to the social organism to be secured for it by a natural selection of ideas. Holmes seized the opportunity now to render possibly his finest statement from the high court, an eloquent expression of intellectual Darwinism: "When men have realized that time has upset many fighting faiths," he wrote, "they may come to believe even more than they believe the very foundations of their own conduct that the ultimate good desired is better reached by free trade in ideas—the best test of truth is the power of the thought to get itself accepted in the competition of the market, and that truth is the only ground upon which their wishes safely can be carried out. That at any rate is the theory of our Constitution. It is an experiment, as all life is an experiment."

Thus, Thorstein Veblen and Oliver Wendell Holmes Jr., two Darwinian thinkers, worked within two different fields of intellectual inquiry. One would be at great pains to extract from their body of works a comprehensive system of thought, some overriding ideology or metaphysics, some unifying synthesis that conjoins the parts of their thinking, some comprehensive whole. Their Darwinian persuasion set Veblen and Holmes against any such intellectual endeavors. In an open-ended system they could find no telos or governing design by which to relate or integrate the separate parts. Instead, the Darwinian framework provided each with tools of analysis, avenues of insight, into human behavior. It provided them methodologies for explaining behavior in the marketplace or in the path of the law. To be sure, it also gave them openings for judgment. We sensed it in Veblen's leisure class depictions and we have just seen it in Holmes's judicial dissents. They all had help from Darwinian insights.

BIBLIOGRAPHY

Baker, Liva. *The Justice from Beacon Hill: The Life and Times of Oliver Wendell Holmes.* New York: HarperCollins, 1991.

Diggins, John. *The Bard of Savagery: Thorstein Veblen and Modern Social Theory.* New York: Seabury, 1978.

Grey, Thomas C. "Holmes and Legal Pragmatism." *Stanford Law Review* 41 (1989): 786–870.

Horowitz, Irving Louis, ed. *Veblen's Century: A Collective Portrait.* New Brunswick, NJ: Transaction, 2002.

Lerner, Max, ed. *The Portable Veblen.* New York: Viking, 1948.

Menand, Louis. *The Metaphysical Club: A Story of Ideas in America.* New York: Farrar, Straus and Giroux, 2001.

Tilman, Rick. *The Intellectual Legacy of Thorstein Veblen: Unsolved Issues.* Westport, CT: Greenwood, 1996.

——. *Thorstein Veblen and His Critics, 1891–1963: Conservative, Liberal, and Radical Perspectives.* Princeton: Princeton University Press, 1992.

White, G. Edward. *Justice Oliver Wendell Holmes: Law and the Inner Self.* New York: Oxford University Press, 1993.

PHILOSOPHY

William James and John Dewey

Darwinism, so worldly a world outlook, entered nonetheless into the rarified realms of philosophy. And its entrance produced one of the most exciting episodes in American intellectual history. Observers have often said that in the school of pragmatic thinkers America began to speak philosophically, that the pragmatists gave voice to an American mentality that has flourished over the course of American history, from farmyard to factory shop. The late nineteenth and early twentieth centuries have won the label "the golden age of American philosophy." The era furnishes the names of Charles Sanders Peirce, Chauncey Wright, William James, Josiah Royce, George Santayana, John Dewey, and others. All registered and expanded evolutionary thinking. Our modest effort must limit discussion to two of these thinkers. In William James and John Dewey we see two varieties of evolutionary philosophy, richly formulated and profoundly suggestive.

A DARWINIAN VIEW OF MIND

William James was ever the cosmopolitan, and ever the tolerant one. Much of that character derived from his father. Henry James Sr. became a follower of Emanuel Swedenborg in the 1840s, part of a small American cult of this eighteenth-century mystic. Swedenborg, who lived from 1688 to 1772, combined God and science in an expansive cosmology, one without creed or dogma. Swedenborgians in turn welcomed new devices like mesmerism and psychic healing as means to affirm and experience spiritual reality, the invisible realm that motivated Swedenborg's great quest. William James himself would later take much interest in hypnotism and in the otherworldly insights of mind-expanding drugs. Father Henry welcomed Swedenborg's expansive religiosity as a means to pursue his own spiritual quest. To this extent he broke radically from his own background. He was the son of William James, the "William of Albany," who, beginning as an immigrant from County Cavan, Ireland, in 1789, had amassed much wealth in several mercantile activities. He and his wife, Catherine, raised their children in the Calvinist Presbyterianism of their Scotch-Irish ancestry. He supported a strict Sabbatarianism and she supervised the family's considerable commitments to charity and philanthropy. Henry James grew increasingly alienated from the family religion, though he had carried it through study at Princeton Theological Seminary. The Swedenborgian break came from a final loss of faith in dogmatic Christianity and in any kind of institutional religion. He passed on no orthodoxy or church loyalties to his own family.

Independently wealthy, Henry James had the means to educate his children widely. William, born in 1842, and younger brother Henry attended schools in New York, Geneva, Paris, London, Boston, and points in-between. William found the relocations and discontinuities frustrating, to be sure. His schooling never amounted to anything like a uniform or standard curriculum, but, on the other hand, he never inherited an academic orthodoxy. He came to any intellectual subject open to new methodologies for understanding it. Nevertheless, for all his cosmopolitanism, William James injected into his writings a distinct American voice. His ideas have suggested to many observers the peculiarities of new-world America—individualism, openness, pluralism, change, fluidity, and newness. "Chance," "flux," "variety," and "novelty,"—Jamesian descriptions that recur in his philosophy—seem to convey normative American realities and ideals.

James's celebration of the "open universe" parallels the open society of an idealized classless America. And who but an American philosopher would champion so brazenly the "cash value" of an idea? William James wrote with a lively prose; he had an ear for the catchy phrase and the pithy expression. Indeed it has been said of younger brother Henry, the novelist, that he wrote literature like a philosopher, and William wrote philosophy like a novelist!

William James, beginning with his entry into Harvard's Lawrence Scientific School in 1861, pursued a career in science. He did not arrive easily to that path, however. He had first undertaken a career in art, even studying painting with William Morris Hunt at Newport. The senior Henry, however, greatly mistrusted art. Human artifacts, he believed, could not be a vehicle of the spiritual; they did not assist in the transcendent connections vital to a high spirituality. Henry relocated the family from Newport to break up his son's new commitment. The father did, on the other hand, welcome the new course in science that William took on at Harvard. He may have had only contempt for positivism and little respect for experimental science, but Swedenborg's doctrine of correspondences led James to recognize in the study of nature an access to the divine. This influence may explain why William James would himself always recoil from science when understood in a deterministic manner; and he wished to puncture science's exclusive or narrow claims to truth. He strove always to leave room for spiritual reality and the validity of religious belief. He would read evolution in a way that affirmed freedom, spontaneity, and open-ended processes. Nothing chilled him more than philosophies of the absolute. No teleologies, no grand designs or systems, no inviolate chain of cause and effect for James. A notion of truth rooted in subjectivity made James also the philosopher of American individualism.

Matters, however, did not go easily for James. It required a life's struggle to reach the conclusions he did in the later, philosophical phase of his career. One turning point stands out. James, in his late twenties, experienced a profound mental crisis. He would describe it as an acute and painful depression. He felt himself caught in a rigid chain of events, a deterministic universe in which his will, indeed, his life, meant nothing. He lived, as he later wrote, with "the horrible fear of my own existence." He could not work and could not define any purpose for his life. Then, in a remarkable way, he broke out of his depression. The occasion, he described, was his reading the works of the French philosopher Charles Renouvier, particularly his views on freedom of the will.

Renouvier, a Protestant, assailed the determinist position by arguing that if all beliefs are determined, then so, too, for all we know, is the belief that all beliefs are determined. Ultimately, Renouvier convinced James that all the intellectual disputation in the world would not answer the question whether we are free or not. How then, can one resolve the matter? By an act of will, Renouvier postulated. We will never know if we have freedom of will until we test that proposition by an act of faith that we do have it, that is, by acting on the affirmative of the proposition. James's reading of Renouvier occurred on April 29, 1870, a date he memorialized the rest of his life. He later described the conclusion that he rejoiced to affirm: "My first act of free will shall be to believe in free will . . . ; believe in my individual reality and creative power. . . . I will posit life . . . in the self-determining *resistance* of the ego to the world." It is not an oversimplification to say that James, in his career in psychology and then in philosophy, sought to understand why such a proposition has merit. In what kind of reality, in what kind of universe, in what kind of Darwinian arena do we live that confirms the reality and efficacy of individual faith of the kind that saw James through his personal crisis?

James studied medicine at Harvard and in 1872 began an appointment to teach anatomy and physiology there. In 1878 he commenced his monumental project, the most comprehensive work of psychology yet produced in the United States and a landmark document for that emerging academic discipline. *The Principles of Psychology* appeared in 1890, in two volumes. It offered a complete biological explanation of the mind as James joined others in the field in breaking from the hard mind/body dualism inherited from Scottish realism in the eighteenth century. Paul Boller has described James's volumes as "the first fully developed evolutionary psychology in which the implications of Darwinism for man's mental life were fully explored." But as James's psychology shunned dualism it also faulted all theories of behaviorism. James meant to discredit materialists who accepted an automaton theory of mind, by which mental life becomes the reflexive, mechanical register of external stimuli. James faulted thinkers like Thomas Huxley who reduced consciousness to "molecular changes of the brain-substance" and rendered it the passive agency of a controlling environment. No, James would make consciousness a dynamic process, product of evolutionary drive and the survival functions of the human organism.

James described consciousness as the teleological agent of the brain. We exist in a vast milieu of sense data, he explained; in any situation we find ourselves surrounded by visual, auditory, and tactile impressions, so vast that we may "take in" but a small fraction of this sensory environment. Why, then, do we take cognizance of this small fraction only? Here James expounded brilliantly on the selective role of the human mind. The thinking being is driven by survival needs, he said; it makes its way through a vast network of sense data focusing on the compelling and vital data that address the organism's immediate needs. Consciousness reflects the demands and purposes, the ends that we pursue. This "autotelic" quality of consciousness, its intense, selective processes, places the whole evolution of the human species, as James saw, into the Darwinian understanding of life.

James's *Principles of Psychology* will challenge its readers with much technical material. One would probably best read it selectively. One particularly suggestive chapter, that illustrates the issue just addressed, has the title "Attention." James began this chapter by noting the general neglect of this subject among epistemologists. He had in mind particularly his rival school, the empiricists. These thinkers, from John Locke to David Hume to John Stuart Mill and Herbert Spencer, had tried to root all mental life in sense data. Locke's famous account of the mind as a tabula rasa that receives impressions from the outside, signified to James an all too passive description of the mind, an error perpetuated by the other members of this tradition. James wrote: "Such an empiricist writer as Mr.

Spencer, for example, regards the creature as absolutely passive clay, upon which 'experience' rains down." Attention, however, because it "breaks through the cycle of pure receptivity which constitutes 'experience,'" James wrote, "upsets the empiricists' apple cart," and hence they generally ignore the subject.

James, then, wanted to add agency and subjectivity to mind, to break a deterministic correlation between mind and external data, one wherein the weight of sense data proportionately shapes the mind and supplies its contents. Here again he challenged the empiricists: "Millions of items of the outward order are present to my senses which never properly enter into my experience. Why? Because they have no *interest* for me. *My experience is what I agree to attend to.* Only those items which I *notice* shape my mind—without selective interest, experience is an utter chaos. Interest alone gives accent and emphasis, light and shade, background and foreground—intelligible perspective, in a word." How many times might we walk into a room and not notice the pattern within the tiles of the ceiling? They are, after all, within plain sight of us. We do not notice because the patterns have nothing at stake for us, no advantage or disadvantage, or, in other words, no survival value. We focus, instead, on the professor giving a lecture in the room. On that individual, after all, depends our getting into the law school we hope so much to attend. Women, James believed, train their peripheral attention greater than men. A woman asleep in her bed, her window open on a hot summer night when sounds from the outside intrude at all hours, may sleep well; if her baby in the next room coughs, she awakens.

The Principles of Psychology, as this discussion suggests, is also a book of philosophy and as such anticipates James's career after its publication. James took up many classical philosophical questions, including the one stated in the chapter titled, "Necessary Truths and the Effects of Experience." He concluded his study by examining a great issue in philosophy. John Locke in the late seventeenth century discredited the notion of innate ideas, truths born into the mind and connected to some transcendent realm of being, often described as their source. The mind, instead, Locke stated, receives data from the external world and subsequently orders it into meaningful patterns. But it can form no knowledge, Locke insisted, without first receiving the sense impressions. Empiricism reached its radical extreme in David Hume, who insisted that we know only impressions and that even "mind" is but the loose affiliation of these perceptions in an insubstantial location, not a fixed, knowing entity.

Of course, these confounding conclusions inspired the effort of Immanuel Kant to reestablish the active agency of mind. Kant's celebrated *Critique of Pure Reason* in 1787 tried to demonstrate that we can have no knowledge without experience, but that meaningful knowledge derives from the mind's role in organizing all the data of experience. The organizing principles, which Kant labeled the "forms of intuition," do not themselves derive from experience; they are contributions of the mind. Thus, we do not experience space and time as objects of experience; we know them only in and through experience, always accompanied, that is, by sense data. Therefore, we have no knowledge of things except within space and time, constructs supplied by the mind, the forms of intuition. Thus, experience has no useful relation for us until the mind, by means of the forms (which include causality as well), structures it for us.

James took a great interest in these questions. In addressing them he highlighted the revisions made to the subject by Herbert Spencer. Spencer allowed the mind an organizing role and thus acknowledged the forms of intuition as necessary additives to the array of sense data that forces itself onto our minds. But he could not allow that the forms are the innate or original endowments of the human mind; rather, they were themselves product of an evolutionary process, by which they reflect a remote parallel in the earliest, primitive organisms, and rise in perfection as humans evolve from them. Passed on from one generation of the race to another, they appear to be axiomatic. "Being the *constant and infinitely-repeated* elements of thought," Spencer wrote, "they must become the automatic elements of thought—the elements of thought which it is impossible to get rid of—the 'forms of intuition.'"

James credited Spencer with offering a "brilliant and seductive" statement of this philosophical question. But ultimately he faulted it. Spencer may have invoked an evolutionary explanation of necessary truths but James distinguished, in a revealing categorization, be-tween "pre-Darwinian evolutionists" and authentic Darwinians. In this instance the pre-Darwinian Spencer lapsed into a dangerous de-terminism and once again it put James on red alert. Here James had to note, as the pragmatists generally were wont to do, that some-where in human evolution the human mind emerged as a quantum leap above and beyond any genetic predecessor. James could not un-derstand this leap as a mere derivation from lower organic forms, or as a replica of them. At the critical point human consciousness jumped into a realm beyond any determining connections to sense data or even the immediate physical environment. James described the mind as a dynamic, mercurial phenomenon. These qualities emerge in the deeper recesses of evolution, James admitted, but they transcend all of their founding causes. They come into play only in the most advanced stages of evolution.

Consider the power to create music, or even the appreciation of it. This trait, James said, "has no zoological utility; it corresponds to no object in the natural environment." And it is highly particularized. One brother may have the talents, the other may not. James went even further. "Our higher, æsthetic, moral, and intellectual life seems to be made up of affections of this collateral and incidental sort, which have entered the mind by the back stairs, as it were, or . . . got surreptitiously born in the house." James was always awed by the sheer power and presence of accident—in the human constitution, in human life, and in the cosmos at large. Even the most basic laws by which we understand our world, rules of physics, for example, de-rived, James believed, not from the force of our experiencing them; they began as flashes of insight, "lucky fancies," that proved socially useful because they usefully assisted in processing sense data.

So, to return, finally, to Spencer and the problem of necessary truths. James posed the question, why might those critical forms of intuition not have likewise begun in such manner? "Why may it not have been so of the original elements of consciousness, sensation, time, space, resemblance, difference, and other relations?" May they not also have entered by way of the back door? Why not categorize them as "morphological accidents"? In short, James speculated that it made more sense to consider the very mental constructs by which we order reality as having begun as "spontaneous variations," "accidental events," that turned out by good look to fit with the real world, and help us get along in it. As with any organic mutations, some fit better than others, and some prove wild or foolish fancies. Some, in other words, prove adaptable, demonstrate their survival value to the species, and become permanent forms in its makeup. The idea was thoroughly evolutionary, but in the Darwinian and not the Spencerian sense. James did not lock human mental evolution into a rigid causative trajectory, deriving advanced consciousness and the forms of intuition from a simpler primordial facsimile. Nothing along the evolutionary path could be so predetermined or ordained. James looked at the Darwinian model and saw chance, spontaneity, accident, and novelty everywhere. Nowhere did these characteristics prevail more decisively than in the intellectual evolution of the human species.

A PHILOSOPHY FOR BELIEF

So *Principles of Psychology* offers philosophical speculations aplenty. James took increasing interest in these questions and moved over to teach in the philosophy department at Harvard. Here he made major contributions to American philosophy with such provocative essays as "What Pragmatism Means," "The Will to Believe," "The Sentiment of Rationality," "Does Consciousness Exist?" "The Stream of Thought," and "The One and the Many." James committed to philosophy because his Darwinian views demanded that he do so. For to philosophize, he believed, is something that the live human organism, the thinking being, must do. We think at all levels of our lives, from the moment in the morning when we must decide what shoes we will wear for the day to the more reflective moments when we reflect on momentous issues about what is good or whether God exists. Even in those moments, however, such thinking could not count for James as mere idle speculation, a delving into the realm of abstractions and remoter realities for the mere pleasure of contemplation. Philosophy for

James always signified something urgent, something all-defining for us, and for each thinking individual a "psychic necessity." For the live individual thrives within an acute environmental milieu through which it must find its way. We adapt to survive. We ask spiritual questions whose answers help us through these challenges. Under this consideration, James could marvelously call philosophy our individual way of feeling "the push and presence of the cosmos." Philosophy happens to that species that lives on the highest level of the evolutionary scale.

Philosophy for James always signified something intensely and unavoidably personal. He observed that all people tend to fall more or less into one of two ways of looking at things. Many philosophers, as the record will show, construct elaborate systems, comprehensive treatises that contain or interrelate all aspects of being. They create vast truth-systems. James described this urge as "the sentiment of rationality." These thinkers are compelled, it seems, to reduce the disparate facts of the world to order, to melt down vast multiplicities into unity and coherence. On the other hand, other thinkers have a "passion for distinguishing," the proclivity to analyze, to break down wholes, to see the unique minutiae of the sensual world up close and clear. In each of these activities, however, we see at work the full play of the individual personality. "A man's philosophic attitude," James wrote, "is determined by the balance in him of these two cravings." And we need no further explanation other than to recognize that we create our truths often from some "dumb conviction" that they must lie here rather than there. It is our base personalities that so dictate. "Idealism will be chosen by a man of one emotional conviction, materialism by another," James wrote. He added: "Pretend what we may, the whole man within us is at work when we form our philosophical opinions. Intellect, will, taste, and passion co-operate just as they do in practical affairs."

Within these parameters James made another distinction—between monistic and pluralistic philosophies. And he urged strongly for the pluralistic. By "monism" James meant any system that located one cause, one substance, one underlying intelligence or spirit as the full explanation of reality. Pluralism, on the other hand, James wrote, sees a reality that exists, as it were, "distributively." James discussed these distinctions in his essay "The One and the Many." And he defined the alternative between monism and pluralism as "the most pregnant of all the dilemmas of philosophy." James granted that the monistic philosophy had great appeal; it offered assuring theistic comfort. As with Spinoza, for example, "monism likes to believe that all things follow from the essence of God." James's colleague and intellectual sparring partner at Harvard, Josiah Royce, united all reality under the absolute, a form of idealistic monism that vexed James. This type also recalled the Swedenborgianism of his father.

In the essay James faulted monism on several counts. But more than intellectual contest motivated him. James simply *had* to believe in a pluralistic universe. Monism signified to him a "block universe"; it meant fatalism, enclosure, constraint, determinism. The monistic universe, James wrote in 1884, "seems to suffocate me within its infallible impeccable all-pervasiveness. Its necessity, with no possibilities; its relations with no subjects, make me feel as if I had entered into a contract with no reserved rights." To resign himself to any intellectual system conveying that sense would mean for James a loss of personal freedom, a destruction of the integrity of his own individual being, a spiritual death.

James thoroughly defended freedom of the will, and he made as its intellectual foundation the fact, the reality, of a pluralistic universe. That universe showed novelty and difference. "'Free will,'" James wrote, "means nothing but real novelty; so pluralism accepts the notion of free will." Pluralism sees a world unfinished, with all its doors and windows open to possibilities. Instead of a brittle causal chain, chance proliferates in the sequence of events and experiences. A universe unshaped may yet be shaped and thus James could insist that each individual may author a novelty.

James's early intellectual career, and the entire direction of his future thought, place him within a major intellectual shift that forms an important context for understanding him. As described by historians like James Kloppenberg, Paul Jerome Croce, and James Turner, this shift, prevalent in Europe and the United States, introduced new attitudes toward science. We enter a culture of uncertainty, a view of life that sees all of nature as understandable more in terms of plausibility than certainty, of tendencies more than laws, fluidity more than category. Both the natural sciences and the social sciences assumed more of a "probabilistic methodology," to use the term employed by Croce, who recognizes the influence of Darwin in the new culture, and especially its role in shaping William James's thinking. Croce writes: "As William James and a few other science watchers noticed, the persuasive power of natural selection resided on a theoretical uncertainty—even if it was an enormously plausible proposition. Because James assimilated Darwinism in a probabilistic way, he turned toward uncertainty not in spite of Darwinism but because of it."

James's conception of a pluralistic universe, we can now see, has clear Darwinian ingredients. In fact, James took the Darwinian description of evolution in biological specimens and rendered it analogously into a model of reality itself. James's pragmatism constituted a Darwinian metaphysics. For Darwin, we recall, made evolution emphatically nonteleological; it proceeded by chance occurrence, by the accident of mutations, in a manner that could point to no inevitable end points, no final causes. An authentic philosophy, then, cannot impose an inflexible order onto this process, cannot bottle up and package the universe. Darwinism made James averse to all universal principles, all enclosed systems of thought. These systems certified to him nothing but abstractions, elixirs fashioned for our assurance against the ever-shifting elements of our changing, confusing experience.

Does the Darwinian construction of reality, then, leave us in a world without truth, values, and religious validity? James answered no, quite the contrary. He took up the question of "truth," a matter always in the focus of philosophers. Within the American pragmatism movement, Charles Sanders Peirce had tried to clarify the issue with his famous 1878 essay in *Popular Science Monthly*, "How to Make Our Ideas Clear." We know any phenomenon by its sensible effects, he argued, so that we may inquire whether this diamond is hard by imagining a sensible test of that notion. If it is hard, he pointed out, we could not, for example, cut it with a knife. Peirce tried to uphold objective standards in his idea of truth, so that truth is what will ultimately be agreed upon by a community of investigators. A number of demonstrations would certify to all, for example, that water will boil at a temperature of 212 degrees Fahrenheit.

James, however, wanted to give a more urgent and personal meaning to truth, taking the matter beyond where Peirce would allow, into questions of morality and religious faith. He began again with the live human organism. It is a being confronted constantly with the challenges of its environmental milieu. It must reason, anticipate, calculate, and judge at every awakened moment of its existence. So thought itself becomes an instrument of adaptation and survival. It gets us from one part of our experience to another. As it does so, we make judgments about the "truth" of those ideas we have put into action. Have they helped us negotiate our way though our experiences? Do they bring us into a satisfactory relationship with our environment? In this way we establish a more personal and subjective notion of truth. How has it worked for *me*? What are the consequences of *my* acting on any particular idea? Is it better to stay up all night and study for my morning examination, or go to bed earlier and get a good night's sleep before taking it? By the time one is a senior in college, one may have established a very personal answer to that question. In doing so, James would say, that individual has established a useful truth for herself.

Here is James's formulation: "Grant an idea or belief to be true, what concrete difference will its being true make in any one's actual life; how will the truth be realized?" James had little interest in truth as first principles, abstractions, or universals suspended in some nether reality detached from individuals' lives, and he further doubted that the mind could at all undertake such abstract questions. Truth for him lay always suspended, awaiting its realization as measured by its value to an individual's experience. Truth, James wrote in another piquant phrase, "is something that happens to an idea." Only then can we assign it its "cash value." And we get close to the important issue for James when we consider such a statement as "I believe that God exists." Under the Peircean standard we would want to ask, what do you mean by the words "that God exists"? By what sensible effects would we know God or what conceivable actions would we take to clarify the meaning of the word "God"? Could we devise a test like that concerning the diamond? For James, on the other hand, the key part of the statement is the words "I believe." He would want to know what consequences *for me* follow from my conviction that God exists. Where does it take me in my personal life and what consequences follow for me in acting on this faith?

James could turn the question this way because he believed so emphatically in an open universe. Our reality does not yield permanent things, neither in biological species nor in truth systems. James wrote in "What Pragmatism Means" that "Darwinism has once and for all displaced design from the minds of the 'scientific.'" So we, live organisms that we are, seek the knowledge, the hypotheses, the convictions we need to make our way through a wilderness of uncertainties. Peirce believed that because we cannot test the sensible meaning of God we cannot include that notion as a truth. (This, even though Peirce's evolutionary system had definite theistic implications.) James countered that because an open universe leaves truth in suspension, we have every right to act on faith. Here James spoke of what he called "live options," those momentous questions that life raises for us and which no thinking person can ignore. We *must* decide the religion question one way or the other. Even to avow atheism, he said, affirms some deep psychic need on the part of the disbeliever. The believer, however, James insisted, has just as much right to answer a personal need by affirming faith in God. And for familiar pragmatic reasons, too. "If theological ideas prove to have a value for concrete life," James wrote, "they will be true, for pragmatism, in the sense of being good for so much."

Here James the psychologist joined James the philosopher. His earlier studies confirmed for him the power of the healthy mind for the live organism. He had seen and described many times the efficacy of religious faith in alleviating the sick soul, in redefining people's lives to a triumphant purposefulness. But James had learned, too, from that Darwinian reality of openness, flux, novelty, and change that individuals, and the human species collectively, help shape reality, give it its form and character. For the universe is always making itself and humans are agents of the process. Faith is an orientation toward the world and to the seen and unseen parts of a large cosmic expanse. "I confess," James wrote, "that I do not see why the very existence of an invisible world may not in part depend on the personal response which any one of us may make to the religious appeal. God himself, in short, may draw vital strength and increase of very being from our fidelity." So for all we know, James urged, our belief in God may bring to us an awareness of, and contact with, a spiritual realm that would otherwise remain obscured to us. For all of a life in science, James always found religion a consuming, personal interest. He bequeathed to the subject his remarkable work of 1902, *The Varieties of Religious Experience*.

Many have seen in the Darwinian form of evolutionary theory an ironclad naturalism. Its history shows the vehement rejection of Darwinism by individuals committed to Christianity and others who insist that we live in a purposeful world that reflects an intelligent design. William James seized on the Darwinian model of scientific explanation and derived from it a world open to flux, to change and spontaneity, all assuring individual freedom, personal significance, and empowerment. Out of it he validated the religious life. Of course, his speculations do not give the theist any guarantees. And to many his ideas have seemed too permissive, too unempirical; to others they are murky and indefinite. Secularist and spiritualist alike have so judged them. James, Darwinian-like, wanted us to fight on our own, work our way to our own best results. If we had the opportunity to press him to a more definitive statement about God, we might want to say, "Tell us, sir, does God really exist or not?" He would have to answer: "Not as long as you are asking the question." So much had evolution shaped the human mind that James allowed it such power to shape reality itself.

AN EARLY IDEALIST

John Dewey named William James as a major influence on his career in philosophy. That influence came, however, in the midst of a long development in Dewey's ideas. He came from an intellectual background—absolute idealism—quite removed from pragmatism, and he took pragmatism in a direction quite beyond James. Dewey in fact became America's complete Darwinian thinker. He most widely carried out the naturalistic implications of Darwinism and situated philosophy further from accommodation with religion than any of the pragmatists. Dewey felt he had to effect the disconnection in order for philosophy to do what religion had once done. It would have to make nature yield an ethical life as humans confronted nature and judged their experiences in interaction with it. Dewey built on Darwinism to construct a more authoritative organic system, one that no longer needed the props of an absolute mind to make it hang together. But as absolute idealism had connected the individual self to a universal self, a naturalist philosophy would connect the individual self to the social body, the community, the state. On this basis Dewey also laid the foundations of modern political liberalism as solidly as any other American thinker. Altogether it's an intriguing story. We have here the evolution of an evolutionist.

Dewey came from New England. Born in Burlington, Vermont, in 1859, the year of Darwin's publication of the *Origin*, as often noticed, Dewey lived there through his collegiate years. Both his parents descended from old New England stock. His father, Archibald, had a congenial personality but little ambition of the commercial kind. He ran a grocery store with only modest success. On the other hand, Dewey could draw on much idealism in his family. When the Civil War broke out, Archibald, a staunch Republican and passionate against slavery, volunteered for service in the Union army, relocating the family to Virginia. Dewey's mother, Lucina, came from a family of higher social standing than her husband and displayed a stronger religiosity than he. She had moved from Universalism to Congregationalism and worked among the city's poor. And she guarded with vigilance the soul status of her children. Dewey recalled how readily she made them feel guilty for their transgressions, however minor. She had great ambitions for the education of John and his brother Davis; all the males in her family had gone to college.

Burlington had moved beyond its earlier history as a small New England town reflective of local grassroots democracy. Dewey grew up in the leading commercial city in the state, its population marked by ethnic diversity and class divisions. Early on he glimpsed the social pathologies of industrial America that would challenge his thinking and inspire his reform ideas. Dewey also felt the cold religious atmosphere of a place still caught in the moral severity of historic Puritanism. His mother's church, however, appealed to him for its opening to religious liberalism as expounded by the minister Lewis Brastow. Also, on the positive side, Dewey would always cherish from his boyhood his local neighborhood—friendly, supportive, and exemplary of an organic community that Dewey championed against the raw and isolating effects of a celebrated American individualism.

Dewey and his brother entered the University of Vermont in Burlington in 1875. John pursued what passed generally for a standard college education there, except for two influences of lasting note. In his second year, Dewey took a course in geology that used Thomas Huxley's book *Elements of Physiology*. It introduced the young scholar to evolutionary theory. Dewey recalled years later that the book awakened him to a sense of the interrelatedness of all things, a new sense of life that "gave form to intellectual stirrings that had been previously inchoate, and created a kind or type of model of a view of things to which material in any field ought to conform." Hereinafter Dewey set himself toward such a realization. He was far from Huxley himself or Darwin at this time. A long passage lay ahead. But at Vermont, Dewey read the Victorian periodicals and followed the debates about evolutionary biology with keen interest.

Second, Dewey remembered the university for its "liberal Christian orthodoxy." The professors reflected it, and many attended Brastow's church. This affiliation also showed the continuing influence at the college of the remarkable James Marsh. Born in Hartford, Vermont, in 1794, Marsh graduated from Dartmouth College and went on to Andover Theological Seminary. He became the University of Vermont's president in 1826, served to 1833, and remained as philosophy professor until 1842, the year of his death. Marsh made a singular contribution to American philosophy in 1829 by bringing out an edition of Samuel Taylor Coleridge's *Aids to Reflection*, offering with it his own introductory essay. The publication helped initiate the movement in American transcendentalism, as it influenced Ralph Waldo Emerson and others. The revolutionary movement in German idealism thus came indirectly to the United States, but it would have profound reverberations. It lingered at the university while Dewey was there taking courses from H. A. P. ("Happy") Torrey, who extended the German reach at Vermont.

Late in his life, Dewey wrote an essay titled "From Idealism to Experimentalism" that recounts his own intellectual trajectory. "Idealism" refers to a kind of phase one in Dewey's career and it also references a major philosophical battle that took place in the late nineteenth century in the United States. Dewey played a vigorously partisan role in it. Furthermore, his commitments established in him the intellectual outline of an evolutionary view of life that he did not abandon as he left phase one later. He did change the content significantly, as we shall see.

Marsh broke through to German idealism because he felt undernourished by the long and dominant strain of empiricism in American philosophy. That strain registered the influence especially of John Locke, but in the American colleges it reflected the orthodoxy of the Scottish Common Sense school of thinkers, Thomas Reid and Dugald Stewart mostly. Dewey had much appreciation for Marsh. He called him "probably the first American scholar to have an intimate first-hand acquaintance with the writings of Immanuel Kant." As Dewey later wrote of Marsh: He wanted to inspire "a truly spiritual Religion which had been obscured and depressed under the influence of the prevalent philosophies of John Locke and the Scottish school. It was as an ally of spiritual and personal religion that he turned to the German philosophy, actuated by the conviction that the same evils which Coleridge found in England were also found in his own country." In fact, Marsh wanted to shore up Christianity with a stronger philosophical ally than the empiricists could furnish. He wanted more internal convictions of spiritual reality than external ones.

Two other matters about Marsh we should note. On the one hand, he contained Kant within a Christian orthodoxy that contrasted with directions, often pantheistic, taken by other American romantics. Emerson's transcendentalism thus earned reproach from Christian Unitarians as "the latest form of infidelity." On the other hand, Marsh ignored all the stop signs that Kant had posted. The forms of intuition, the German philosopher insisted, organize the world of experience for us, but they do not give us access to ultimate truth. They confine knowledge within the sense data thus arranged ("phenomena"), but do not give us the *ding an sich*, the "thing-in-itself." Marsh drove through the barriers and allowed an intuitional insight into the hidden "noumenal" realm, the realm of spiritual and moral truth. As Dewey wrote: Marsh "never even refers to the Kantian limitation of knowledge to phenomena." Thus, Marsh dissolved the barriers Kant had imposed between the natural and the supernatural, the worldly and the transcendent. He embraced a large and comprehensive vision that saw far behind the sense data, perceptions, and common sense truisms of the empiricists. As Dewey put it: "He wanted to see the universe and all phases of life as whole."

Dewey left Vermont after his graduation and spent three years teaching high school in Oil City, Pennsylvania. In the raw heart of the oil industry and its cutthroat competition, he had a further education in American capitalism. But his thought focused on higher things. He returned to Vermont and for a year studied philosophy with Torrey and perfected his German in the process, for Kant and the neo-Kantians remained his preoccupation. He had in the meantime submitted an essay to William Torrey Harris, editor of the *Journal of Speculative Philosophy* and leading voice among the American Hegelians. Harris gave the essay high marks and published it in 1882; it bore the title "The Metaphysical Assumptions of Materialism." That fall Dewey enrolled as a graduate student in Johns Hopkins University, studying philosophy and psychology. This institution, founded in Baltimore in 1876, represented, as noted earlier, America's new departure in higher education, an approximation of the German model in which scholarship—research and the advancement of new knowledge—marked the real purposes of a university. Dewey rejoiced to be a part of the new adventure.

At Johns Hopkins Dewey came immediately under the influence of George Sylvester Morris. Morris, in fact, had a double impact. His own ideas greatly affected Dewey's early thinking, but he also introduced Dewey to the works of the British philosopher Thomas Hill Green, who died the year of Dewey's relocation to Baltimore. Green played a major role in the idealist resurgence against empiricism among English-speaking philosophers. His first work, *Prolegomena to Ethics,* delivered a frontal assault against that tradition from Locke to Hume. The idealists were fighting on an extended front against the empiricist ranks that now included John Stuart Mill and Herbert Spencer. The latter had established an unbridgeable gap between human knowledge and ultimate reality, the "unknowable" in Spencer's language. Green, as Dewey explained in an informative article on him, posited a single permanent consciousness that forms the bond of all sensuous and intellectual relations, "an eternal intelligence realized in the related facts of the world," as Green described it. This intelligence forms a constitutive part of each individual being; we all reproduce in us the universal mind. Green wanted to reconcile science and religion, to bring all science under a large spiritual principle that underscores all experience. Empiricism could not grasp this comprehensive unity, he insisted. Green, finally, believed that an idealist philosophy so understood allied with Christianity as the religious expression of these philosophical truths. Dewey called Green "the prophet of our times."

Not surprisingly, Dewey wrote his doctoral dissertation on Kant. However, he wrote on Kant from the critical perspective of Hegel. Dewey's thesis registered the now more direct influence of his Johns Hopkins professor. Morris was another Vermonter, born in Norwich in 1840. He graduated from Dartmouth College and then Union Theological Seminary in New York City. Morris counted himself an empiricist at this point, but he then undertook philosophical studies in Germany, with Friedrich Adolph Trandelenburg in Berlin and Hermann Ulrici in Halle. He emerged an idealist and his work established him as a foremost Hegelian in the United States. He taught at the University of Michigan and then at Johns Hopkins. Morris considered Hegel "the most profound and comprehensive of modern thinkers." Dewey biographer Robert Westbrook points out that Dewey did not need Morris alone to confirm the young scholar in idealism. Morris was only "symptomatic of the growing influence of post-Kantian idealism on American philosophy," against which William James recoiled in horror. Morris, too, wanted philosophy to support Christianity, and Dewey observed that the two individuals Morris most often cited were Plato and St. John of the Gospels. Morris and the idealists gave a strong fortification to Protestant Liberalism in the late nineteenth century.

Morris wanted to establish an organic unity of man with nature and God. To do so he had to certify the existence of an Absolute Mind. He wrote: "The very sense of philosophical idealism is to put and represent man in direct relation with the Absolute Mind so that its light is his light and its strength is made his." Morris described the natural as only the partial and dependent manifestation of the spiritual. And Morris understood all history—the evolution of art, religion, the state—under this theory. Such a grand synthesis of life immensely appealed to the young Dewey. He later recounted how his New England experience had left him with a sense of isolation of the self from the world, "an inward laceration." Hegel's grand scheme, as Morris championed it, came to Dewey as "an immense release, a liberation." He would move far from idealism later, but Dewey had to acknowledge that the "acquaintance with Hegel left a permanent deposit in my thinking."

Morris left Johns Hopkins in 1884 and returned to Michigan. Dewey followed him there. Dewey also taught briefly in Minnesota, then, on Morris's untimely death in 1889, became chair of the Philosophy Department at Michigan. He took over from Morris the courses in Kant and Hegel and also taught ethics and political theory. The ten years Dewey had at Michigan were productive ones. He published essays in psychology, which he now defined as a key battlefield for a defense of idealist philosophy. Thus his early writings in this field argue that the empirical study of human nature led assuredly toward a concept of the Absolute. Dewey also wrote a small book on the German philosopher Leibniz, whom he championed for his profoundly conceived organic view of life and whom Dewey hailed for his attack on Locke. Dewey's early essays, one notes, appeared in such publications as the *Andover Review* and *Bibliotheca Sacra*, major theological journals of liberal Protestantism. In fact, Dewey taught Sunday school at Ann Arbor, and, as Alan Ryan affirms, "until he was thirty-five years old [Dewey] wrote in a distinctly Christian idiom." In 1886 he married Alice Chipman and they began a family shortly thereafter.

Dewey in the Michigan years had the subject of evolution very much on his mind. It could hardly have been otherwise given Dewey's Hegelianism. It highlighted the centrality of the dialectical process and described history as the incidence of the Absolute's self-conscious activity in the world. But how did Dewey move from Hegel to Darwin? One essay from these early years has particular interest to us for this question. Dewey called it "Ethics and Physical Science," and it appeared in an 1887 issue of the *Andover Review*. He cited at the outset the great implications that developments in the physical sciences, "and of the theory of evolution in particular," had for moral philosophy. The new ideas pose for us critical questions, Dewey wrote: "Is man the last outcome of a series of physical changes following mechanical laws, or is he the spiritual end which nature in all her processes has been aiming towards? Is man one of the forms which the kaleidoscope of animal life has assumed, is he one of the transitory varieties in which the type has embodied itself; or is his origin from God, that in his very life in nature he may yet find a way to make life divine and Godlike?"

In the essay Dewey remarked on a trend of the last five years in which men of science, instead of claiming their domain as exclusive of religion, now read into nature a progressive ethical advancement propelled by humans' recognition of their place within a large, inclusive scheme of life. Dewey formulated the categorical imperative that emerged from this evolutionary ethics: "Teach man the unity of his nature with that of the world, make him realize that he is an outgrowth of development, show him, in particular, his oneness with the social organism, foster in him the idea and the feeling that his good is the good of this larger whole and its detriment his loss" and the moral progress of the race is assured. Dewey saw the "scientific men" here proclaiming a more certain authority for their ethics, one rooted in natural reality, than any like system founded in theological speculation or creedal affirmation. Thus the scientific men would insist that nature offers all the moral instruction we need, that evolution shows us the tendencies of the universe and the means by which it is realizing its own teleological program.

Dewey, however, found himself "unmoved" by these proclamations. And he made a response surprisingly Darwinian in content. Nature, he said, cannot generate an ethical system. Even if we admit that the physical universe is evolving toward a certain goal or end, it has no necessary relation to man. Man may be some means to nature's end, he said, but he is not an end of or for nature. Furthermore, he asked, what does nature show us as its means toward its ends? Scientists themselves, Dewey asserted, have now demonstrated that nature works through combat and competition; it yields the "survival of the fittest." "Rivalry, struggle, is thus the very heart of the physical process." These conditions hardly supply us with an ethical system, Dewey asserted. The ethical laws honor unity and mutual assistance. So Dewey could write: "There is presented to us the difficulty, not only of getting the moral out of the non-moral, but out of that which, if it be in the ethical sphere at all, is immoral. The ideal of the physical world is superiority of strength or skill; the ideal in the ethical world is community of good, moral equality."

Dewey went further. He was prepared to disavow in physical nature any end or purpose whatsoever. He rejected any teleological reading of nature's processes, any final causes in evolution. His words sounded very Darwinian. "There is in nature, as natural," he wrote, "no end; there is no final result; there is no outcome; there is no tendency." Nature reveals change only, ongoing, unpredictable change, a continual flux. So Dewey believed that nature, read only as physical, as mechanical, can supply no ethics. But Dewey did hold to idealism to the extent that he insisted that reality in its whole has a spiritual dimension in it and that this presence alone assures us of a purposeful cosmos. "We shall have to show," Dewey wrote, "that [ethics] are compatible only with a spiritual interpretation [of reality], which in its broad and essential features is identical with the theological teachings of Christianity." One is led to ask, however, was Dewey not employing a clear dualism here of nature and spirit, one that would seem to compromise or weaken his idealism? Soon the uneasy tension would be too much for him to sustain. Soon he would try to show that if nature yields no ethical system, then human intelligence, in interaction with nature, must derive one. An overriding spiritual reality would lose its place in his thinking and fade from his focus.

That rethinking accelerated after Dewey accepted a new appointment. In the 1890s John D. Rockefeller, oil magnate and dedicated Baptist, was helping to transform a small denominational school in Chicago into America's largest university. New president William Rainey Harper used Rockefeller's millions to hire leading academics to join this enterprise and he named Dewey as chair of the Philosophy Department at the University of Chicago. Dewey and his family arrived in the city in 1894, right in the middle of the Pullman workers' strike against the railroad industry, an event that awakened Dewey to the stark realities of labor strife and class conflict in the United States. His soon growing friendship with Jane Addams and his appreciation of her pioneering social work at Hull House expanded Dewey's commitments on the social question that agitated and troubled many Americans in the late Gilded Age. Dewey's writings did not suddenly turn "political" at this time. Rather, his enlarged awareness led him to interrogate the current situation in philosophy. He wanted more of a reality principle. He wanted philosophy to have a greater relevance to the industrial world and the social challenges it posed. His thinking became noticeably more this-worldly. He did not join a church in Chicago, as he had always done in other places. The alliance that he had supported between religion and philosophy lost its priority in his thinking.

At Chicago, Dewey gave much attention to education, in 1896 opening the Laboratory School at the university. That work, and his voluminous writings on educational theory and practice, would make him known worldwide. Less obvious, but equally decisive, was the intellectual shift. Dewey described it later as a slow "drifting away" from idealism. He had fallen much under the influence of William James, who helped him see the biological nature of intelligence, its problem-solving character, and its creative purposes. So he grew vexed at the notion that reality is embraced in its fullest meaning by some transcendent mind, some supra natural principle or entity that unites all the diverse and discordant pieces of empirical realities and alone assures them some ultimate meaning. That shift now made Dewey critical of Hegelianism. Here we have the irony, he wrote, that a dialectical system that describes change and conflict as integral to the universe, ends in delivering to us a universe wholly fixed, an "eternally self-luminous rational world." This system attributes knowledge and truth to a knower "set over against the world." For humans, such a world, Dewey wrote, dries up thought as its very beginning. Later in his 1917 essay "The Need for a Recovery of Philosophy," Dewey admonished the dwindling adherents to philosophical idealism. To pursue a remote and extraterrestrial source of truth, he wrote, "is to testify that one has still to learn the lesson of evolution in its application to the affairs in hand." Dewey had moved completely toward a philosophy of the near-at-hand, a problem-solving view of intelligence.

A PHILOSOPHY OF EXPERIENCE

Dewey thus broke his ties to idealism, but he still contended with his rivals in empiricism. Here Dewey delighted to note another irony: The attempt by John Locke to secure our knowledge of the world outside us had fixed on the hard data of experience, transmitted by the senses; but the new empiricism led to George Berkeley and David Hume and landed in profound skepticism. It yielded an acute doubt that we really know anything beyond the impressions that define our consciousness. That unhappy state cried out for a larger principle or being to contain them, so empiricism and idealism actually reinforced one another.

All empiricists, Dewey charged, betrayed a fundamental error. They misconstrued the nature of experience and the nature of the mind. Here Dewey extended the pragmatic critique of empiricism that we saw in James. Empiricism locks us into sense impressions, Dewey said, but the mind confronts the world and makes connections. Empiricism simply bound together the hard-and-fast and separate data of experience in a quite mechanical operation. Knowledge then becomes but a reflection of a ready-made reality, bloodless and passionless, Dewey wrote, a "kodak reflection" of the world. The live organism, however, does not experience the world this way. The mind projects itself into an always unstable, fluid, changing environment. It must perceive interconnections and organize and direct them. "Experience in its vital form," Dewey wrote, "is experimental, an effort to change the given . . . connection with a future is its salient trait." Thought is always forward-looking, anticipatory. It does not merely register past facts, Dewey insisted, but confronts all sense data manipulatively with the end in view of successful adaptation of the organism to its environment. Herewith the pragmatist understanding. In a later essay Dewey summarized: "Pragmatism, thus, presents itself as an extension of historical empiricism, but with the fundamental difference, that it does not insist upon antecedent phenomena but upon consequent phenomena; not upon the precedents but upon the possibilities of action. And this change in viewpoint is almost revolutionary in its consequences."

In the early twentieth century Dewey identified himself with the new directions in philosophy taken by Peirce and James, and he made himself public defender for philosophical pragmatism. Dewey had moved from Chicago to Columbia University in New York City in 1904, and he remained there to the end of his teaching career. Peirce and James had shifted American philosophy in the direction of a Darwinian input that Dewey now reinforced and extended. He gave philosophy a more literal Darwinian reading to the extent that he tied it to Darwin's naturalism. Dewey abandoned idealism partly because he had acquired the confidence that naturalism did not mean a negation of values and it did not signify a deterministic view of life. Rather, he now arrived to an optimistic understanding of evolution, one that looked to human intelligence as the creator of values, the shaper of experience, and the secure intellectual foundation of American democracy.

Dewey named his version of pragmatism instrumentalism. His philosophy now focused on the nature of the mind, which he understood in Darwinian terms as an instrument of adaptation. Intelligence, for human beings, supplied the key device of adaptation. What were reflex actions and instincts in lower organisms evolved to thought in man, a critical and decisive turn. For this species now responds constructively and creatively to its changing milieu. We owe this insight, Dewey urged, to the "progress of biology"; it represents the "chief impact of the evolutionary movement." The mind, biology informs us, is a "method of adjustment." It reads nature as a sign and thinks in terms of potentialities. It cannot settle on stable facts or truths, but must take cognizance of processes, read and anticipate their directions. Thought constitutes this reading and directs the actions needed to shape and configure them to useful purposes. "To anticipate the consequence of processes going on," Dewey wrote, "is precisely what is meant by 'ideas,' by 'intelligence.'"

The pragmatist's view of intelligence coincides with another key fact—the nature of nature. If reality, our world, were permanently fixed in all aspects, Dewey argued, there would be no occasion for thinking. If reality, our world, were all chaotic, subject to no laws and immune to any intervention, there would also be no occasion for thinking. In both instances thought could have no consequences. But Dewey looked to the vast domain of experience that he called the "problematical." It describes the fluid, unstable, undetermined aspects of things. Confronting this character of our experiences we are compelled to think. And herein the drama of life takes place, in the interplay of a universe that is partly closed and partly open. As Peirce had explained, thought begins because the uncertain nature of the undetermined leaves us in doubt, and that situation demands that we contrive a response that will lead us to a temporary truth. Thought, Dewey wrote, begins as a response to the "doubtful as such." And the greater the indeterminateness of a situation, the greater the intellectual and cognitive quality of that experience. For here we are dealing with potentialities. Thought addresses those problematic situations of experience, "the outcome of which is not yet determined."

For Dewey, Darwinism taught that the universe was an unfinished product, open-ended and without teleological meaning. Furthermore, nature is essentially indifferent to human purposes. Concretely, it may be more hostile than benevolent, for everywhere it challenges human beings to reshape it or perish in its midst. The very unfriendliness, however, stimulates thinking and assures progress. The human species has as its only recourse its thinking function, the essential business of the live organism. "Its activities," Dewey wrote, "must change the changes going on around it; they must neutralize hostile occurrences; they must transform neutral events into cooperative factors." In an open universe, thought makes the world different from what it would have been if thought had not intervened.

REVISING WESTERN PHILOSOPHY

These points had vast implications for Dewey as a philosopher, and he sought to use them in a thoroughgoing revision of modern philosophy. He gave an address at Columbia on the subject of Charles Darwin and published it in 1909 as "The Influence of Darwin on Philosophy." It is a major document of Darwin's influence in the United States. The essay might well have had the alternate title "The Influence of Darwin on John Dewey." He referred to Darwin specifically in his essay, not to evolution simply. Dewey meant emphatically that the Darwinian form of evolution furnished the keys to a needed reformulation of Western thinking in its entirety.

So Dewey began with a look back at the Greeks. Plato and Aristotle, he wrote, bestowed on Western thinking a certain habit of thought, a dangerous one. The first clue came in Aristotelian science. All things, Aristotle asserted, have an end or higher realization ascribed to their identities. Each organism conceals in its appearance a larger, controlling form, what later assumed the name "species." And each organism disclosed a "telos," or end, that signified its fullest meaning. The end of an acorn is the oak tree, for example. These categories, as the Greeks understood them, had stable and permanent features, reflecting as they did higher forms. This fixation on forms always obviated any consideration of forms merging or changing, one out of the other. Greek science saw fixity amid the teleologies.

The fundamental Greek error, Dewey believed, lay in projecting this format into all of reality. Thus Greek metaphysics saw nature as a progressive realization of purpose; everything took place within a comprehensive cosmic order, a temporal process that linked earthly particulars and heavenly ideals. Profound consequences followed from this understanding. Dewey explained that under the Greek formulation, to know something is always to know it in terms of the higher order, to locate it within the comprehensive scheme of things, the higher realities. Dewey often referred to the "spectator" view of knowledge; to know is to grasp in a single vision the all-integrating, all-comprehensive design of reality. And, inheriting from the Greeks the teleological bias, Western thinking became focused also on primal origins and ultimate ends, or "final causes." Thus, we do not know fully by knowing mere particulars; they acquire meaning only within the larger parameters of origins and ends.

Modern science, Dewey believed, disabuses us of this notion of true knowledge. The Greek view, and the long legacy of it in Western thinking, misconstrues reality, he argued. Under the evolutionary view, under Darwinism, that is, we see reality in terms of flux, openness, and possibility. We see forms, species, as unstable, always breaking their boundaries and mutating into new forms. Philosophy now follows this lead, Dewey proclaimed. It abandons the quest for first causes and final ends. It does not seek to explain things in terms of absolutes or inclusive principles. Intelligence redefines its functions and purposes. In a world of flux and change, it settles for a program of managed growth, problem solving, redirecting of the problematic aspects of things into satisfactory reconstructions. Darwinism, in fact, redefines the meaning of intelligence. It shifts from the idea of a higher, controlling intelligence, the way of the idealists, to an intelligence that is immediate and practical. Explaining the Darwinian turn in philo-sophical thinking, Dewey wrote: "Interest shifts from the wholesale essence back of special changes to changes that serve and defeat our immediate purposes." He opted, of course, for the newer understand-ing, derived from evolution. The older habits, he said, prevent us from looking reality in the face, from confronting the immediate, the prob-lematic. In short, they circumvent the evolutionary purpose of think-ing, the adaptive imperative of intelligence.

This distinction described for John Dewey another bad legacy of the Greeks and the program of damage control that modern philos-ophy must undertake. We have inherited from the Greeks, Dewey argued, a bifurcated reality. One realm gives us changelessness, per-fection, permanence. It is the realm of the spiritual, the transcen-dent, the divine. The other realm is that of earthly things. It is tran-sient, flawed, deficient, human, and inherently unsatisfying. In fact, the first realm has always served as a refuge from the other. We have made that higher realm the location of religion, the locus of re-demption for the fallen persons and things that inhabit the lower earthly realm.

Dewey charged to this stark dualism the many and wrong-headed invidious divisions that follow from it. Everywhere he found di-chotomous habits of thinking; they were rife in the Western intel-lect. They have given us the mind/matter division, also the spirit/ body, man/nature, ideal/real, means/ends, individual/society, and state/people divisions. Modern science, Dewey believed, should have rendered all of these brittle categories suspect. Evolution shows the interrelatedness of all things; it breaks down hard cate-gories; it places human beings into the large complexities of a chang-ing nature.

In other essays like "Evolution and Ethics" and "Intelligence and Morals" Dewey gave further illustrations. Western thinking, he ob-served, has long searched for the essentially good, the principles of absolute worth and intrinsic right. Often that quest has led to identi-fication of a moral faculty, or conscience, in our makeup, an infalli-ble guide to that moral essence. The habit derives from our dualistic thinking; we are led in the quest for the good to move outside the confinements of tangible experience and quotidian activities. We have made the ethical an aspect of some higher reality. Dewey located the corrective to this errant thinking. "The progress of biology," he wrote, "has accustomed our minds to the notion that intelligence is not an outside power presiding supremely but statically over the desires and efforts of man." The "evolutionary method" further informs us, he added, that "there is no separate body of moral rules . . . no separate subject-matter of moral knowledge, and hence no such thing as an isolated ethical science." Dewey thereby located the moral life, and the source of its direction, within the large social environment in which human beings negotiate their choices and ends. Ethics then affixes its quest to an extended body of related learning, derived from anthropology, psychology, law, politics, and economics. Within this larger intellectual milieu, ethics becomes the construction of intelligent methods for improving the social organism.

A PHILOSOPHY FOR SOCIETY

And in that direction, Dewey believed, philosophy should go. He judged philosophy by its social usefulness. Of all the American pragmatists, Dewey most deliberately took his thinking into the social and political realms. His writings over decades address the changing industrial order in the United States; they reflect his public commitments—to civil rights, women's suffrage, the American Civil Liberties Union, and the American Association of University Professors. Dewey secured a liberal political program within a larger philosophical system. The work to which we turn in a concluding section is Dewey's book of 1920, the terminal date of this study. He titled it *Reconstruction in Philosophy*. It is a book about ideas and history, philosophy and its social consequences. Like so many of Dewey's writings it reflects his Darwinian view.

Dewey begins by positing "natural man." Natural man, he says, lives in simple contact with nature. Intellect, as evolution dictates, helps him to perform basic tasks of survival. It reflects a practical intelligence. Original man also follows his social nature, living in groups in a cooperative economy. But the leap of mind that marked the distinctively human phase of evolution sets thoughts in other directions. While it enhances creative thinking it also gives new room to the imagination. That exercise represents a response to the unknown and to the fear associated with what individuals cannot explain by simple causal behavior. To secure explanations and to allay fears, a belief system emerges, codified in mythology, religion, or dogma. Invention of these religions has important social effects in Dewey's account. They bring about a priestly class that serves as the protector of sacred knowledge and moral codes. Priestly officials claim monopoly of this saving knowledge and turn to the political establishment as its ally in perpetuating and enforcing it by law and punishment. The dominant powers in the social order maintain their privileged positions by means of an expansive edifice of higher truth.

Dewey always read social consequences into all belief systems. The establishment of higher truth and esoteric knowledge led to invidious distinctions, he claimed, a dangerous social dualism, in fact. There resulted two kinds of knowledge: the "higher" knowledge associated with the ruling classes and the dominant social institutions of church and state, and a "lower" knowledge. This kind of knowledge constituted practical science, manual skills, mechanical technology, in short, the word of menial laborers, the broad masses of the society whose daily activity confines them to the mundane, practical realities of bodily labor in its manifold forms. One realm of knowledge had its transactions with permanent things, abstract realms, higher gods and goddesses, churchly rites and rituals of a sacred nature. The business of the higher knowledge is otherworldly. The lower knowledge, by contrast, functions among transient and impermanent things, perishable entities. It deals with worldly facts in all their fallen estates. It denotes the work done in the ordinary lives of the underprivileged in the social hierarchy.

The Greeks represent both the culmination of this trend, in the elaborate mythology of their religion, and a new departure. The Greek philosophers, seeing the dysfunctional turn in the state religions, sought, Dewey explained, to secure the higher truth on a more purely intellectual basis, and in the manner described above. This new stage carried through to its political perfection in the Middle Ages. Here a class-bound society, topped by an alliance of church, state, and aristocracy, dominated, its authority extending down to the local parish priest. A universal ecclesiastical order prevailed, bringing the masses into its ritualistic complexities and dogmatic authority. The universities, with their vast scholastic enterprise, made philosophy the intellectual props of a recondite scholastic system jealously guarded by the priesthood and by whose mysteries alone the vulgar mass found salvation. Briefly summarized, this long process signified to Dewey the terrible heritage of Western philosophy. The most noble intellectual efforts of Western thinkers attached themselves to an external cosmic order. They deflected thought from doubt and inquiry, from practical intelligence and from experimentation within the immediate social environment.

The hope for a counter force against this heritage Dewey found in modern science and technology, and the associated application of the scientific method. They give new and liberating power, he believed, to critical thinking, to functional intelligence, to the problem-solving mentality that was evolution's major gift to the human species. Technology, with its extensive social effects, Dewey believed, could reintegrate human society, breaking down the rigid class system. Schools, as the large literature that Dewey contributed on them elaborated, could accelerate this improving trend, by emphasizing collective learning and an education in practical skills. All of these activities fell under the larger idea of the scientific method. Against dogma, abstract values, and inherited truths, that method emphasized empirical observation, experimentation, and the conclusions drawn from them. As science and technology reinforced such habits of thinking, Dewey hoped that they would gradually undermine the regimes supported by the higher thinking, both intellectually and in the political consequences that had followed. Dewey celebrated pragmatism as having precisely this role in the contemporary struggles. Under pragmatism, he wrote in his essay "Intelligence and Morals," thought "has descended from its lonely isolation in the remote edge of things, whence it operated as unmoved mover and ultimate good, to take its seat in the moving affairs of men."

Those consequences had their fullest expression for Dewey in effective democracy. Dewey gave much more attention to social and political issues in the years after *Reconstruction*, but that book laid those writings on a firm foundation. Democracy had concerned Dewey in the early phase of his philosophical idealism, particularly in his important essay "Ethics of Democracy" in 1888. Here Dewey certified the social nature of human beings, relating the individual to the social complex as he did individual realities and experiences to the absolute mind in which they find a larger meaning. Here again evolution easily supplemented and then replaced idealism, for Dewey stressed heavily that for human beings the social environment became, in evolution, the great adaptive challenge for the race. All the more important, then, was the role of collective intelligence, embodied in government and the state.

As such, the challenge for any social organism lay in its utilization of critical intelligence through application of the scientific method. That method, to ensure its success, must address as wide an array of data, of information, as it can in order to make judgments about the right course of action to solve the problem under consideration. That procedure applied also to the functioning of government, Dewey urged. How might society draw upon the widest data bases possible in order to plan and program? Dewey answered, only by establishing as wide a social base as it can, by becoming, in short, a wholly inclusive society. Dewey saw in the United States, and even more so elsewhere, a political arrangement much too narrowly based. It excluded females from the voting booth and disenfranchised most of the black population. No state thus organized could truly speak for its society as its collective intelligence. It could draw on only a narrow base of information input; its response to social needs could be only partial and ultimately ineffective.

Here the full pattern of Dewey's social philosophy emerged in outline. Where an absolutist and authoritarian system of thought prevails, so will an absolutist and authoritarian system of state. A truly evolutionary philosophy, based on the recognized realities of change, flux, newness, and variety, will influence an open and democratic society. Thus, for John Dewey, democracy is that system that embraces in the real world the concept of an open universe in the intellectual world.

Finally, Dewey related pragmatism directly to the American experience. In all his ruminations on philosophical systems he made associations between them and the nationalities in which they flourished. Greek philosophy had answered immediate social needs. British empiricism and its appeal to the static past reflected the habits of a tradition-minded nation. During World War I, Dewey pondered the legacy of German philosophy, in its neo-Kantian forms particularly, to explain Germans' supreme loyalty to their state and that state's dangerous aggressiveness in 1914. He found it not accidental that pragmatism had American origins. It suited a people who had always confronted new environments in their history, who, removed from traditional social patterns, had to turn unstable situations into orderly arrangements. Instrumentalism, he believed, suited the temperaments of a present-minded people who see the world as always in a state of continuous reformation and welcome the challenge to rethink each situation afresh. "Our life," Dewey wrote, "has no background of sanctified categories upon which we may fall back; we rely upon precedent and authority only to our undoing." Pragmatism spoke to celebrated American traits, Dewey assured. "We pride ourselves upon being realistic," he proclaimed, "desiring a hard-headed cognizance of facts, and devoted to mastering the means of life. We pride ourselves on a practical idealism, a lively and easily moved faith in possibilities as yet unrealized." In John Dewey, as much as any thinker, we have the Americanization of Darwinism.

BIBLIOGRAPHY

Barzun, Jacques. *A Stroll with William James*. Chicago: University of Chicago Press, 1983.

Boller, Paul, Jr. *American Thought in Transition: The Impact of Evolutionary Naturalism, 1865–1900*. Chicago: Rand McNally, 1969.

Cotkin, George. *Reluctant Modernism: American Thought and Culture, 1880–1900.* New York: Twayne, 1992.

——. *William James: Public Philosopher.* Baltimore: Johns Hopkins University Press, 1990.

Coughlan, Neil. *Young John Dewey.* Chicago: University of Chicago Press, 1974.

Croce, Paul Jerome. *Science and Religion in the Era of William James.* Vol. 1. *Eclipse of Certainty, 1820–1880.* Chapel Hill: University of North Carolina Press, 1995.

Diggins, John Patrick. *The Promise of Pragmatism: Modernism and the Crisis of Knowledge and Authority.* Chicago: University of Chicago Press, 1994.

Dykhuizen, George. *The Life and Mind of John Dewey.* Carbondale: Southern Illinois University Press, 1974.

Feinstein, Howard M. *Becoming William James.* Ithaca: Cornell University Press, 1984.

Hollinger, David. "The Problem of Pragmatism in American History." *Journal of American History* 67 (1980): 88–107.

Kloppenberg, James T. *Uncertain Victory: Social Democracy and Progressivism in European and American Thought, 1870–1920.* New York: Oxford University Press, 1986.

Kuklick, Bruce. *The Rise of American Philosophy: Cambridge, Massachusetts, 1860–1930.* New Haven: Yale University Press, 1977.

McDermott, John J. *The Writings of William James: A Comprehensive Edition.* New York: The Modern Library, 1968.

Myers, Gerald E. *William James: His Life and Thought.* New Haven: Yale University Press, 1986.

Perry, Ralph Barton. *The Thought and Character of William James.* 2 vols. Boston: Little, Brown, 1935.

Ryan, Alan. *John Dewey and the High Tide of American Liberalism.* New York: Norton, 1995.

Turner, James. *Without God, without Creed: The Origins of Unbelief in America.* Baltimore: Johns Hopkins University Press, 1985.

Westbrook, Robert B. *John Dewey and American Democracy.* Ithaca: Cornell University Press, 1991.

POSTSCRIPT, 2006

Darwinism was big news in 2005. It's news in any year in the United States, but it was really big in that year. A measure of the attention it received came from popular magazines. *National Geographic* jumped the gun in November 2004 with its cover-story question, "Was Darwin Wrong?" Inside, readers found that the answer was "no, he was right." In August 2005, *TIME* magazine placed on its cover the headline "Evolution Wars," following with a story on the prevailing efforts around the country to force intelligent design into public school curricula. The same month the *New Republic* also placed evolution in its lead article, with the label "Unintelligent Design," a thoroughgoing defense of Darwinian evolution. In December the *Economist*, with a humorous depiction of the ascent of woman, offered another attack on intelligent design and the covert religious agenda its proponents sponsor. And on its cover the same month, the *Christian Century* posed the question, "Intelligent Design?" The conservatives weighed in the next summer. George Gilder delivered an assault on Darwinism in the July 17, 2006, issue of *National Review*.

Science magazine, a publication of the American Association for the Advancement of Science, also kicked in. As per tradition, it announced in its December 2005 issue its annual "Breakthrough" recognition of the most significant advance in science during the previous year. *Science* announced that in 2005 it was honoring "Evolution in Action." Its editorial described several new biological studies in this "exploding science." One concerned the European blackcap, "a species of warbler that spends the winter in two separate places but then reunites to breed, with birds selecting mates from those who shared the same wintering ground." Eventually, species differentiation occurred. Another example involved the small stickleback fish and its relocations from the sea into freshwater. In these occurrences, the editorial explained, the fish shed the rather heavy armor plates that protect them from their predators, and attain an advantageous mobility in the new waters. "New species have been generated in each invasion, always in the same way: by rapid evolutionary selection of the same rare and ancient gene," the journal reported. Scientists, in another study, also found that the sequencing of the chimpanzee genome, which allowed them to compare it with human DNA, showed only a 4 percent differentiation between the two. Impressed by the new studies, the magazine added that "the exciting thing about evolution is not that our understanding is perfect or complete but that it is the foundation stone for the rest of biology."

This attention to evolution concurred with a renewed fight against it in America's public schools. These activities won national attention, in several states, but especially two. After a protracted fight, and re-elections over several years, the Kansas State School Board in 2005 voted to exclude evolution from its new, approved state standards for science in Kansas public schools. It allowed local options for teachers to teach so-called intelligent design, the idea that some natural phenomena, such as the eye, are so complex that we can explain them only by invoking a special designer. William Paley's watch was still ticking. And in Pennsylvania, the Dover Area School Board ordered that its biology curriculum must include a statement that the earth's creation derived from an unidentified intelligent cause (though not necessarily "God"). Federal judge John E. Jones III, however, after a six-week trial and after board members who supported the new policy were voted out of office, returned a 139-page judgment, a strong rebuke to the earlier school board. His ruling affirmed that the driving cause behind the individuals promoting intelligent design was their own intention to promote religion in the public schools.

Of course, no one expected that this "second Scopes trial" would end the debate and the politics about evolution and the classroom science program. A guest discussant on the Larry King television show lamented (paraphrasing) that "I can't believe that here in 2005 in the United States we are still debating Darwinian evolution." But many clearly had little concern for scientific standards or scientific research in settling their minds about evolution. A woman board member who helped secure the Kansas directive expunging Darwinism from the state standards said she had never seen natural selection at work so why should she believe it. She clearly felt no compulsion to state whether she had ever seen gravity or whether she had ever seen an atom, or even whether she had ever seen God. For most people who have a visceral opposition to Darwin, one thing stands most clear: their loyalty to the book of Genesis and the Bible story of creation. Kent Hovind, the popular television guru and Darwin-slayer, who denounces all Darwinism in textbooks as "lies," insists that God created the earth in six days and that humans once walked with dinosaurs.

The story from 1920, where the main story of this book ends, to 2007, of course, has many missing links. But this book is not intended to adjudicate all the quarrels of religion and science that have fueled America's ongoing "culture wars" over the many decades. This is a book about history, the sixty years or so in which evolution presented to American thinkers a fresh way of looking at life and a new way of understanding reality. Many Americans wrote about evolution and applied it where they saw opportunities. In doing so, they discussed the subject at the level of grand ideas that addressed questions about God and nature, design and purpose, social formulations for human progress, and new devices for explaining human behavior. Since the first decades, of course, in the natural sciences and the social sciences, evolutionary studies have become much more empirical, and much more technical.

But some historical reflection on the early studies might offer some help, perhaps some perspective on the issues that divide Americans so much today. Darwinism will always threaten many people with the prospect of a meaningless cosmos, of a universe without purpose or plan. Others will take offense because of more specifically dogmatic reasons, such as the Genesis account. Nor should anyone give a facile dismissal of these concerns. Darwin's theory emphatically does threaten theism; it gets along very well without final causes and without a teleology. And logically, too, there surely is a burden on those Darwinians who explain all by chance and spontaneity to show how order and equilibrium prevail in nature, for in fact all is not chaos and confusion. One would hope only that these questions not impede science's continuing inquiries into how life forms change and how organs, like the eye, acquire their wonderful abilities. None can say today that tomorrow will not have natural explanations for today's many questions.

Again on science and religion. Might it not do all parties well, in the face of such bitter contention today, to consider what this book describes? It describes a generation of religious thinkers who examined evolution and saw in it new space for God's activities. The liberal Protestants believed that evolution gave them every right to portray a more active God, a more omniscient deity. They never doubted that religion could only gain, and expand its domain, from the new perspectives that modern evolutionary science offered them. Of course, they also wished to redefine Christianity to accommodate the new learning. They would have to argue that their faith, their church, is also an evolution, a growth that comes from new understandings of how God works in the world. Often, that turn meant that Genesis and other biblical accounts would lose their authority. Biblical literalism remains the major sticking point in the evolutionary quarrels of today. But evolutionary thinking also had its unexpected twists. The two scientists studied in chapter 3 were profoundly religious individuals. And even Darwinism itself, as we saw in the example of William James, could also open up to religious possibilities. Personal faith, given the Darwinian reality of an "open universe," supplies us personal truths, legitimate truths, that sustain our lives and open us up to the unseen, spiritual dimensions of reality. James found his way to this understanding of things through a life's work in evolutionary science.

INDEX

Abbott, Lawrence, 54
Abbott, Lyman, 103, 105
Abrams v. United States, 208
Agassiz, Elizabeth Cabot Cary, 55
Agassiz, Louis, 47, 67–68, 72, 85,
  196, 197; career of, 51–55, 75;
  *Contributions to the Natural
  History of the United States*, 58;
  and Darwin, 51, 58–61; "Essay
  on Classification," 58; *Études sur
  les glaciers*, 53; "Evolution and
  Permanence of Type," 61–62;
  and glaciers, 53–54; and
  Naturphilosophie, 52, 55; on
  polygenism, 56–57; on race,
  56–57; *Système glaciate*, 53
Ahlstrom, Sydney, 103
Alexander, Archibald, 79, 82
American Academy of Science, 67
American Association for the
  Advancement of Science,
  247–48
American Association of University
  Professors, 241

American Civil Liberties Union,
  241
American Economic Association,
  181, 182
American Historical Association,
  182
American Law Review, 198
American Political Science
  Association, 182, 184
Amherst College, 109, 113
Andover Review, 232
Andover Theological Seminary,
  104, 122, 227
Anglicanism, 12, 28, 29, 34, 84,
  104, 135
Aristotle, 2, 238
artificial selection, 37, 152
Athens, 174
Auburn Theological seminary, 122

Bacon, Francis, 81, 90
Baker, Live, 193, 198, 199
Baptism (denomination), 82, 104,
  234

Baron d'Holbach, 13

Bartram, John, 5

Bartram, William, 5

Bascom, Abby Burt, 122

Bascom, Emma Eustis, 122

Bascom, John (father of the evolutionist), 122

Bascom, John, 104, 179; career of, 122–23; and evangelicalism, 123–30; and evolution, 123–30; on government and the state, 127–28, 130; *Natural Theology*, 124; and philosophy, 123–24; *The Philosophy of Prohibition*, 128; and social issues, 127–29; and sociology, 126–28; *Sociology*, 127, 129; *Things Learned by Living*, 124; at University of Wisconsin, 123, 27, 128, 129

Bascom, Laura Woodbridge, 122

Bascom, Mary, 122

The Beagle, 30–34, 36

Bederman, Gail, 158

Beecher, Charlotte, 108, 109, 157

Beecher, Harriet (Stowe), 108, 109, 157, 160

Beecher, Henry Ward, 103, 157, 179; in Brooklyn, 111; career of, 108–11; on Darwin, 111; and evolution, 110, 114–16, 119–22; *Evolution and Religion*, 104, 110, 121; *Lectures to Young Men*, 111; *Norwood*, 114–15, 117, 119; at Plymouth Church, 110, 112, 114–15; and race issues, 113–14, 120; on science and technology, 118; and social issues, 116–22

Beecher, Lyman, 108–10

Bellamy, Edward, 160, *Looking Backward*, 160

Berkeley, George, 82

biblical flood, 7, 8, 20, 75

Biblical Repertory and Princeton Review, 79–80

Bibliotheca Sacra, 232

Bill of Rights, 207

Blackstone, William, 198

Boller, Paul, 214

Bonnet, Charles, 10

Boston University, 104

Botanical Society of Edinburgh, 92

Bowen, Francis, 196

Bowler, Peter J., 13

Bowne, Borden P., 106

Bozeman, Theodore Dwight, 81

Brastow, Lewis, 227

Briggs, Asa, 104, 105

Broad Church movement, 104

Brown, Janet, 26

Büchner, Ludwig, 85

Buck v. Bell, 205

Buckle, Thomas Henry, 146, 174

Buffon, Compte de, 7–10; *Epochs of Nature*, 9–10, 14, 15

Bureau of Statistics, 145

Burlington, VT, 226, 227

Bushnell, Horace, 79, 104; *Christian Nurture*, 104; *Nature and the Supernatural*, 104

Calvinism, 12, 63, 64, 77, 91, 95–96, 100–101, 109, 113, 116, 121, 123, 136, 142, 193

Cambridge Philosophical Society, 29

Cambridge Scientific Club, 67

Cambridge University, 28–30

Campbell, George (Duke of Argyll), 87; *The Reign of Law,* 87

Campbell, Helen, 159

Cape Verde, 31

Carnegie, Andrew, 134

catastrophism, 7, 15, 18, 20, 53, 89

Chambers, Robert, 21–22, 41, 42, 53, 65, 95; *Vestiges of the Natural History of Creation,* 21–22, 23, 53, 65, 95

Chandler, Shattuck, and Thayer (law firm), 197

Christ, Jesus, 99, 150, 174

Christian Century, 247

Church of England. *See* Anglicanism

Church of Scotland, 91–92

Clark, Clifford, 118

Clark, William, 15

Colden, Cadwallader, 5

Coleridge, Samuel Taylor, 55, 228; *Aids to Reflection,* 228

Colgate Theological Seminary, 104

College of New Jersey (Princeton), 78, 90, 95–96

collocation, 93, 185

Columbia College (Washington, DC), 145

Columbia University, 236

Commager, Henry Steele, 143, 154

Compromise of 1850, 113

Comte, August, 146

Congregationalism, 104, 123, 226

Cornell University, 180

Creation Science, ix

Croce, Paul Jerome, 21–22

Cuvier, Georges, 17–19, 52–53, 57, 61, 89; *Theory of the Earth,* 17

Dana, James Dwight, 115

Dartmouth College, 227, 229, 230

Darwin, Annie, 37

Darwin, Charles, ix–xii, 1, 14, 17, 20, 49, 55, 63, 66, 67, 69, 71, 74, 77, 80, 83, 101, 105–6, 146, 149, 196; and Agassiz, 51, 58–62; and Buffon, 9–10; and Chambers, 22; and controversies in 2006, 247–50; Dennett on, 25; *Descent of Man,* 85, 169; development of theory of evolution, 36–38, 40–41; and Dewey, 226, 227, 236–38, 238–41; early life, 25–26; education, 27–30; and Emma Wedgwood Darwin, 34; and Gamble, 169–77; geological studies of, 31, 35; and Gilman, 161–68; and Gray, 60, 62–64, 67, 68–75; and Hodge, 83, 84–90; and Holmes, 195, 196, 197, 198, 200, 203–4, 207–9; and Huxley, 43–44; and W. James, 218–20, 222, 224–25; and Lamarck, 16, 41–42, 44; and Lyle, 19–20, 38, 42, 60; and Malthus, 35–36; and McCosh, 97; *Origin of Species,* 25, 40, 51, 66, 69, 71, 85; and Owen, 45–46, 47; on race, 33; reactions to his theory of evolution, 38–47, 51; on religion, 47–48; 71–72; and Spencer, 23, 41; and Sumner, 133–35, 141–42; and uniformitarianism, 31; *The Variation of Animals and Plants under Domestication,* 74; and Veblen, 182–88; voyage of the *Beagle,* 30–34, 36; *Voyage of a Naturalist,* 85; and Wallace, 39;

and Ward, 147, 153; and
  Wilberforce, 43, 45; in year 2006
Darwin, Emma Wedgwood, 34
Darwin, Erasmus, 16, 25; *Zoonamia,
  or, the Laws of Organic Life*, 16
Darwin, Robert Waring, 25–26, 28,
  30–31
Darwin, Susanna Wedgwood, 26
Darwin, William, 34
David, F. D., 23
Deland, Margaret, 168
Dennett, Daniel, C., 25
design. *See* evolution and religion;
  religion and science; teleology
development. *See* evolution
Dewey, Alice Chipman, 232
Dewey, Archibald, 226
Dewey, Davis, 226
Dewey, John, xii, 183, 196, 202,
  204, 211; career of, 226–27,
  229–30, 231–32, 236; and
  Darwin, 226, 227, 232–38,
  238–41; 244–45; on dualism,
  240; on early human society,
  241–42; on empiricism, 236,
  245; "Ethics and Physical
  Science," 232; "Ethics of
  Democracy," 244; "Evolution
  and Ethics," 240–41; "From
  Idealism to Experimentalism,"
  228; on government and the
  state, 244; on Greek philosophy,
  238–41, 245; "The Influence of
  Darwin on Philosophy," 238–41;
  and instrumentalism, 237; on
  intellect and social classes,
  242–32; "Intelligence and
  Morals," 243–44; and Kant, 230;
  and liberalism, 226, 244–45;

"The Metaphysical Assumptions
  of Materialism," 229–30; and
  Morris, 230–31; "The Need for a
  Recovery of Philosophy," 235;
  and philosophical idealism,
  228–29, 230–34, 235; on the
  problematical, 237–38;
  Reconstruction in Philosophy,
  241–43, 244; and religion, 227,
  232, 234, 239–40; on science
  and technology, 243–44; on
  World War I, 245
Dewey, Lucina, 226, 227
Dickie, George, 92–93; *Typical
  Forms and Special Ends in
  Creation*, 92–95
Diderot, Dennis, 13; *Encyclopedia*,
  13
Douglas, Stephen, 113
Downe, England, 35
Duffield, Thomas, 95–96
Dupree, A. Hunter, 66
Dwight, Timothy, 109

The *Economist*, 247
Edwards, Jonathan, 91
Eiseley, Loren, 4

Ely, Richard T., 143, 150
Emancipation Proclamation, 66,
  144
Emerson, Ralph Waldo, 54, 193,
  228
Enlightenment, 12, 13, 19. *See also*
  Scottish Enlightenment
Episcopalians, 104
Espionage Act of 1917, 207–8
evangelicalism: and Bascom,
  123–24; and Beecher, 108, 111,

121–22; and McCosh, 96–101; and Protestant Liberalism, 107–8; in Scotland, 91–92, 93–94

Everett, Edward, 54

evolution, ix–xi, 19; and Agassiz, 58–62; and Bascom, 123–30; and H. W. Beecher, 110–11, 114–22; and Buffon, 7–10; and Chambers, 21–22; and Cuvier, 17–19; and Erasmus Darwin, 16; and Dewey, 232–34, 235, 238–41, 244–45; and Gilman, 162–68; and Gray, 68–75; and Hodge, 84–90; and Holmes, 203–4, 207–9; and Hutton, 10–14; and Huxley, 42–44; and William James, 214–15, 218–19, 222; and Lamarck, 16–17; and Lyle, 19–20, 44; and McCosh, 94–101; and Owen, 45–47; and W. Smith, 15; and Spencer, 22–23, 107; and Sumner, 137–42; and Veblen, 182–93; and Ward, 147–55. *See also* Darwin, Charles

evolution and feminism. *See* Gilman, Charlotte Perkins; Gamble, Eliza Burt

evolution and religion, x; in 2005, 246–50; Abbott on, 105–6; Agassiz on, 55–56, 58; Bascom on, 123–30; Beecher on, 114–16, 119–22; Dewey and, 227, 232, 234, 239–40; in early America, 77–78; in England, 44–45; Gray on, 60–66, 71–75; Hodge on, 84–90; Hutton on, 12; James on, 222–25, 250; Lyell on, 44; McCosh on, 101; Sumner on,

141, 143; Wallace on, 39–40; Ward on, 143,151

Evolutionists, xi

Ferguson, Adam, 12, 91

Fichte, 124

final causes. *See* evolution and religion

Finney, Charles Grandison, 79, 126

Fisk, John, 146

FitzRoy, Capt. Robert, 30, 31–32

fossils, 15, 17–19, 44

Fourteenth Amendment, 206

Franklin, Benjamin, 5, 80, 146

Free Church of Scotland, 100

French Revolution, 14

Fuegians, 33

Fugitive Slave Law, 113

Fuller, Margaret, 193

Galápagos Islands, 32

Galilei, Galileo, 146

Gamble, Eliza Burt, 179; career of, 168–69; on Christianity and gender, 174; and Darwin, 169–70; *Evolution of Woman*, 169, 173; on gender in history, 173; on human evolution, 170–71; on male supremacy, 172–75; on marriage, 173; on progress, 175–76; on sex differentiation, 170–71, 172; *The Sexes in Science and History*, 169; and women's rights, 176–77

Gamble, James, 169

Garden, Alexander, 5

Genesis, Book of, 44–45, 55, 89, 96, 249, 250

Giddings, Franklin, 143

Gillispie, Charles Coulston, 17

Gilman, Charlotte Perkins, 143, 179; career of, 157–61; on the family, 167–68; on marriage, 159, 167; on motherhood, 159, 166–67; on race, 162; and radical politics, 159–60; on sex differentiation, 163–66; and Lester Frank Ward, 160, 162; on women and evolution, 160–68, 176–77; *Women and Economics*, 161, 165; on women and industrialism, 162–63

Gilman, George Houghton, 159

Gladden, George, 57, 65; *The Types of Mankind*, 58

glaciers, 53, 58, 66

Gothic architecture, 117

government, 127–28, 130, 138–39, 150, 152–53, 244–45

Grant, Robert, 16

Gray, Asa, 60, 115; and Agassiz, 65–67; career of, 62–65; and Darwin, 38, 39, 67, 68–75; *Darwiniana*, 69; on design in nature, 68–75; on flora, 66–67, 68; *Flora of North America*, 63; on *Naturphilosophie*, 67–68; and religion, 64–65, 73; on species, 67, 69–71; "Statistics of the Flora of the Northern Unites States," 68

Gray, Jane Lathrop Loring, 65

Gray, Moses Wiley, 63

Gray, Roxanna Howard, 63

Gray, Sarah Miller, 63

Great Chain of Being, 1–5, 16, 18

Green, Ashbel, 78

Green, Nicholas St. John, 199

Green, Thomas Hill, 230; *Prolegomena to Ethics*, 230

Grey, Thomas, 197

Hacking, Ian, 23

Hadley, James, 63

Haeckel, Ernst, 85

Hall, G. Stanley, 161

Hamilton, Sir William, 83, 91

Harper, William Rainey, 234

Harris, George, 103

Harris, William Torrey, 229

Harvard College (University), 54–55, 64, 123, 193, 194, 213

Harvard Divinity School, 104

Harvard Law School, 195, 196–97

Harvard Medical School, 194

Hawthorne, Nathaniel, 193

Hegel, G. W. F., 83, 104, 124, 185, 229, 231, 232, 235

Henry, Joseph, 80

Henslow, John Stevens, 29, 30

Herschel, John, 29

Hickok, Laurens Perseus, 124

Himmelfarb, Gertrude, 27, 36, 74

historicism, 83

Hodge, Charles, 95, 96, 97, 101, 103; and Baconian methodology, 81, 90; on biblical authority, 83–89; career of, 78–80; on Darwin, 85–89; on design, 88; on religion and science, 80–82; *Systematic Theology*, 79, 82; *What is Darwinism?*, 81, 84–85, 89, 97

Hodge, Mary Blanchard, 78

Hodge, Sarah Bache, 80

Hofstadter, Richard, 142

Holmes, Abiel, 194

Holmes, Amelia Jackson, 194

Holmes, David, 194

Holmes, Fanny Bowditch Dixwell, 195

Holmes, Oliver Wendell (Dr.), 194, 195

Holmes, Oliver Wendell Jr., 193; and anti-trust laws, 205–6; career of, 194–97, 201, 205; *The Common Law*, 199–201; as conservative, 205; and Darwin, 195, 196, 197, 198, 200, 203–4, 207–9; on freedom of speech, 207–9; on individual rights, 204; on judicial restraint, 203–4; on the law, 197–98, 199–200, 202–3; as liberal, 201–3; on social regulations, 205, 206–7

Hooker, Joseph, 39, 64, 69; *Flora of New Zealand*, 68

Hooker, Richard, 29, 68

Hope, Thomas, 28

Hovind, Kent, 249

Howe, Frederick, 154

Hull, David, 62

Humboldt, Alexander von, 146

Hume, David, 82, 215, 216, 230, 235

Hunt, William Morris, 213

Hutcheson, Francis, 11, 91

Hutton, James, 10–12, 88; *Theory of the Earth*, 10–11

Huxley, Thomas, 42–44, 45–47, 72, 85, 99–101, 215, 227; *Elements of Physiology*, 227; *Man's Place in Nature*, 56

hybridization, 66

The Iconoclast, 145

The Impress, 160

Indianapolis, 110

Institut International de Sociologie, 154

"Intelligent Design," 247

Irvine, William, 44, 48

Jackson, Andrew, 140

Jackson, Charles, 194

James, Henry, 212–13

James, Henry, Sr., 211–12

James, William (grandfather of the evolutionist), 212

James, William, 60, 199, 204, 225, 231, 236; on accident and chance, 212, 218–19, 222; on attention, 215; career of, 211–14; on consciousness, 215, 218–19; and Darwin, 214–15, 218–20, 222; on empiricism, 216–17; on freedom of the will, 214, 221; on monism, 220–21; and need for philosophy, 219; "The One and the Many," 221; on pluralism, 220–21, 222; *The Principles of Psychology*, 214–19; and psychology, 214–19; and religion, 222–225, 250; on science, 213; on truth, 223–24; *The Varieties of Religious Experience*, 225; "What Pragmatism Means," 224

Jameson, Robert, 13–14, 28, 92; *System of Mineralogy*, 13

Janet, Paul, 85

Jefferson, Thomas, 14–15, 64, 142, 176–77

John (New Testament), 231

Johns Hopkins University, 180, 181, 231

Jones, John E. III, 248

Kansas-Nebraska Act, 113
Kansas State School Board, 248–49
Kant, Immanuel, 55–56, 83, 180, 217, 228–29, 231, 245; *Critique of Pure Reason*, 217
Kent, Joseph, 198–99; *Commentaries on American Law*, 198
King, Larry, 249
Kirwan, Richard, 12–12
Kloppenberg, James, 221
Knapp, Adeline, 159
Knights of Labor, 159
Kuklick, Bruce, 90

La Follete, Robert, 131
laissez-faire economics, 23
Lamarck, Jean-Baptiste, 16–17, 19, 23
Langdell, Christopher Columbus, 196–98, 200
Lawrence Scientific School, 54, 65
Lawrenceburg, Indiana, 110
Lecky, W. E. H., 174
Leibniz, 2, 232
Letourneau, Charles, 171; *The Evolution of Marriage and the Family*, 171
Lewis, Meriwether, 15
liberalism, (political), 143, 226, 244–45. *See also* Dewey, John; Ward, Lester Frank
libertarianism, 204. *See also,* Sumner, William Graham
Lincoln, Abraham, 66, 144, 145
Linnaeus, Carolus, 3–5, 10; *Systema Nature*, 4, 10
The Living Church, 135
Lochner v. New York, 206–7

Locke, John, 215, 216, 228, 230, 235
Longfellow, Henry Wadsworth, 193
Lovejoy, Arthur, 2
Lowell, James Russell, 193
Lowell, John, 54
Luther, Martha, 159
Lyell, Charles, 19–20, 32, 36, 38, 39, 42, 44, 60, 89; *Antiquity of Man*, 44; *Principles of Geology*, 19, 31, 69

Maine, Sir Henry, 174
Malthus, Thomas, 35–36, 135, 138; *Essay on the Principle of Population*, 35–36
Mansel, Henry, 83
Marsh, James, 55, 227–29
Massachusetts Supreme Judicial Court, 195, 209
Maurice, Frederick D., 104
Marx, Karl, 182, 185–87
McCosh, James, 78, 103, 115, 179, 185; career of, 91–92, 95–96; *Christianity and Positivism*, 98–100; and collocation, 93, 98; and Darwin, 98–100; and evolution, 96–101; and Hodge, 90; and homologies, 93–95; on Liberal Protestantism, 100–101; *The Method of the Divine Government*, 92; and morphology, 92–95; *The Religious Aspects of Evolution*, 97; *Typical Forms and Special Ends in Creation*, 92–95
McLaughlin, William, 110, 118
Melville, Herman, 193
Menand, Louis, 195

Mercersburg Theological Seminary, 84
Metaphysical Club, 199
Methodism, 82, 104, 144
de la Mettrie, Julien Offray, 13
Meyer, D. H. 106
Mexican War, 113
Mill, John Stuart, 111, 146, 148, 215, 230
missing link, 73
Moderate Party (Church of Scotland), 91, 100
Monboddo, Lord, 10
monogenism, 56
Moore, James R., 107
Morgan, J. P., 189, 191
Morgan, Lewis Henry, 171
morphology, 45
Morris, George Sylvester, 230–32
Munger, Theodore, 106
Museum of Comparative Zoology, 54

National Geographic, 247
natural selection, 33, 72; Chambers on, 44; Darwin on, 36–37, 40–41, 46, 69, 74, 85–86, 179, 249; Gamble on, 169–71; Gilman on, 164; Gray on, 71, 72–73, 75; Hodge on, 86; Holmes on, 198, 209; James on, 222; Lyell on, 44; McCosh on, 98, 100; Owen on, 46; Sumner on, 138, 140; Ward on, 148, 152; Wilberforce on, 46; Veblen on, 186
Naturphilosophie, 52, 53, 55, 94
Neander, Augustus, 84
Neptunists, 6–7, 10
Nevin, John W., 79, 84

New England intellect, 193
New Republic, 247
New York City, 117
Newport, R. I., 213
Newton, Sir Isaac, 149; The Types of Mankind, 58
Northern Securities Case, 205
Norton, Andrews, 79
Nott, Josiah, 57, 65

Oberlin College, 113
Oil City, PA, 229
Oken, Lorenz, 52
ontogeny, 21, 61, 86; Lehrbuch der Naturphilosophie, 52
Owen, Richard, 45–47, 58, 64, 93–94; On the Archetype and Homologies of the Vertebrate Skeleton, 93
Oxford movement, 84

Paley, William, 29, 93, 248; Natural Theology, 29, 93, 94
Patten, Simon, 143
Paul (apostle), 174
Peacock, George, 30
Peckham, Rufus, 206
The People, 159
Peirce, Charles Sanders, 199, 204, 211, 224, 236, 237; "How to Make Our Ideas Clear," 222; on meaning and truth, 222–23
Perkins, Frederick, 157
Perkins, Mary Westcott, 158
phylogeny, 21, 61, 86
Plato, 2, 231
Playfair, John, 14, 92
Plymouth Church (Brooklyn Heights), 110, 114, 115, 118

polygenism, 56
Popular Science Monthly, 158, 222
Porter, Noah, 135
Powell John Wesley, 145
pragmatism, 195, 204. *See also*
    James, William; Dewey, John
Presbyterianism, 64, 78, 100, 104
Princeton Review, 79–80, 81, 123
Princeton Theological Seminary,
    78, 79, 82, 90, 95, 212
probabilistic methodology, 222
Progressivism, 130–31, 202, 206
Protestant Liberalism, 100, 104,
    231. *See also* Beecher, Henry
    Ward; Bascom, John

Queen's College, Belfast, 92

race: Agassiz on, 56–58; Beecher
    and, 113; Darwin on, 33; Gilman
    on, 158, 162; Gray on, 65–66
Rafferty, Edward, 146, 154
Ray, John, 3–4; *The Wisdom of God
    Manifested in the Works of the
    Creation*, 3–4
recapitulation. *See* ontogeny;
    phylogeny
reform Darwinism. *See* Ward,
    Lester Frank
Reformed theology. *See* Calvinism
Reid, Thomas, 11, 55, 82, 91, 228
religion and science, 1–3; Agassiz
    on, 55–56, 58–62; Beecher on,
    110–11; Buffon on, 7–8;
    Chambers on, 22; Cuvier on, 18;
    Diderot on, 13; Duffield on,
    95–96; Gray on, 64; Hodge on,
    80–82, 83, 86; Hutton on, 11–12;
    Huxley on, 43–44, 72; Kirwan

on, 12–13; Linnaeus on, 3–5;
    Lyell on, 19; McCosh on, 97;
    Playfair on, 14; Wilberforce on,
    45. *See also*, religion and
    evolution
Renouvier, Charles, 214
Ricardo, David, 135
Rockefeller, John D., 130, 205, 234
romanticism, 84. *See also*
    transcendentalism
Rome, 174
Roosevelt, Theodore, 205–6
Ross, Dorothy, 154
Ross Edward, A., 143
Rousseau, Jean-Jacques, 10
Royce, Josiah, 211, 221
Ruse, Michael, 52
Ruskin, John, 117
Ryan, Alan, 232

Santayana, George, 211
Savage, Minot J., 103
Schaff, Philip, 79, 84
Schenck v. United States, 207–8
Schelling, Friedrich, 52, 124
Science magazine, 247–48
Scottish Common Sense
    Philosophy. *See* Scottish
    Enlightenment
Scottish Enlightenment, 11, 12, 55,
    79, 82, 91, 124, 228
Sedgwick, Adam, 29
Seneca Falls ("Declaration of
    Sentiments"), 176–77
Shedd, William, G. T., 124
Sherman Anti-Trust Act, 204, 206
slavery, 65–66, 80, 108, 113–14
Smith, Adam, 12, 91, 135, 182,
    184–87, 187

Smith, Samuel Stanhope, 78
Smith, William, 15, 19; *The Stratigraphical System of Organized Fossils*, 15
social Darwinism, 133, 141, 142, 152, 154. *See also* Sumner, William Graham
Social Gospel, 150
socialism, 139, 186
sociocracy, 146, 152–53
sociology, 126–28, 133. *See also* Sumner, William Graham; Ward, Lester Frank
species, 179; Agassiz on, 52, 58, 59–60; Buffon on, 9–10; Chambers on, 21; Cuvier on, 17–19; Gray on, 69–70; Hodge on, 90; Huxley on, 43–44; Jefferson on, 15; Linnaeus on, 10; Lyell on, 20, 44; McCosh on, 93–95, 98
Spencer, Herbert, 22–23, 41, 83, 107, 111, 134, 135, 141, 146, 148, 207, 215–16, 217–18, 230; *Social Statics*, 107; *Synthetic Philosophy*, 107
Stanford University, 180
the state. *See* government, 127–29
Stetson, Charles Walter, 159
Stetson, Katherine, 159
Stewart, Dugald, 11, 55, 82, 228
Stewart, John W., 80, 84, 91
Strauss, David, 83–84, 104, 105; *Das Leben Jesu*, 83–84, 104
Sumner, Sarah, 134
Sumner, Jeannie Elliott, 135
Sumner, Thomas, 134
Sumner, William Graham, 133–34, 142, 179, 180, 182; on capitalism, 136; career of, 134–35; and classical economics, 135; and Darwin, 137–38; on the "Forgotten Man," 140–41; on government, 138–40; moral judgments of, 136–37, 138–39, 141; on natural rights, 142; on progress, 141; on social evolution, 139; on socialism, 138; on tariffs, 140; at Yale, 134, 135; *Folkways*, 135; *Protectionism*, 140; *What Social Classes Owe to Each Other*, 135
survival of the fittest: Darwin on, 40–41; Dewey on, 233; Lamarck on, 17; Sumner on, 138–39; Ward on, 149–50
Swedenborgianism, 158, 211–12, 213, 221

Tappan, Lewis, 113
Taylor, Nathaniel William, 79, 109
teleology: Beecher and, 110, 116; Chambers and, 22; Darwin and, 41, 85, 87; Dewey and, 233, 238, 239; Gray and, 72; Hodge and, 87; James and, 222; Protestant Liberalism and, 104–5; Spencer and, 23; Sumner and, 141; Ward and, 143; Veblen and, 183, 185, 186. *See also* evolution and religion
telic evolution, 151
Tennyson, Alfred Lord, 106
Thayer, Nathaniel, 60
Thoreau, Henry David, 193
Tierra del Fuego, 33
TIME magazine, 247
Torrey, H. A. P., 228, 229

Torrey, John, 63
Tractarians, 84
Trandelenburg, Friedrich Adolph, 230
transcendentalism, 55, 82, 115, 228
Turner, James, 80, 221
Tyndall, John, 111, 146

Ulrici, Hermann, 230
uniformitarianism, 10, 12–13, 15, 19
Union Theological Seminary, 230
Unitarianism, 55, 65, 82, 88, 123, 193, 196, 229
United States Geological Survey, 145
United States Supreme Court, 205–9
Universalism, 226
University of Chicago, 104, 234–35, 237
University of Michigan, 231
University of Vermont, 227–28, 229
University of Wisconsin, 129, 130–31

Van Hise, Charles, 131
Veblen, Thorstein, 201, 209; career of, 180–81; and Darwin, 182–83; on early habits of thinking, 182–83; on "economic man," 187–88; on early human society, 189–90; *The Higher Learning in America*, 181; on leisure class behavior, 189–93; on Marx, 185–87; on religion, 182–83, 192; on Adam Smith, 184–85, 187; "Why Is Economics Not an

Evolutionary Science?", 182–84
Voltaire, 19
Vulcanists, 28. *See also* uniformitarianism

Wallace, Alfred Russel, xi, 39, 85, 89, 99, 172; *The Malay Archipelago*, 172
Ward, Cyrenus, 144, 155
Ward, Justus, 143
Ward, Lester Frank, 133, 142, 160, 162, 179, 182, 202; on the artificial over the natural, 148, 152; career of, 143–45, 154; and Darwin, 146, 147–48, 153; *Dynamic Sociology*, 148; on evolution, 147–55; on government, 144, 147–48, 150; on nature, 146–47; and the Positive Philosophy, 145–46; *The Psychic Factors of Civilization*, 153–54; and reform Darwinism, 149–53, 155; on social revolution, 155; and sociocracy, 152–53; on telic evolution, 151–52
Ward, Lizzie (Elizabeth) Vought, 144, 145
Ward, Silence Rolph, 143
Warner, Joseph Bangs, 199
Wayland, Francis, 182; *The Elements of Moral Science*, 182
Wedgwood, Josiah, 31
Werner, Abraham Gottlob, 6–7, 13–14
Westbrook, Robert, 231
Whewell, William, 29, 37
Whiston, William, 8

White, Edward G., 195, 200
White, Michael, 28
Whitefield, George, 65
Wilberforce, Samuel, 43
Williams College, 122, 123
"Wisconsin Idea," 130–31
Witherspoon, John, 78–79, 82, 95
women's rights movement: Bascom
    and, 129–30; Dewey and, 241;

Gamble and, 176; Gilman and,
    176–77; Ward and, 145
World War I, 245
Wright, Charles, 66
Wright, Chuancey, 199, 211

Yale College (and University), 109,
    134–35, 180
Yale Divinity School, 104

ABOUT THE AUTHOR

J. David Hoeveler is professor of history at the University of Wisconsin–Milwaukee. His previous books include *The New Humanism: A Critique of Modern American, 1900–1940*; *James McCosh and the Scottish Intellectual Tradition*; *Watch on the Right: Conservative Intellectuals in the Reagan Era*; *The Postmodernist Turn: American Thought and Culture in the 1970*; and *Creating the American Mind: Intellect and Politics in the Colonial Colleges*.